SexPressions

By: Te'an Swington

Cover Design by Marquecia Jordan of EMJAY INC.

©2006 by Te'an Swington
All rights reserved.

ISBN 0-6151-3631-8

Published in the United States of America

Cover Design by Marquecia Jordan of EMJAY INC.

Table of Contents

Introduction	i
Acknowledgments	iii
Peeping Tom	1
Habitual Secrets	35
Hardcore Criminals	41
My Two Wives	61
Room Service	89
The Bitch and the Best Friend	93
Late Night Stop Over	101
Dale's Passion	107
A Simple Dinner Date	113
New in Town	129
The Secrets	135
The Compromise	147
Conjagal Visit	153
Table For Two	157
Glen's Guest Room	161
The Games	197
Old School Love	203
To the Max	213
Between Sisters	217
Chains and All	221
The Baritone Voice	235
Vacation in the Keys	239
Aries Birthday	253
Bruised	287
Old Friends; New Lover	313
Yellow and the Drum	343
Trouble With Hanna	373
Sunni and Lorraine	381
Sneaking Off	397
The First Time	411
Thug Love	423

Introduction

Thank you for purchasing this book. I labored over these stories and it's a relief to finally have them out for you, the reader, to enjoy. I want to explain a few things about these stories and this book. First I want to say, or ask that you save any criticism of the stories for me. I was the one who rushed and I don't want that blame to be place anywhere but where it belongs and that's on me. So don't take it out on my characters, editors, or any one other than me. I left some of the miscues in to show growth. That leads me to another thing. The reason for calling it the green book, instead of volume one. I chose the color green for two reasons. One reason is, outside of money no one says green is their favorite color. Green is a queer, odd color which brings me to my second reason. Green is the color of new life and growth. When something or someone is new they are called green and to writing I'm very green. So as you read this I want you to see growth. See my green-ness. I also want you to see how odd some of the characters or the situations they are put in are. I know there are some grammatical errors in the book. Some are mistakes and some are on purpose, but the way I see it, if you are correcting this book instead of enjoying the juicy escapades, then you really are doing something wrong and you need his book more than you know. Sex(Fucking) isn't always correctly formed and placed neatly in a bow. Most of the time(if its done right) it is nasty and crude. There are errors and miscues the entire time. If you don't believe me think about the first time. Then think about the best times. Then think about the other 85% of times you have sex. Now you see what I mean? Sex (fucking) is usually unedited. But that's what makes it fun. And if you don't believe that look at your children and ask yourself how many were planned. As I re-read the stories I didn't notice the miscues, but I've been looking at them for close to six years and I can't see the bad. So just read the book and enjoy.

Now another thing, I hope I stayed true to is the unfantastic fantasies. Normally A story is only good if the main characters are these "story book" people who you never really meet or see. That's bullshit. There is a fat waitress and a skinny broke janitor having some great sweaty sex. I want to write about that kind of thing. I'm a normal dude and I know I'm hardly represented by most authors. Neither are the people I know and the women I like. So I'm writing for us. So if you've been reading books and can't find you and what you like to do in them this is for you and me. We are Freak Nasty(the original title) people. I hope you, the reader, are satisfied with what I've given you. I hope it encourages you to have better(SAFE) sex. I hope it sparks conversation at work and on the bus. I hope somebody uses this book to get somebody sprung. Hell I hope a few babies are the result of this book. I hope somebody puts it down half way through a story and touches themselves. I hope it causes you to want me to write another. So enjoy this gift I'm sharing with you.

AMANI NA BARAKA.
GET TESTED FOR HIV AND ANY OTHER STD'S. HAVE RESPONSIBLE SEX AND OWN UP TO THE RESULTS. SOME MISCUES GROW UP AND CHANGE THE WORLD.
BlackWriter12
Te'an L. Swington

Acknowledgements

Well this is what all the fuss has been about. This book, these pages, this ink and these characters are what I've devoted a good portion of my time and energy doing. I've met a lot of people, in person and on the internet, that have been waiting to see how this would come to pass. Honesty I've been waiting even longer and hoping harder than anyone else that this would work. So before I do anything else I want to exhale (aight I'm doing the happy dance too). Seeing as how I'm from the Hip-Hop generation and I may never get an album cover to say my Thank You's I'll do it here.

First I want to thank the Creator. Thank YOU for everything I've done and will do. For what I am now and what I should have been. Thank YOU for that dirty little freaky part of my mind and the ability to turn those thoughts into written words. Your son is grateful for being the vessel you chose to work through. And before anyone says anything crazy about this genre think about the motivation it took to make you. Enuff said.

Okay I'd like to thank my characters now. I want to thank them for voicing their lives through my pen. I've often told people that writing for me is like listening to a conversation. Getting a phone call from someone about some real nasty shit and then I'm allowed to write it down. So when people tell me that I should write more about them it isn't for me to say. That's all of the story I was given. Oh yeah, with the exception of a few stories, most of these aren't about any one living. If you've met me and find some connection to these characters it truly is coincidental. Plus they live a better sexual life than I ever could.

I want to praise those that have gone before me. PEACEFUL JOURNEY to My Grandparents; Eddie Lee and Mary Cox Smith. Ya'll left this heavy burden for me to carry and I haven't drop it once. Read my back when I sleep and you can see. I love you both. To my aunt Irene. I was an asshole and a very, very disrespectful boy then. I should have told you this before but I see what was being taught and now I'm teaching. To David Riley and Tony Haney. Dave we tried our best to reach old age before we saw you again but it didn't work out that way. Tony I wasn't there when you left us. I'm grateful for you dude. You are a good dude and I was BLESSED to know you. You will always be my blessing HOMIE.

To my Mother Sharon. Look what ya boy has done. You always knew I was mannish and nasty-minded. Guess how many dresses I can look up now. To my father Rodney; I see ya pops. To my uncle Edward... We should talk more. Oh yeah...I'm Percy Lee Jr. now... Love you for the guidance. You made sure that your baby sister's boy grew into a man. For real that was big. And thanx for showing me he light. Thank you to my sisters Juretha(four-thirty for real huh?) and Java-Shaqui. Look what ya' brother did. AAAaahhh HHhaaaa. To Patrice Hanes. Honey we have to do something and do it fast. I love you. (yeah "those" stories are about you). To my kids Tierra and Donovan. One day you'll see somebody reading this book and think that's yo daddy's book. You may laugh or you may think it's nasty that your friends are reading it, either way look what We did. And when Ya'll old enough to read it, let me know what ya think. To my niece and nephews... What happen, who getting money? Uncle Tank is doing the damn thang. To Linc, Lawrence, Maltese, Gina, and Mya; we always had love. We Family and we never forgot that(and before ya'll ask I ain't got no money laffing)

To Miguel and Marcel...Dude it's going down. Rio, look at me grind cuz. I still want a free hair cut. Kahly (thanx for looking out for my boy) Ant, Uncle Willy, Bill, Chris Illa, Sherice, Jill, Joe, Malik, Jamaican Mike, Jazzy Belle and my lil Brother Kelly, What the hell now? Everybody at General Jones Armory and all the joes in 1/178 and the 2/122... Damn all those deployments paid off, huh? Gotta say what the hell up to everybody on 81st and May Street and the Wild

Hundreds... To the entire SouthSide of Chicago and the other three sides. Thank you to the liquor that got me drunk and the things I drank after I gave up that crutch. To Sonya Thomas and Michelle Muhammad; I should have been more careful with ya'll love. Sonya I found you when I was really lost and you allowed me to learn to love. Michelle you taught me a lot about being a man in a relationship. I was listening when you were talking and I'm still taking notes. Ruth Williams damn love thank you for helping me tighten this down. I know I couldn't have done it with out you. Thais Mills and Mr. Lyrik(can't believe you tried to fight that big ass dog...never forget RDDB), Hey Boss Lady. Thank you for the exposure you and ya radio show(LIPSERVICEINK.COM). The next sound you hear will be you blowing up. I will never forget the Milan's thing either. And we going to New Orleans to do a book signing, I want to thank my editors over at Eve's Literary Service. Ya'll did "write" by me. It don't hurt that both you ladies are beautiful and sexy. Marquecia Jordan, glad you came when you did. The cover is banging(I saw yo' nipple in the other one...laffing that'll be the cover for the next one). Tell the photographer he has that eye. Sorry for spilling coffee on ya desk.

I want to thank BlackVoices, Blackplanet, & AFF/Passion.com. Everybody in every room I've chatted with thank you. We some nasty minded folks(rotflmao). Big up to Myspace. Thank you to every hip-hop artist (Common..dude I needed Electric Circus... Lupe Fiasco, Kanye West, Shawnna, Twista, Rhymefest, Bump J and Jap...), jazz, r&b(R.Kelly, Dave Hollister, Dwele, J.E., Jill Scott, India Arie, Maxwell, Goapele, Ron Isley, Lenny Williams,,,still can't believe the Boss Lady had you call me at 1 a.m. ... Anthony Hamilton, and Carl Thomas.) reggae(Bounty Killa and Beenie Man), and blues singers ever. Thank you to the strippers that I've helped put through school. To anybody doing something that inspires. I would like to thank all the authors past, present and future. We owe it to people to do good things with a pen. Let's stop being lazy and put out good shit.

And lastly I'd like to thank you the reader. Hell without you I would still be trying to do something. I know how hard times are and for you to drop a few dollars to buy this book means a lot. Email me @ bw_wuntu@yahoo.com or catch up with me on myspace @ tean_swington/myspace.com and tell me what you think. Whether

there was something that moved you. That one of these stories got you to thinking about you and yours. Hell, tell me if you think I can't write. You paid the cash and I'll listen. And if I see you on the bus reading this I may even ask if I can sign it.
Peace and Blessings
B.W. WUNTU(BlackWriter12)
Tean L. Swington

PEEPING TOM

Voyeurism. I laugh every time I hear the word. That's one of the reasons I like these more modern, hip times in which we live. Everything has a new, sexier label; butt fucking is now called anal sex, blowjobs are referred to as oral sex, and faggots are homosexuals. What's next? Sex with a midget - wait they're called little people - being called miniature intercourse?

At least I know what I am; I'm a Peeping Tom. I can't help it. I like watching people doing things. I'd rather it be sex that I am watching, but I'll watch people doing just about anything. I really can't think of the last time I *peeped*. Looking through my telescope is the closest I've ever come to doing that. And even then I'm not *peeping*. I have an expensive set up with a lens that allows me to see in the dark. I got it at a Fishing and Hunting Convention. I really wasn't aware of the big need to fish and hunt at night, but I guess these are the times we live in.

Being a Peeping Tom is also the reason I bought my condominium downtown. With all these high-rises, a person is bound to see something of interest sooner or later. When I first moved here, I was disappointed. But after studying my favorite people, I soon learned when and where to look and

SexPressions

that's when everything fell into place. After finding targets for my obsession, I acquired a routine. I turn my radio on to a smooth jazz station, adjust my lights and blinds and begin to watch. I'd like to lie and say this helps me think, but the truth is I'm a Peeping Tom, plain and simple, who gets his jollies from watching other people "get down".

When I first started, I'd leave the light in my living room on and people would notice me watching. It took several occasions of me getting caught in the act for me to learn to be more discreet. Now I close my blinds slightly and turn the lights off. It may not seem like a lot, but you would be surprised at how many other "Toms" I see through my telescope looking back at me, standing in a full picture window with every light in the apartment lit. When our lenses connected, most would become embarrassed and hide their face. Although one, a female, has chosen to turn her lights off as well. We wave at each other every now and then, but no other contact is made. Maybe it's for the best. I really can't see myself dating someone as nosy as that. Not to mention, I'm not really into white women. It's not that there aren't any that I find attractive. I just know there are a lot of sexy single sisters in the world, and I prefer to give them my attention.

As a matter of fact, one of my favorite people to watch is a tall caramel-brown skinned sister. She's a straight-laced, tight-buttoned kind of woman most of the time. She usually wears business suits where the hems fall consistently right above the knee. Her hair is set in tight neat braids that hang evenly on her shoulders. The thing that makes her my favorite is that she only goes out on Tuesday nights. It's on those nights that she transforms

Peeping Tom

from a kitten to a wild cat. That's how I noticed her. I was scanning the window of one of the taller neighboring buildings when I caught a glimpse of red. I brought the window into focus and that's when I saw her, a dangerously sexy woman dressed in a fire-engine red leather outfit. The clothes fit her body so tight, it looked as if she had dove into a pool of red paint. I didn't know it then, but she wore a red wig, with the same color lipstick covering her full lips. She wore a one-piece suit that allowed her breast to push their way out of the top be seen. I don't honestly think I've ever had an erection that was as hard for so long as it was the first time I saw her.

I watched her move around her apartment for a few more minutes before leaving for the night. I fell asleep soon after that. When I woke, it was early the next morning. I checked the windows, hoping to catch a glimpse of my lady in red. But by the time I got the lens to focus, all I could see was her sprawled out across her couch, lying atop a dark naked male body. I smiled myself to sleep imagining what had happened in her living room that night.

One week later, I saw her transform again and leave for her night's activities. This time I stayed awake long enough to see her return with a young brother as her guest. He looked like the kind of guy who orders martinis and only learned to play golf to please the corporate big-wigs whom he lets beat him every chance he gets. He looked exactly like a victim, a lamb being coaxed into a wolf's kitchen. She even turned toward the window, every now and then, unknowingly facing me, and she cursed her lips with a wicked smile. She then ran her hands slowly along her exposed cleavage before blowing a seductive kiss towards

SexPressions

the dark night sky. I felt my manhood rise as I watched her. Then she turned away from me and faced her "lamb". I noticed he held his glass with shaking hands, and he swallowed hard while accepting her glance. She slowly moved toward him. I felt my eyelids grow heavy with each step she took. By the time she reached him and they kissed, my lids were nearly sealed shut. I forced them open long enough to see her down her drink and grab him by his timid balls. I don't remember falling asleep, nor do I remember pushing my pants to my ankles and jerking my dick, but the dry drool on my face and the sticky cum all over my legs and hands told me I'd done both. Although, I've watched her devour a lot of men since then, I've always wondered what happened that night. Fantasizing about her and him together, visible only through the soft light coming from behind her blinds, has been the basis of many an erotic thought for me.

Shaun had to admit it, he was impressed. He'd met a lot of people in his life that talked a good game. But when it was time to show some substance they mostly fell short. They didn't know it, but it was the details that gave them away as frauds. That's what impressed Shaun about the long-legged sister. She dotted her "i's and crossed her t's." Shaun thought she was lying about her view of the city, and since they never talked about what they both did for a living; all he had to go on was what she said. Shaun had spent the entire evening trying to find flaws in her game. Now he stood in her immaculate apartment, which was decorated with an air of sophistication. The woman stood before him dressed entirely in white. Shaun never got her to say her name, which was another detail she didn't slip up on. She had on a trendy wig, he knew it was a wig, but he didn't mind, it added to the excitement. She wore a long white

Peeping Tom

dress, which clung snugly against her body and showed every curve to tease her prey. The nails on her hands and feet were done in a simple, but sexy French manicure. Her erotic image against the white and brown color scheme of her apartment was intoxicating. Shaun was sure a woman of her caliber wore clothes of various colors and styles, but the sight of everything in the room composed of either white or brown, including the liquor that sat at her bar, was truly impressive. Most people gave up on the attempt to keep the décor and to maintain the flow of the ambiance, but not her. That's really what did it for Shaun. This woman was different.

"So do you always stand around with your mouth open not saying much?" She asked Shaun, turning away from her apartment's large picture window. "Or are you just scared?"

"Yes!" Shaun wanted to yell. "I'm scared as hell!"

Only serial killers and account-types were this anal, this meticulous, this frighteningly arousing. Half of him was scared that she was a vampire. The other half hoped what he was encountering was real.

"No just taking it all in." Shaun said trying not to flinch. "They can smell fear." He thought to himself and whispered to his mind.

She walked over to him, each step forcing small shivers through his spine. Shaun's tie instantly felt like a noose. He wanted to put his arm out to stop her forward progress. He wanted to halt his erection from slithering down his leg. But he couldn't. Shaun was just as frozen as the ice that clanked against the glass he held.

"Just taking it all in, huh?" Her words blew against his face like mean-spirited smoke from a cigarette.

"Well hopefully, I can take this all in, *Punk.*" With that, the woman grabbed Shaun fiercely by his dick with one had and gulped down her glass of rum with the other. He closed his eyes and quivered, thinking the word *"Punk"* never sounded so seductive.

"So finish your drink so I can fuck you and send you home."

Shaun's ass cheeks clenched together. Normally, he would've told this broad to "Kiss his chubby ass." But he knew this wasn't a normal situation. Shaun sipped his drink quickly. The sweet taste of the rum precluded the warm fuzzy feeling that ravaged his belly. The quick rush of the liquor gave him a feeling that normally would have turned his stomach. But looking into her eyes steadied him, and he believed she would kick his ass and force him to maintain his alcoholic composure if he couldn't maintain it on his own.

The woman wrapped Shaun's tie around her hand and jerked it, pulling him behind her. The effect wasn't lost on Shaun.

"Lead me into temptation." Shaun thought as they neared the bedroom.

Peeping Tom

"So what can I call you?" Shaun asked, trying not to let the fear and excitement show in his voice.

"Tomorrow, if you're good enough." She spat back over her shoulder." "Until then, don't say shit."

She pushed the bedroom door open. The room's color scheme was red, or at least the red lava lamp that sat on the nightstand, covered everything in a red hue. Shawn felt drugged; sex usually gave him that feeling. At least good sex did, anyway. The woman pulled Shaun to the bed, forcing him to crawl.

"Undress slowly, punk!" She ordered, standing at the foot of the bed.

The red spell of the room changed her white outfit to slightly pink. Shaun slowly loosened his tie, trying to keep his eyes interlocked with hers. His heart rate quickened. Shaun felt his nipples stiffen and grow warm. A harsh pulsation began in his groin. Shaun's hands trembled as he fumbled with his shirt buttons. The woman hung her head as if she were slightly disgusted. Shaun truly felt like a punk.

The woman slowly moved around the bed, eyeing Shaun and his activity. She reached beneath the bed and pulled out a small white whip. Shaun wrestled to remove his suit jacket and shirt together. He tried to undo his buckle, when he felt the sting of her whip swat his hands away.

"Damn Punk, you move too slow!" The woman kicked her shoes off and crawled slowly across the bed until

SexPressions

she hovered over Shaun.

"Open up." She ordered, leaning close enough for Shaun to smell the sweet smell of the Jamaican rum. She placed the whip into Shaun's open mouth. Shaun grunted as he bit down on the leather-braided handle. He held the whip in his mouth and tried to sit up. His actions were met with the woman pushing his head backward; forcing him onto the bed.

"Lay the fuck back." She ordered before grabbing his shirt and ripping it open, exposing his chest and plump belly. The woman kissed, Shaun on his exposed skin. He hummed softly, the feeling of her soft thick lips tickling his sexual flesh. The woman bit his nipples and moved lower. She worked her hand quickly removing his belt and pants. She alternately worked the pants with each hand, moving them side to side along with his thin underwear until they were past his ass and hips. Shaun's hidden erection shot up, gently brushing the woman's chin. She raised her left eyebrow and shot him a scornful look, then kissed the head of his penis. Shaun resisted the urge to cum. The woman pulled the pants free of his legs. Then she reached behind her and undid the single clasp that held her clothing in place and slowly removed the dress from her body. A thin gold chain hugging her ample waist was all that she wore beneath the whiteness. She kneeled again, this time returning with a small square package. She used her teeth to quickly open the small wrapper and pulled out a red, Shaun was sure it was red, latex condom. The woman stalked over Shaun with the condom in her mouth, grabbing his erect penis by its fat base. Artfully using her mouth and tongue; she skillfully lowered the condom on the tip of Shaun's penis, as she

Peeping Tom

glided her lips down the shaft.

The fit was exact, as if it were tailored to him. He wondered if she was happy with his size, but embarrassment suffocated the question. He felt her hum, but couldn't determine if it was out of pleasure or contempt. The woman snaked her hand over Shaun's trembling torso while slowly easing his penis up and down in her mouth's warm cavity. Shaun gasped as the woman sucked harder and yanked the whip from his teeth. The woman re-positioned herself so that she could easily fill her mouth with Shaun's length. She struck Shaun's chest and nipples with a quick, hard snap. He tried not to lose his composure, as the conflicting sensation of joy and pain overtook him. She stroked and sucked his sex while still striking him with the whip. He moved softly in pleasure, unsure which feeling he liked more, but as his penis jumped with each touch whip's sting he knew that feeling was more dominant. It was a new feeling. The raw feeling of an erotic intruder against his senses. Shaun had always wondered what someone got out of being spanked or bitten. Now he couldn't understand why he had lived this long without the pleasure of pain. He felt himself turning into a living stone inside of the latex wrapping. Once again his ass cheeks tightened and became warm, as a faint smell of strawberry tiptoed over his nose. He instinctively licked his lips, trying to taste the smell. The woman moved her tongue along his shaft and down to his balls; he arched his back in anticipation. The woman purred at the sweet taste from the homemade soap Shaun used.

"The dick tastes sweet, punk."

Instantly Shaun was pleased he had begun using the

SexPressions

soap his sister brought him back from her vacation in the Virgin Islands. She reached beneath Shaun and caressed his ass cheeks roughly; brushing her fingers against his brown rear hole. He wanted to protest. He wanted to push her off him and storm out of her detailed world. But he was enjoying it. The woman struck him quickly twice on his tight round belly. Shaun ran his fingers lightly over her head, as she slowly moved him in and out of her mouth. He winced when she purposely raked her teeth against his flesh. He grinned when he felt his body shudder. She smacked the side of his buttocks, and slowly moved him from her mouth, and slowly began to crawl up and over him again. She stopped abruptly and began to stare at Shaun with deeply seductive bedroom eyes. Shaun smiled at her, instantly regretting the gesture. The woman frowned slightly and mouthed the word "*punk*" softly. She moved quickly, and replaced the red condom with another and straddled him. Shaun moved his hands to the sides of her face, then to her shoulders, and finally setting them on her hips and waist.

The woman kissed Shaun on his soft, chubby chest. He felt a little embarrassed and wondered if she viewed them as man-titties. He gasped softly as she pressed her vaginal warmth against his thick penis. She reached between her hot thighs and grabbed him firmly by his sex. She moved the head of his sex around her cream-covered, swollen clitoris before slowly sliding it deep into her. She was warm and comforting. The woman rotated her hips slowly, getting her mahogany walls accustom to the fit. Shaun moaned gingerly. The woman moaned at the surprisingly tight feel of him inside of her

"He isn't big", she thought, "but he is more than enough."

Peeping Tom

The woman placed her hand on Shaun's chest and moved to a squatting position. She slowly moved up and down onto him. He slowly began to pump upward into her warmth. The electric sensation of his orgasm sizzled deep within him. He smiled at the sight of her body working in sexual earnest, forcing him to hold her tighter. He filled his palms with as much of her flesh as he could. She began moving faster. She spitefully smacked the whipped across Shaun's chest (man-titties). Her nipples began to swell and protrude from her red-tinted brown skin. She curses wickedly, holding Shaun by the shoulders and pressing her pelvis against his. Shaun sat forward and sucked hard on her breast. Sweat began to form on his forehead and covered his face.

"This is some good dick/pussy." The woman/Shaun moaned, bodies alternating between quivers.

He held her by her buttocks and pulled her into him with each of his strokes.

"Yeah... fuck me *punk*." She panted loudly. The woman pulled Shaun upright and slowly began rocking against his deep pumping. Her fingertips began tingling, the pinkie first, then the rest. She increased her pace forcing him deeper inside her still. He did believe he could grow any harder, but his penis proved him wrong; and suddenly a pulsating wave began to roll through him. Shaun scolded himself, alerting the woman.

"Nooo..... Not yet, mutha-fucka!" She howled, addressing Shaun by something other than *punk*.

SexPressions

He tried to rally more stamina but the effort was futile. He felt the force of his orgasm stiffen his penis inside of the condom. Shaun felt a "fuck-face" grow tightly over his face as his entire body tightened. The woman pumped furiously, attempting to catch up. After shocks made Shaun tremble beneath her movements. She reached between her thighs and massaged her clitoris. Her orgasm arrived like a sexual hurricane crashing against her helpless sexual shores. A feeling of light-headedness swarmed her. She moaned into his ear as wave after wave of her liquid sex moved from her. She slowly rotated her pelvis, smearing sex cream over Shaun's pelvis. A smile slowly grew over his lips. He felt he could get used to this type of sex, even if he had to pay for it. He welcomed the soft tingling that whispered to him. The woman held onto the back of his head; digging her nails into his shoulders, bracing herself against the convulsions that followed her orgasm. She lay motionless atop of him, riding the rise and fall of his breathing. She felt her own breath rush from her lungs and roar lightly past her lips.

"I may even keep this *punk*." She thought to herself, allowing Shaun's limp penis to slide from within her. She sat up, straddling his heavy torso; a smile wicked and knowing in nature; on her face.

"Well?" Shaun asked, hoping for an ego stroking answer. He could feel his penis's strength returning.

A small sign of being disturbed eased across her face. The woman shook it off and allowed her smile to return. She pushed herself from atop of him. She tossed her leg over his and reached around his girth to playfully rub his belly.

Peeping Tom

"Well?" Shaun said repeating his one-word question.

"Damn *Punk*!" You're okay, now shut the fuck up and let me enjoy it." She said, spitting the words out in slight disgust. "Be happy I haven't put yo' ass out."

Shaun smiled telling himself she was pleased. She could play tough all she wanted, he knew the truth. He felt her move closer to his body. A warm ticklish feeling caused him to squirm and fidget. Shaun enjoyed the feel of the woman's touch against his neck and back, as it ushered him to sleep. He smiled as she traced random patterns.

Shaun was suddenly awakened by the sound of the woman's voice.

"Its time to take yo' snoring ass home." The woman said, standing over him dressed only in a pair of bikini-cut panties. Shaun sat up in the bed; the effects of the alcohol and good sex had taken their toll. He was groggy, but he gathered his clothing, got dressed and began walking toward the door. The woman followed close behind, lightly hitting her hand with the small white whip.

"Hey Shaun," she said as he turned the door knob, "Meet me back at the same bar next week."

Shaun smiled and disappeared into the hallway.

Shaun stood in front of his bathroom mirror, supporting himself with the sink. He told himself he'd never drink rum again. No matter how sexy the sister who drank with him happened to be. He tossed two extra strength painkillers in his mouth. He prayed the numbing effect of the medicine would take him soon.

"So who's Madeleine?"

Shaun caught the reflection of his wife in the mirror. She leaned against the doorframe, jaw held tightly closed.

"Don't know, why?"

Shaun clearly wasn't in the mood for this so early in the morning.

"Because "Madeleine was here" is written on your back in lipstick."

Shaun instantly felt like vomiting.

Sometimes I wish I could talk to the people I watch. I find myself yelling at them. Like those folks in the movies who yell at the screen. Mostly I offer encouragement. You know, shit like, "Fuck the shit outta her, bruh!" Or, "Nutt in her face fool!" Hell once I saw a chick going through a guy's pockets while he showered. I would've warned him or at least told her where the good stuff was hidden.

There's this one cat I watch, a young brother, who I call the *Champ*. I can tell when he has done a good job; because he stands over each woman he's had sex with, arms over his head, foot on their chest. I cheer every time I see him do it. Hell, it's something I'd even like to try myself to see how the women respond to it. They must take it personal because they always try to redeem themselves, like

Peeping Tom

it's a personal attack on their pride. But they never seem to beat the *Champ*. He never disappoints. Sometimes the "fights go longer than expected, but he always knocks them out.

You talk a lot of shit, you know that?" April smiled as she spoke. She wouldn't admit it to him, but that one of the reason she liked him so much. Terrell was an ass hole. He bragged constantly about his sexual conquest, and April had been the middle-woman between Terrell and a few friends and family. Well actually more than a few. The funny part was they all said the same thing. That Terrell **was** the" Champion of the Coochie". April laughed the first time she heard a woman repeat the phrase Terrell used. The fool even had a large wrestling-style belt made. And since she would never get a chance to find out, April would have to take the word of two sisters, one cousin, four co-workers, seven sorority sisters, and one jealous neighbor who thought she was stealing April's man. Terrell was truly "The Champ" in their eyes. But now really wasn't the time for Terrell to break his arm patting himself on the back. April had come by to vent; not listen to the latest report of Terrell and his prize-fighting penis.

"But I can back it up, though." He answered; arms spread out in a wide "I'm the Man" manner.

"Whatever." April shot back, waving her hand in disgust. They both chuckled before moving around the apartment. April stood and moved to the large window that faced the city, while Terrell went into the kitchen. April looked out of the large thick glass, crossed her arms and fought off the feeling of dizziness that massaged her brain.

SexPressions

She'd always been scared of heights and couldn't imagine what made Terrell's scary ass live so high off the ground. April stared across at the building facing Terrell's and was overcome by an alarming thought.

"Ain't you scared of people looking at you?" She said, over her shoulder.

"I hope somebody is looking." Terrell answered, handing April a bottle of beer," But I do think there is somebody looking at me."

Terrell stood next to April and pointed across to the tall building. She suddenly felt excited and violated, as if anybody watching them could read her thoughts as well. Terrell moved the bottle of Red Stripe beer to his lips, before humming.

"So where are we going; since you're taking me out." April asked, falling onto the sofa and curling her legs beneath her.

"I feel like some Reggae music."

Terrell said, sipping from his beer, before moving his hips like the dancers April had seen in a few of the Reggae videos.

"But I have to work!" April protested, secretly lying to herself and Terrell. What she really wanted to say was, "Tee, I'm not really in the mood to get high, meet a sexy, drunk Jamaican dude, and not give him any." When she and Terrell went to the Reggae club, they normally went all the way out. Ganja included. She wasn't sure if she was up for it.

Peeping Tom

She felt like sulking and it's hard to sulk when you've burned down a small Caribbean forest. She began to concoct other excuses, as Terrell pulled her from the sofa, slowly winding his waist.

"Me not kare!" He said, using his best Jamaican accent, which sounded pretty good against April's ear. It wasn't the accent, that was actually corny, but it was the heat of his breath that melted her reserve. And with that, April knew arguing was just as in effective as a knife in a gunfight.

"I think she likes you." April said, leaning in close, so she didn't need to yell.

Terrell looked over her shoulder at the woman who had just left the dance floor. Terrell had to admit it she was fine. She had move behind Terrell and slowly moved her hips in close vicinity and unison with his. As a matter of fact, Terrell thought, she only left when April had returned from the restroom.

"You scared her off." Terrell smiled, voicing his opinion.

They both moved with the music, positioning themselves so they could spy on the woman. April began evaluating her features. The woman's skin was in a darkish brown color. The color one thought of when they heard Afro centric poetry. At that moment, for the first time in her life; April had to admit she found another woman sexually attractive. The woman was taller than April, but shorter than Terrell, who stood close to six feet three inches tall.

SexPressions

Her breasts were a large C-cup or a small D-cup.

"Nice shapely ass." April thought; much better shape than her own. She looked to April to be the kind of woman who had five piercing; except you could only see the two in her ears. April didn't know if it was the potent marijuana she and Terrell had smoked, or if it was that she'd heard that women were better at eating pussy than men, but she winked and waved. The woman returned the gesture; freezing April's heart beat for a second or two.

"It looks like she likes both of us." Terrell laughed, penis pushing out in anticipation.

April secretly hoped she did. The woman waved for them to join her at her table. She erotically smiled as they approached. The woman pushed one of the four chairs away and maneuvered her chair so that she faced the two remaining ones. Terrell raised his hand to smooth down the sides of his goatee and he inhaled a hint of her fragrance. His groin tingled, as the sweet robust smell of her body oil coated his nasal passage. He nearly cried when she crossed her legs allowing her smooth thighs to peek out from the split in her long dress. He coughed, trying to hide the fact that he'd just had his breath stolen. April watched the entire exchange, smiling the whole time, becoming aroused and envious.

"She is pure sex appeal." April thought. The kind of woman, who if she stole your man, you couldn't truly be upset. The kind of woman other women called "Bitch", but secretly wanted to know how she pulled it off. April knew this woman was the kind of woman who could send her

Peeping Tom

from bi-curious to very bi-serious.

"Hello." April said, extending her hand. The woman delicately received her hand, gently shook it, held it then lightly squeezed.

Hello, I'm Sephia." The woman said, momentarily eclipsing the clubs strobe lights. .

"Sorry about dancing so close to your man," Sephia started, "But I thought he was alone."

"Don't worry, girl. It's only dancing." April sang back, never correcting her on her slight placement of Terrell's sexual ownership.

"Well that dancing got me hot." Sephia thought, trying to squelch the small rumbling coming from between her thighs. Sephia continued smiling, as April introduced Terrell.

"Not only is he a good dancer, he's a *"Champion Lover.""* April mocked Terrell.

Both Sephia and Terrell blushed, before he gave an explanation. Giggling at her friend's nervousness, April waved the waitress over.

"Sounds like a challenge to me!" She said, before taking the liberty of ordering drinks for everyone.

Sephia stood close behind Terrell, making his attempt to open his apartment door even that much more of a chore.

SexPressions

Terrell had spent most of the night drinking and dancing and sometime during the night he'd been seduced by these two women. He caught a glimpse of April staring at him, drunken bedroom eyes in full effect. Terrell had always found April attractive sexually, and any other "ly" for that matter. But her new bi-curiousness, still somewhat of a shock to him, drove him crazy. He thought about turning his friend down. Giving her the *"we're just friends"* speech. But being in love with her and having the chance to have a threesome caused him to hold his tongue.

"Staaaahhhhpah!" Terrell said, playfully scolding Sephia.

"I know' *The Champ*' un lovah's not ticklish." She said, Caribbean accent no longer suppressed.

"Yes, he is." April said, joining in the assault. She winked at Sephia, who ran her hand softly across April's cheek.

Terrell held onto the doorknob, closed his eyes and commanded his urges to stay in check. His nipples and penis disobeyed the command, and grew with tingling excitement. His bladder seemed to be the only organ that followed orders, but Terrell wasn't sure how long it would hold up. He pushed into the apartment, sending the three of them laughing at some unspoken; yet shared punch line. He made a beeline for the large sofa and plunged into its plush ness.

"Ya'll too much for me." He panted, the effect of being drunk and tickled stealing his breath. He could hear the women talking around him. They'd sandwiched him in,

Peeping Tom

April on the right and Sephia on the left. Terrell felt his head begin to get heavy.

"So ya'll gonna double team me, huh?" He said, not sure if it sounded the same on the outside of his head as it did on the inside.

Terrell listened to the two women kiss softly against the sides of his face. April gently pulled his ear between her lips, while Sephia brushed her lips against his neck, just under his jaw line. Terrell wanted to laugh, but with his eyes slowly closing and his dick slowly growing, he knew this wasn't a laughing matter.

"Dayum..." Terrell mumbled, as the power of drunken slumber overtook his sexual desires.

Terrell told his eyes to open. His other four senses were hard at work. He could feel a damp, warmth over his exposed erection (he really wasn't sure when he'd gotten undressed). He smelled the very distinct aroma of highly aroused vagina, the taste of which was now coating his sound asleep, yet still licking, tongue. He heard two women moaning. Now all he had to do was get his eyes to show him what he'd gotten himself into. Maybe if he could move, his eyes would, get the message. Terrell moved his hand to where his erection should be and felt a soft braided quaff slowly bobbing to an unheard tune. He used his other hand to slowly caress the thigh and buttocks of the woman who stood over him. He tried to listen for the moans. He moved his tongue around her clitoris. The woman's pubic hairs were soft and neatly trimmed. A sweet thick creaminess covered Terrell's tongue and chin. He wondered how long he'd been

SexPressions

licking, but quickly told himself it didn't really matter. His eyelids slowly became unglued. He eased them open. First he focused on the woman in front of him. Her pubic hair was fashioned in the shape of a heart that seem to hang under a slightly chubby stomach. Terrell moved his head so that he could see this woman's belly button.

"So this is what you taste like." He said, as he peered up at April, who held Terrell by his head to balance herself.

Terrell smiled intently and lightly slapped her buttocks. She smiled with acceptance. He kissed her flush on her vaginal lips, and then looked down. He was surprised to see that for the most part he wasn't as naked as he thought. His pants were just open enough to give Sephia clear access to his penis. He continued caressing her head. He tried to think of something cool to say. It wasn't everyday two women seduced him, but he thought better of it. No need sounding like a fool. Also the only sound he could muster was a hard moan. Terrell relaxed while each woman continued working her sexual endeavors, before putting an end to their fun. He gently pushed April from atop of him, and then coaxed Sephia from working her oral magic.

"Let's get ready to rumble." Terrell thought, using his inner "Michael Buffer" voice.

Once he got to his feet, Terrell slowly began undressing. He removed his shirt and flexed and posed. He wasn't much of a body builder, still both women smiled. He slowly removed his bikini underwear and pants, quickly pulled off his socks, so he would not look goofy, like the

Peeping Tom

guys in the porn movies. Still the women smiled, not in delight or disgust, but in eager readiness. Terrell moved toward his bedroom, stopping long enough to turn on the stereo; setting the mood music. He disappeared into the bedroom and after a few moments returned with three large candles and a black bag. He placed the candles around the room, lit them then turned the lights off. All the while, the woman sat on the sofa watching his actions. Each woman had removed her remaining clothing and slowly traced her own body's curves.

Terrell cleared the large wooden coffee table and covered it with a plush blanket that had laid over the love seat. He fashioned the blanket so that it adequately cushioned the table, then Terrell stood and faced the women.

"You first!" He pointed at April. "Lay down on your back."

She was reluctant at first, but April slowly moved to the table, sat on the edge and laid back. The table easily accommodated her body without anything hanging off. April smiled at the picture of her naked best friend standing over her; seeing his erect penis hang, firm and heavy, from his body. April knew why he'd been so cocky.

Terrell motioned for Sephia to come closer. He grinned at her as if they were wolves and he was telling her a new way to eat fox. Terrell stood back and watched the slow event he'd put into motion. Sephia kneeled before April's brown quivering legs. She looked up to April and winked. She kissed her just above her left knee, sending fingers of uneasy excitement to April's brain. April allowed

SexPressions

her hands to layover her pelvis and slowly curled her fingers into relaxed fists. Her legs spread on their own. Sephia knew where to go, what to do, and April let her. She treated April's inner thighs to the feel of her thin elongated tongue and thick lips. April cringed away from the feel of her touch. Sephia's braid's brushed lightly against April's just-kissed thighs, tickling her closer to an orgasm.

"What the fuck?" April moaned.

Sephia's tongue lead the way to her sexual epicenter. April drew her lips into her mouth and moaned. Sephia pushed her bent legs apart, while April allowed them to fall open, causing her vagina to blossom to its full sexual form. Her mind teased her body, as it tried to slink away from Sephia's tongue.

"Yes!" April's body whispered, celebrating the moment and he feel of Sephia's full tongue against her labia. If there was a man's tongue whose tongular touch was this gentle, this firm, and this experienced, April prayed she'd find him soon. She immediately despised her straight friends for lying to her. She felt as if she could scratch out their eyes. This was how pussy should be eaten. She was defenseless against Sephia's tongue. She let her eyes droop nearly close and caressed her face in surrender. Terrell stood just within her vision, smiling and stroking his long, thin sex.

She mouthed, "Thank You", before cursing and allowed her eyes to close. Sephia moved April's labia apart with her thumbs, and slid her tongue over her creamy pinkness. She sucked very gently against April's clitoris and

Peeping Tom

vaginal opening. The sounds of April groaning, panting and humming cascaded against her ears, filling her own nipples with fiery arrogance.

"Ya damn right this feels good." Her inner lesbian said, answering April's pants.

She drew light, figure eights over April's trembling sex. She pushed her hands over April's body, enjoying the feel of April's warm skin beneath her touch. Sephia easily found herself beginning engrossed with April's taste and feel. Her own vagina quivered and throbbed between her thighs. She lost herself in her lust and pulled April with her. Neither of the women noticed Terrell sneak off to the kitchen and return with a small jar of warm honey. Sephia, who had briefly moved her tongue over April's torso, was drawing circles around her navel, when sweet honey ran against her tongue. Both women moaned; Sephia from the combined tastes, and April from the feel. A small orgasm moved throughout April. She opened her eyes to the sight of Terrell standing, naked, over her holding a jar.

"Say ahh." Terrell said in his deepest, most suave voice. April obeyed, not daring to spoil the moment, tilting her head back. He placed the head of his penis against her tongue, then poured the honey down the base of his shaft and allowed it to flow into April's mouth. April lapped at the sweet thickness that flowed over her tongue and Terrell's sex. He continued slowly pouring and began softly moving his honey-covered erection in and out of April's mouth. April began slowly swallowing the honey as he inched his way deeper into her mouth. Each gentle thrust moved him further into her, and before either of them could stop

SexPressions

themselves, Terrell felt April's nose tickle the underside of his penis.

"Dayum." They both thought, as the sight of the other overwhelmed them. He felt himself throbbing and pulsating inside of her mouth, praying his orgasm's arrival hadn't cursed them. He slowly began withdrawing his penis from her reluctant mouth. She sucked and licked each retreating inch of his brown flesh.

"Turn over." He said, pulling his muscle free.

She smiled, obeying this order. She eased her way into a sitting position; stopping briefly to exchange the taste of Terrell's penis from her tongue with the taste of her own sexual residue nom Sephia's, then gently turned on all fours. April giggled softly as she wiggled her ass. She moved forward on to the table coming dick-to-face with Terrell's sex. She held him in place, before feeding him into her mouth again. This time Terrell moaned and steadied himself against his buckling knees, by holding onto April's shoulders. Her hand moved in a piston-like motion opposite of her mouth. She worked her tongue around the head of his penis, teasing quivers and moans from his mouth.
She told herself, "I'll be damned if I pass up the chance to make Terrell's knees buckle."

It wasn't everyday that someone gets the chance to have a threesome with their best friend and a sexy brown one-night-stand. Because that's what Sephia would be after tonight. Although the touch of her tongue between her spread butt cheeks told April to not to be so hasty.

Peeping Tom

Terrell slowly rotated his hips and moved himself in and out of her mouth. He scolded himself for losing control. April smacked him sharply on his ass, palmed his left cheek and pulled him forward. Her soft moans soon turned into greedy slurps. She didn't know why she wanted to move faster and suck harder. Then she realized Sephia's tongue was making her light-headed, signaling she was close to exploding. April removed Terrell from her mouth. Her body became hysterical, as April's her impending orgasm neared. She involuntarily tightened her grip around his girth and bit her lip.

"What the fuck is this bitch doing to me?" April asked herself, as her orgasm's warm front stored her sexual beach.

Her vagina contracted and relaxed against Sephia's tongue. She felt herself trembling throughout her entire body. April told herself she would definitely keep in contact with Sephia. She saw no reason to deprive herself of yet another expert tongue. April wasn't sure if her orgasms would ever cease, so she crawled from the table and lay on the warm carpeted floor of Terrell's apartment.

Sephia smiled as she watched April slowly float to the floor. Alcohol and a powerful orgasm usually did that to a person. Sephia smiled across the table at Terrell and his swollen penis. Honey and a pre-cum mixture slowly dripped from the head. She slowly stalked onto the table, kissed the head of Terrell's sex before turning the other way. She had enjoyed the taste and feel of Terrell inside of her mouth, now she wanted to feel him deep within her. He stuffed her mouth and Sephia was eager to see if he could do the same to her Caribbean pussy. Terrell smiled with erotically evil intent. Sephia eased herself backward, position herself nearly perfect to the height of Terrell's dangling sex. Terrell traced her tattoo of the Island of Jamaica, kissing it where a star sat above the word "Ocho Rios".

Terrell reached into the black bag and fished out a condom. He removed the small latex ring from its wrapping and rolled it down his length. Small "feelers" covered the outside of the condom. Terrell smiled to himself about the little surprise. He held his penis by its base and introduced his head to the opening of Sephia's vagina. Sephia hummed from the welcoming heat and snug fit. She contracted her vaginal muscles teasing Terrell's timid approach. Terrell still smirked as he placed his other hand on her lower back, pressed down and slowly pushed himself into her warm warmth. Ticklish electricity shot through Sephia's sex. She cursed in a mixture of English and Pathos. The small ticklers on the condom ignited thousands of individual internal sex nerves. She'd told herself she was ready for the "surprises" he had in store. First Sephia tried bracing herself against Terrell's powerful thrust. She gripped the front of the table and lied to herself with false confidence.

"Me pussy can beat dis!" She said, hoping to motivate herself. She pushed her pelvis back against Terrell's thrust.

"Take that!" She taunted back at Terrell, before quickly realizing that her out bursts only doubled the sensation. Each thrust stole Sephia's voice. And the only thing Sephia thought to do was run. She put her hands on her the floor and slowly clawed at the carpet, pulling herself slowly from Terrell. But as her breast cleared the table's edge Sephia cursed the glorious mistake. Her new angle

Peeping Tom

exposed her hidden spot to the pressure and to the fall of his sexual onslaught. Sephia felt like she had to pee. Terrell held onto Sephia's waist and drove his sex into her with powerful determination. The alcohol had numbed his penis after it had reached its maximum girth and he was determined to punish the women for his inability to climax. Terrell grunted with beastly affirmation. Sweat began covering his face and chest. Terrell alternated the speed and depth of his thrust, but not the force. This was what it was like when you fuck *The Champ*. He reached forward and grabbed a fist full of her braids and roughly forced a wet finger into her puckering asshole.

"Who's *The Champ*?" He grunted at Sephia, while looking at April.

Sephia couldn't speak; only grunts and passionate howls came from her mouth. She hated herself for not remembering his name. He smacked her on her raised ass cheeks and repeated the question.

Yooouuu. Mahn." She spat in defeat.

He pushed further into her; happy with the angle she'd trapped herself in.
"Ty'rell's The Champ'un." She panted, finally remembering the name of the man who had just re-introduced her to her sexual self.

She felt weak and light. She wasn't sure if she could hold herself up, then realized she no longer was supporting herself. Terrell held her onto his penis. She felt her body trembling and involuntarily twitching, and wondered how she missed her own orgasm. She felt her clitoris pulsating and Terrell continued moving further into her.

'Please!" Sephia whispered, unable to finish the request.

But she didn't have to say it; her body had finished the question. She'd had enough.

"Nothing should feel this good." She thought to herself. "Not even sex.

Terrell pushed into her one last time and pushed her forward off his sex. The small ticklers moved against the sensitive surface of her vaginal walls, causing an immediate powerful orgasm. Sephia howled and moaned as the waves of her climax flowed from her like urine. She pushed her hands to her pussy and held it firmly in disbelief. Her sexual muscles twitched and convulsed, leaking white fluid over her tingling finger. She licked her lips, swallowed hard and waited for her breath to return.

Terrell now turned his attention to April, who still lay on the floor. Terrell removed the condom from his penis, tied a knot into the open end and replaced it within new one. April had been laying on her stomach, half sleeping and half watching. Terrell slowly moved over her, gently kissing her on her back. April stirred beneath him, rising slightly to meet his warmth. Terrell slowly ran his fingers along her side. She purred softly. April could feel his breath across her neck. Shivers skipped down her spine. She smiled as Terrell massaged her buttocks. Her brown hole became warm. She grinned. She didn't know his touch would be so soft, so gentle. She could fell feel the tip of the latex covering over

Peeping Tom

his penis move slowly around her vaginal hole. Smiling, April held her eyes closed and bit her lip. She moved her hand beneath her and slowly rubbed her clitoris. She wiggled beneath Terrell's slow grinding weight, happy with the warm buzzing that hummed within her kitty.

Terrell kissed April gently on her exposed neck and moved himself into position. He had often dreamt of this moment. He wanted to make passionate love to her as well as fuck her brains out. Often he'd imagine that the women he was with; was April. Terrell placed his hand over April's raised buttocks. He pushed down on her brown rear exit and lifted forward. The slight pressure caused her to gasp as her vagina's pinkness exposed her sex spot. He slowly began feeding his thick se deep inside of her. She lifted her head and opened her mouth in a silent yell. His penis pushed against the tightness of her recently divorced vagina. He slowly pulled himself halfway from April's, the prickly knobs on the condom massaging, tickling and taunting her inner walls.

She fell flat on the floor, trying to escape the overwhelmingly good feeling. He pushed deep within her again, rotated his hips and slowly, yet powerfully, began his stroke. He placed his legs on the outside of hers forcing her tightness, to be tighter. He gasped harshly and searched for her voice. Terrell's thrusts felt mean-spirited, as they hunted for her g-spot. He often switched positions, moving side-to-side and higher or lower. All the while his stroke and force constant, staying of his breath. She felt new inside of her skin as he moved inside of her. Terrell eased his legs between hers and pulled her up on all fours. April wasn't sure, but he felt like he was growing larger, longer. She could feel more of his moving in her depth. He held her the waist as he pulled and pushed himself into her, the soft latex knobs teasing and taunting April's tightness. She clawed at the plush carpet. Sephia crawled closer to April and caressed the sides of her face. April tried to push backward, hoping to ease the wickedly sweet feeling, but she was in her place. Terrell kissed the small of her back, and then continued his sex-assault. April mumbled a prayer for her orgasm to rescue her, to end this. Terrell began panting a rough sounding cadence, increasing his force and tempo.

"Say it!" Terrell grunted, "Say it. I'm *The Champ*."

April hated those words. The truth was so hard to accept. April knew she'd agree to anything to be done with this man and his dick. She shook her head in affirmation. She couldn't speak. Her mouth felt dangerously dry. He repeated his demand, emphasizing each word with an accompanying powerful thrust.

"Yoooouuuu.. *The Champ*!" She finally spat.

A sour light-headedness swarmed April. Queasy warmth tiptoed through her ebony thighs. She felt her eyes slowly roll upward into her head, as her orgasm made its fashionably late arrival. Her legs stiffened and she dropped lower to the floor. Her orgasm moved from her stomach and outward in waves throughout her entire body. She softly howled as her body began relaxing against her orgasm. Terrell slowed his pace, finally pulling from April. Terrell crawled between the two women and began stroking his stiff penis. Each of the women watched him wrestle with his sex. Terrell moaned and buckled as he moved his hand roughly

Peeping Tom

over his own sensitive areas. April ran her hands over his chest and nestled close to him. She cheered his deliberate strokes. He bit his lips and twisted the head of his penis gently. The sensation had immediate results. He felt his orgasm rushing to the head of his rod.

"Dayum!" He barked, as hot black life erupted from his penis. Terrell bucked and contracted, massaging more and more of his sperm from his body. April watched in amazement as more and more of the white, hot liquid spewed from him. She'd never watched a man masturbate and the sight of Terrell pleasing himself made her immediately jealous of his hand. Terrell panted softly as his orgasm eased to a slow pulsation. April nestled close to Terrell's heat. She closed her eyes and surrendered to sleep.

April felt a little pressure on her chest, lightly shaking her awake. She fought through the grogginess to see Terrell standing over her; his left foot between her breasts. He smiled down at her, naked except for a large championship belt around his waist.

"Told you I was *The Champ*!" He said, smiling down at her. Arms over his head in a muscle man pose. April playfully pushed his foot away and returned to sleep.

"You talk a lotta shit." She sang, as the feeling of deep; well-sexed, drunken sleep captured her.

"You talk a lotta shit." She sang, as the feeling of deep; well-sexed, drunken sleep captured her.

Yeah, *The Champ* is one of my favorite people to

SexPressions

watch. Although he's slowing down some, he moved in with a pretty faced, big-booty sister. He still performs for me, I saw him at the deli one day and we struck up a conversation. He told me he was "in love" and all that jazz. But she wants to "take it slow." I felt like telling him, "He was a fool." That he should keep running those fine women in and out of his apartment, so I can continue to re-live my young glory days. Re-live the days when I was a whole man, with two legs that pushed me high into the sky. Re-live the days when I was *The Champ*" and women lined up to be knocked fucking silly by me. Re-live the days before a bullet hit my spine and cursed me to this wheelchair. But instead, I swallowed my pride, froze my tears and listened to the young man talk about the new love of his life. I shook his hand and told him, "I'd see him around." Because I would. I'm a Peeping Tom.

HABITUAL SECRETS

Forward

Kizzy read the cabdriver's eyes through the rearview mirror and answered her gaze with a smile. *Some bitches have all the luck,* those eyes said. Here she was with two men when most sisters can't seem to find one. Darryl and Mikhail were too good to be true. Kizzy met them at the bar near her hotel, and seeing as how she couldn't choose between the two of them, she decided to have them both. It didn't take much to convince them either. The car pulled in front of the hotel just as Kizzy tucked both men's penises back into their now too small trousers.

"Down boys!" Kizzy whispered, giving both men a light pat on their third legs. "Be nice and pay the fare." Kizzy said as she crawled over Darryl's lap.

Kizzy wore an electric green g-string that allowed her labia to peek out from under her too-short skirt. She poked her head back into the cab and smiled.

"And please leave a nice tip for the driver." The men fought amongst themselves to see who could pay first.

"You go girl!" The driver said to Kizzy in a *wish-I-*

SexPressions

were-you voice.

"You go girl indeed." Kizzy thought to herself as she walked ahead into the hotel.

Kizzy could hardly contain her lust. Both men groped and fondled her in the snug confines of the elevator. Darryl's touch was tender and wise. He pressed against her from behind, sneaking hot kisses onto her neck. Mikhail was deliberate and thorough. He sucked curtly on Kizzy's heaving breast, while exploring the territories between her chocolate thighs. Kizzy praised and cursed the arrival of her floor. Her orgasm screamed to be released. Kizzy bit down on her lip to stop it from quivering. The three of them collected themselves, as the elevator doors opened and proceeded to the room. Kizzy was glad her room was close to the elevator. The ride up had taken her to the brink. She unlocked the door and turned to wink at the eager men. Kizzy pushed through the door and felt a pair of strong arms secure her waist. It was Mikhail. His hands went quickly to work. He searched over her body for weaknesses, a chink in her brown armor. He poked, licked, and rubbed. He guided Kizzy toward the large waterbed in the center of the room. He had her bend forward at the waist and kissed her on her thick elevated cheeks. Kizzy giggled as Mikhail's breath tickled the area around her tight hole. She inhaled hard and allowed her legs to give slightly. Another pair of hands went quickly to work, as Darryl began removing her blouse and bra.

Kizzy surrendered to her captors. Her short thick legs never touched the floor as Darryl held her close to him. Kizzy was dark toned, but still she shone in the room's semi-darkness. Darryl rolled her stiff nipples between his fingers.

Habitual Secrets

Darryl, the lighter of the two men, was tall and muscular. His tender touch was deceiving. Kizzy moaned at the feeling that the two tongues and four hands gave to her body. The sensation confused her body with sexual insanity.

Kizzy crawled from between the men and told them both to undress. It was time she took control of the evening. She lay back as both men quickly disrobed, exposing themselves in the darkness. She could easily make out their shapes and sizes. Mikhail's slender build gave no clue to the powerful looking muscle that stood out, at least ten inches, from his body and curved to the left. Darryl on the other hand, was clearly thicker but shorter by an inch or so. Kizzy smiled as her holes leaked sexual cream as she envisioned being filled by these two men.

Kizzy crawled forward and grabbed both men by the base of their dicks. She used her hands to stroke the lengths of their shafts. Both men exhaled and groaned. Starting with Mikhail, Kizzy licked each man's swollen head. The taste of pre sex-cum, danced across Kizzy's tongue, it was warm, salty, and undeniable The taste alone made her give him her full attention. Kizzy slowly inhaled his full length, and Mikhail hummed in delight. It was rare for him to receive oral sex and the unfamiliar sensation caused his knees to buckle slightly. He held onto Kizzy's shoulders for support. His loins filled with an orgasmic riot. Mikhail held the back of Kizzy's head and slowly made love to her mouth. The feeling was too good to be called anything else but love. Kizzy rubbed from rear to front, trying to coax the black life from Mikhail's sack. Mikhail shook in terrific surprise as Darryl watched in awe, knowing he was next. Kizzy felt the quakes that stirred within Mikhail. She grabbed Mikhail's

SexPressions

slim ass cheeks and held him deep within her mouth. She sucked deeper, longer and stronger. Mikhail exhaled and balled his fist in denial, as the first wave engulfed him with force. Kizzy used her free hand and pumped the salty sweetness into her throat. Mikhail whimpered in sexual defeat. The tiger in him was now a kitten. She pushed him away and grinned in the darkness at Darryl. Now that she had satisfied her mouth, she wanted her most intimate place filled.

Kizzy grabbed Darryl's hand and pulled him atop of her. Darryl was breathing hard, and he held the scent of rich mahogany and refined ebony; strong smooth and black. Darryl kissed her neck; his tongue softly introduced itself to her sensitive skin. Kizzy exhaled through clenched teeth. She ran her hands over his back, urging Darryl to extinguish her deep fire. Darryl felt Kizzy grinding slowly under him. He took his cue and slowly moved his hips between hers. He gradually drew more of her cream from her, turning her morning dew into a steady stream. Kizzy bit down on his neck and sucked harshly on his chest. She hoped he'd have a hicky or two in the morning.

"Now!" Kizzy whispered, not wanting to wait another second. Darryl waved his latex-covered sex over her clitoris as if it was a magician's wand, and Kizzy was ready for the magic. She pushed a deep and heavy moan from her throat. The tenderness Darryl displayed made Kizzy cringe. Even the pain was full of pleasure. She kissed Darryl on the lips, caressing his face, before slapping him spitefully on his ass. He was her stallion; and she, his jockey. Darryl increased his pace and Kizzy hung on for the ride. With each powerful

Habitual Secrets

stroke, he drove deeper into Kizzy. He pushed her walls wider and wider. Darryl's moans of passion became grunts of domination. Kizzy heard him growl, "Bitch" into her ear. Her body screamed in agreement. Another slap rippled through Darryl and into her. A sexual revolution began between Kizzy's thighs. The savages had crashed her gates. She whispered a scream to the suffocating darkness, and the orgasm ambushed her. Kizzy dug her nails hard into Darryl's ass and tender back. The ensuing waterfall soaked them both in Kizzy's release. Darryl thundered to an orgasm, exploding deep from his loins. The stallion in Darryl's spirit slowed to a gallop, then a trot, before stopping. Mikhail crawled into the bed and slid into Kizzy's defeated warmth before she could recover. For the rest of the night the three continued. Two on one; one on one; and even a few solo sessions. Kizzy lay between the two prone, sleeping bodies; and smiled the smile of a conqueror.

An alarm blared off in the distant land of Awake ness snatching Sister Kizzy Lee Carter from her deep slumber. She sat up slowly. Her two vibrators lay askew, next to her in the quiet conservative bed. Kizzy quickly tapped the "off button, hushing the alarm before the other nuns were awaken by its sound. She packed away her two "lovers" and changed her soaked sheets. Promising she'd pray hard for restraint from her lust after breakfast, she dashed off to the shower.

And so started her first day at the convent.

HARDCORE CRIMINALS

Dina sat wiggling her legs trying her best to hide the fact that she'd counted the same stack of money three times. The robbery had gone as they'd planned. Well close to how they planned. For starters, they hadn't planned on taking a hostage, and Dina damned sure hadn't planned on being so horny. The excitement of the robbery had gotten her hormones in an uproar. She looked over at the bank guard they'd taken hostage and wondered how long it had been since he'd had sex.

"Ninety-five, ninety-sex," Dina said trying to return to the business at hand, "Ninety-seven, ninety-eight, ninety-nine, one horny!"

Dina looked over at the hostage and fought off the heat that rose deep within her. Maybe it was that she was nervous, or that he was good looking, hell it could even be the fact that she hadn't had a man between her legs in some time, whatever the case, the result was a body in heat. Dina squirmed in her chair as the thought of Duke's last night with her. Her wrist still tingled from being tied to the pole in the basement. Dina glanced over at the man tied in the comer and knew that the reason she couldn't concentrate was the

SexPressions

long, thick lump that she could see lying against his leg. Damn, she thought, if only she could touch it. Then she would be okay.

"Will you stop looking at him and count the money!" Pooh said, pulling Dina back to reality. "He ain't going no where, and you making me nervous."

Dina crossed her legs and tried again to suppress the warmth that grew in her brown sexual oven. She was horny. Really horny, and no amount of money could change that.

"So how long do we have to be here?" Dina asked Pooh and Evelyn. "Because I'm horny as hell!" Dina She said, rubbing her stomach.

Pooh and Evelyn laughed aloud, both shaking their head.

"Damn", Dina thought to herself. "I meant hungry." She giggled, knowing that she only meant to keep being horny to herself.

"So that's why you keep looking at him." Evelyn said still laughing. "Shit I thought it was just me. He is fine ass hell."

The three women turned their heads to look at the man they'd taken as a hostage. He was average height, with a slender athletic build. His lips were thick and soft looking. The kind of lips most men called "DSL's" or *Dick Sucking Lips*, while most women called them very kissable. And if the bulge in his pants was any indication, he wasn't hung

Hardcore Criminals

like a horse but a well-hung donkey wasn't bad either.

"Well?" Dina asked. Half pleading; half demanding.

"I'm cool with it." A deep voice came softly from across the room. The three women turned to look at each other, before turning back to look at their hostage.

"All I ask is that ya'll leave the handcuffs and the blindfold on." The hostage said, tongue slipping from his mouth and covering his lips with an even, light coat of saliva.

"I'm first!" Dina said, as she shot from her chair. Pooh and Evelyn turned their chairs to face the show, as Dina moved slowly across the room.

Dina wasn't tall but she had long legs. Her shapely ass burned with each step. She stopped in front of the man. Fear moistened her panties as a slight grin appeared on her face. Her eyes ran over him, inch by inch. His hands were behind his back and secured to the bottom of the chair, causing his chest to push further out. Dina straddled him gingerly. The faint smell of aftershave ran from her nose, to her nipples, then down between her quivering thighs. The hostage groaned softly as he accepted her weight. He wiggled beneath her, the bulge fitting neatly between Dina buttocks. Dina She wrapped her hands behind his head and leaned in to kiss his lips. Instinctively, the hostage raised his head to meet Dina's mouth. His lips were warm. He kissed softly on her lower lip, before holding it easily between his teeth. Soft pants paraded from Dina's throat as he began kissing her chin. He placed three cotton-soft kisses just under her mouth before returning to her lips.

SexPressions

"The only thing better than a man with a big dick," Pooh whispered loudly, "Is a man with a big dick who can kiss!"

"Thank you!" The hostage laughed, his voice thundering sweetly from within him.

He continued placing delicate kisses over Dina's mouth before slowly moving to her neck. Dina threw her head back and exhaled loudly. She held onto the back of the chair, fearful that she'd fall backward. The Hostage kissed and sucked just under Dina's jaw line. She giggled in ecstasy as his tongue landed against her sensitive area. Dina thought of it as one of her "perfume places". There were four of them really, both wrist and just below the each ear. Most men either didn't know or didn't care about the spots, but the Hostage did.

Dina closed her eyes as a warm lightheadedness swept over her. Soft shivers moved down her back. She hadn't remembered when she began, but she slowly rotated her hips, her swollen clitoris pushing against her labia, which pushed against her silk panties. Finally, and mercifully, the Hostage's lips found their way to Dina's deep cleavage. He playfully allowed his tongue to dart between kisses at her soft brown canvass. The Hostage kissed the exposed area around Dina's her cleavage. Dina cursed herself for wearing a bra. She stood, letting her full breast sit in front of him and quickly removed her shirt and bra. She/He they both moaned as his lips met her now hot breast. The Hostage took each of Dina's nipples into his mouth. One "kiss and suck" after another. He ran his tongue over

Hardcore Criminals

her breast, pulling a slow building orgasm with it.

"What does your tattoo say?" He asked, as he drew circles over the raised area just above her right nipple.

"Ms. Bitch." Dina moaned, with "*how'd he know*" curiosity running through her.

Dina pulled his head deep into her breast. The Hostage sucked hard. Dina's heart rate quickened. Pumping more hot blood through her already overheated body. She bit down on her lip and sucked curtly. Her hips moved to the rhythm of his kisses. Slow and long as first; then quick, short and tender. Dina's soaked panties began to bunch, and with each movement, pressed firmly against her pearl tongue. Her hand trembled with anticipation of her impending orgasm. The Hostage rolled his lips beneath her. His thickness lay hard and throbbing beneath under her.

"Tell me what your friends are doing." The Hostage said, re-alerting Dina to the two women sitting behind her with their hands stuffed down their pants.

"Some hardcore criminals we are." Dina thought as she tried to describe the scene.

I think they're fingering themselves." She panted. Each word followed by a harsh exhale of breath.

Dina let her head fall forward and rest on the Hostage's shoulder and watched as her mends worked themselves into frenzy. Pooh's hand was hidden from the wrist down and moved slowly. While Evelyn's fingers were the only part tucked away, they moved at a more frantic

SexPressions

pace.

"Which one of them is squeaking?" The Hostage asked, his voice in deep heavy moans.

"Evelyn!" Dina sang.

"Good! She can go next."

The Hostage arched his back and pushed his pelvis higher into Dina's grind. Dina she was wearing thin cotton sweat pants, and now they too were soaked in the front. She bit down into his shoulder and rocked back and forth along the Hostage's covered penis. Dina's hand shook as her orgasm's preview slammed her eyes shut.

"Yeah. Just like that." The Hostage said.

His voice boomed softly against her ear, before he kissed her on the upper portion of her breasts. Pooh's moans joined Evelyn's squeaky pants to back up Dina's musical exhales.

Finally Dina could no longer stand the *sex*pense. She stood over the Hostage, her chest rising and falling with giddy pleasure, and pushed her pants to her ankles and stepped free. A thick, warm creamy wetness caused her pubic hair to clump together. Dina gathered her balance and slowly began to undress the Hostage. She tried to unbutton his shirt, but her trembling hands and pleading sex made the task nearly impossible. Dina grabbed the Hostage's uniform shirt and ripped it open, sending buttons and ecstasy flying across the room. And with that a rush swept over Dina her. She ripped his undershirt open; exposing his thin sculpted chest. She pushed the edge of his tattered shirt as far down his arms as it would go. Dina let her hunger take over. She greedily ran her tongue over the Hostage's chest, pausing only long enough to tease his nipples. She playfully tugged on each with her teeth, before she rolled them between her lips. The Hostage hummed in pleasure with each twinge of tenderly torturous pain. He began to squirm beneath Dina in an attempt to straighten himself. Dina placed her hand on his chest to calm him, while trailing kiss after squirm-inducing kiss down to his quivering abdomen. Her own trembling had been passed on to the Hostage. She drew elaborate designs on his stomach with her tongue. The Hostage twitched underneath her, as if trying to dodge her tongue. Dina watched as his face became tense then relaxed under the blindfold. While her tongue assaulted his stomach, Dina allowed her hands to undo his belt and unfastened his pants. The Hostage lifted himself slightly as Dina tugged at his pants. And just as the waist band moved past his large blackness sprung forward like an erotic slinky. Pre-cum glistened on the purplish, swollen head of the hostage's penis, causing Dina and the other women to salivate. Dina held the Hostage's full erect penis in her grasp. It was hot within her palm. Although Dina wasn't good with measurements, she guessed the Hostage pushed a full nine inches of thick pleasure into the air. Dina squatted in front of him and kissed the tip of his sex. The salty, musky taste of his length combined with the faint smell of Egyptian musk body oil made Dina feel warm allover. She softly sucked at the head, still holding his girth. She slowly and softly stroked him guiding him inch by inch into her mouth.

Dina lost herself in the Hostage's moans, not noticing Evelyn, standing naked over them. Dina didn't look up as

SexPressions

Evelyn placed one foot on the side of the chair and stepped up, placing the other foot on the back of the chair. Evelyn looked down at Dina, who by now had the Hostage's fullness, deep within her mouth. The Hostage tossed his head back, cursing softly in bound appreciation. Evelyn leaned forward, bracing herself against the wall behind them with one hand, while using the other to guide the Hostage's face closer to her honey pot. Evelyn was glad the Hostage wasn't bald as she held onto a fistful of his hair. Without a second thought the Hostage began slowly enticing and teasing Evelyn's passion. His tongue was wide and it covered her entire swollen vaginal area, as it passed over. He used a flick of the tip to further drive Evelyn wild. The Hostage sucked and kissed at the cream that covered her pubic hairs and inner thigh. Soon his face was covered in her glaze as her body quickly neared another orgasm. The Hostage's thick tongue dove deep into Evelyn's warmth. Evelyn She moaned harshly and pushed against the wall as the Hostage quickly licked her into an explosively erotic frenzy. Evelyn nearly lost her balance as her orgasm shook her, causing her to close her eyes and inhale deeply. She held the Hostage's head deeply into her plush ness. Just as the last of her waves swept through her body, Evelyn felt/heard heard the Hostage hum and moan rapidly. She looked down and saw Dina's head moving in quick unison with her quick moving hand.

The hostage tossed his head back as his body locked. Dina moved her head in time for Evelyn to watch the fountain of hot life spew from the Hostage's his large blackness.

Dina looked up to her friend, as hot jism ran over her

hand. The Hostage pumped upward into Dina's hand, his still hard erection, twitching from the orgasmic sensitivity. Dina watched Evelyn step down, before again straddling the Hostage, slowly guiding herself over and onto his still throbbing inches.

"Damn!" The Hostage moaned loudly, voice rippling with dominated pleasure. "There you go Mssss B-B-bitch!" He hissed as Dina; slowly at first, moved back and forth.

The Hostage moved his hips upward, pushing deeper into Dina. A small fire quickly turned into an inferno as Dina placed her leg, bent at the knee, on each side of the Hostage and drove him deeper still. His thickness pushed against her walls. Although she felt her heart pounding within her chest, Dina couldn't breathe. She held onto the Hostage's neck and pimped for her life. Dina's inner thighs began twitching rebelliously as her orgasm swirled deep within her, growing more and more wild. Dina's breath finally returned in the form of a scream, as her orgasm forced her walls to clamp tightly around the Hostage's penis. The force of her orgasm shook Dina. She slumped forward; sucked and bit, sucking and biting teasingly into the Hostage's shoulder. Dina heard the Hostage coaching her, still thrusting, rebellious hips.

"Yeah Ms. Bitch! There you go." He whispered into her ear.

Dina panted hard, noticing the slight trembling that flowed through her.

"You heard the man," Evelyn's voice pushed through

SexPressions

Dina's sexually clouded head. "I'm next!" Dina turned her head as Evelyn's a smile blossomed across her Evelyn's face.

Dina slinked away from the Hostage. Sexual exhaustion warmed her body. She smiled smirked as Evelyn passed her. Evelyn winked at Pooh and Dina playfully dangling the key to the handcuffs. Evelyn stood in front of the Hostage and placed her hands above her voluptuous hips.

"Are you going to be a good boy while I undo these handcuffs?" She asked, as she leaned close to the Hostage's face. The Hostage licked his thick lips, savoring the heavy taste of Evelyn's sex fluid.

"Only if I can be a bad boy when you put them back on." Cocking his head to the left, the Hostage smiled. His lips thinned slightly at the edges. Evelyn's nipples grew hard and rigid from the memory of those lips and his tongue.

"You don't mind if I take my shoes and pants off, do you?" The Hostage asked, shifting his legs so that his shoes fell off.

"Let me help." Pooh whispered, moving in closer.

Evelyn moved to the rear of the chair to remove the handcuffs. As she unlocked the first cuff, the Hostage pulled his arm free of his tattered shirt and then shook his other arm free once Evelyn removed that cuff. He stood in front of Pooh and Evelyn; his body tight and covered in sweat from sex. Pooh reached forward and ran her hand over his heaving abdomen. Humming intently as her hand dropped past his six individual sections. She let her hand linger on his mid section, while walking around him. Smacking the Hostage stingingly hard, she leaned in and softly placed his ear between her lips.

"I hope you have enough for me!" Pooh purred, running her hands along the Hostage's side and down to his still firm erection.

The Hostage nodded his head in affirmation and placed his hands in front of him.

"Not so tight this time." He said, stepping free of his pants and underwear that were now bunched at his ankles.

Evelyn secured the restraints and led the Hostage toward the table. Pooh trailed behind them, her hands flowing over the Hostage's chest, stomach, and hips. The Hostage slowed his stride, causing Pooh to press closely against his backside. Evelyn turned as she reached the table, and came face to face with the Hostage. She stared at his lips. She began to tingle with the thought of their juices. Evelyn slowly ran her fingers over the Hostage's plush puckers before kissing him softly on his upper lip. The Hostage moaned softly as he pulled Evelyn's her lower lip over his own. Evelyn rolled her head as the Hostage kissed her chest, chin and the front of her throat. The soft, sweet smell of Evelyn's skin brushed over his nose. The Hostage brought his hands high and softly massaged Evelyn's full C-cup breasts, while she slowly stroked him back to his full length. Pooh massaged the Hostage's shoulders; planting tender pecks on the back of his neck. Her tongue darted

SexPressions

quickly assaulting his sensitive area. The Hostage's nipples began to grow firm; poking out from his chest, as the two women teased and taunted his electrified body. Evelyn ran her free hand over his chest, trapping his stiff nipple, gingerly, between her fingers. The Hostage fought back moans as he absorbed the intense heat Evelyn's body gave off. He continued fondling her breast, guiding her back onto the table. Slowly guiding her to lay down the Hostage kissed and rubbed lower over Evelyn's quivering skin. Evelyn smiled as she lay back onto the table. She released the Hostage's now throbbing, blackness, realizing that it wouldn't grow any further. She caressed the Hostage's head as he kissed and tickled her breast. Evelyn let her legs fall open in ravenous anticipation, welcoming the Hostage's full weight. The heat of her crotch was intense against his sculpted abdomen. Moisture quickly turned to wetness, as Evelyn began grinding beneath the Hostage. He was hard and strong hovering above her. Evelyn looked at the Hostage's sex and wished she were the one who were bound and blindfolded. Evelyn closed her eyes and let herself slip deeper into ecstasy. Her clitoris slowly began to swell and press forward from her thick vaginal petals. Evelyn could hardly stand the attention. Her body began to feel hot and cold. She shivered began to shiver and sweat. Evelyn wondered if she were coming down with something, as the Hostage rose from her and ran his hands over her body. She tossed her hands over her head, and could feel the feeling of moans gathering at the back of her throat, before seeping from between her lips. The Hostage began to massage the tender area of her sex, tickling and rubbing at Evelyn's ever-increasing passion. A wicked grin covered his face as she moved her body to the rhythm of his fingers. The Hostage could feel himself growing thicker and slightly longer until a soft throb signaled his eagerness. He pulled Evelyn closer to the edge of the table, giving him the perfect angle to maximize his sexual girth. He smiled as he slowly introduced "himself' to Evelyn with small circular motions. Evelyn's Her eyes were cemented shut. A tiny squeak danced from her lips. The Hostage began to smile, as he slowly entered Evelyn's warmth. She was tight, yet comforting. The Hostage held her thighs and slowly moved half of himself into her. He entered and exited Evelyn with an upward angle, adding pressure to her very sensitive black pearl. Evelyn opened her mouth to speak, or scream. Hell, she would have settled for a whistle, but nothing came. The Hostage, still only using his first few inches, found a rhythm. It was fast and powerful. With each stroke, he was drawn deeper into Evelyn. Unable to see the effects of his efforts, and if he could; the Hostage would've seen Evelyn biting her lip and holding her large breast as they bounced and jiggled. He moved Evelyn's legs up, resting them on his chest and shoulders. Then pulled Evelyn in place; holding her back into him. The softness of her thighs added a plush increase to the tightness of Evelyn's his warmth. Evelyn squeaked in approval. Each thrust and pump pushed her closer to the edge. The Hostage inched his way closer to her sensitive nerve endings, before finally touching them, then passing them altogether.

Evelyn's fingertips tingled with *sex*citement. She peeked and watched the Hostage push himself deeper into her. He was covered in sweat and his body was aglow with the moisture. Evelyn's heart began pounding harder, threatening to explode. She moaned and squeaked from the feel of the Hostage's movements within her. She was still weak from his tongue and now had no chance against his

SexPressions

full black sex. Evelyn held the sides of the table as the Hostage held her legs, by the ankles, out in front of him. Evelyn could feel the added friction her thighs and buttocks caused. She wanted to scream, but suppressed it. The Hostage continued to push further into her. Soon her squeals turned to screams.

"Damn Bitch!" Pooh said, waiting her turn.

Pooh slapped the Hostage's sweat covered ass cheeks, before turning her attention back to her friend.

"Take this dick!" The Hostage grunted, as he held her legs straight out before him.

He bit down on his lip and thrust, harder and deeper, into Evelyn with determination. Evelyn began to tremble. She clung to her heavy breast with one hand and the table with the other. He pumped at a downward angle, adding more pressure. The Hostage began to grow stiff signaling his own orgasm. Evelyn tried to hold back her squeak-laced moans she felt a knot growing in her belly. Then she felt something in her "pop". A warm lightheaded feeling swept over her as her orgasm froze her body. The Hostage continued pumping deep into her. She softly squeaked as he slowed his pace, before stopping completely. The Hostage pulled himself from within Evelyn, leaving her to her own sexual aftershocks.

"And then there was Pooh!" Pooh said as she hugged the Hostage from behind.

She gingerly wrapped her hands around the Hostage's

hardness, still sticky with Evelyn's juices. Pooh licked her fingers and then the Hostage's ear. The Hostage allowed Pooh to pull his head in her direction. She closed her eyes and let her hands be her vision. She felt how brown he was; strong and lean. The Hostage stood to his full height, absorbing Pooh's touch. Her small breast pressed against his back. The coolness of her nipple ring was the only blemish he could feel. Pooh licked her way down his neck. The Hostage bent forward at the waist, allowing Pooh to plant kisses along his spine. Still holding the Hostage's sex, Pooh slowly began to stroke his full length. A few moans dropped from the Hostage's mouth. He held back on Evelyn, but he decided to give Pooh all he had left.

Pooh could feel the brown firm flesh between her hands stiffen.

"This is what a real dick feels like." Pooh thought to herself.

The Hostage slowly turned to face Pooh, who now was on her knees. She lightly kissed the head of the Hostage's black penis. The combined taste of Evelyn's juices and the Hostage's tart musk, made the area between her smooth thighs grow from luke warm to scalding hot. The Hostage ran his fingers through Pooh's short locks, as the tender sensation of her lips greeted him. He spread his legs apart, accepting the soft warm feeling that began to engulf his head. Pooh ran one hand between his thighs and roughly kneaded his tight buttocks. The Hostage tossed his head back, his body confused by the two different sexual assaults; soft tender warmth in the front and rough hard attention in the rear. He smiled beneath the blindfold. He slowly rotated

SexPressions

his hips, pumping deeper into Pooh's welcoming mouth. Pooh used her tongue to massage the hard long shaft. She moaned as the Hostage pushed another inch over her tongue. Her small breast lightly brushed against the Hostage's legs. Her nipples grew hard and hot, igniting the rest of her sexually flammable body. The kindling that was her vagina soon caught fire. And she wanted the fire within her to burn wild, not to ever be extinguished. She slowly removed the Hostage's member from her mouth, eager to have him it deep within inside her. The Hostage's length fell from Pooh's lips with a forceful pop. He chuckled gently, before stroking Pooh's soft coif. Pooh stood before the Hostage clad in nothing but her panties and bad intentions.

"Fuck me!" She ordered in a commanding whisper.

The Hostage shook his head and stretched his arms out to Pooh.

"Where's the wall?" He asked, penis standing from his body like an erotic directional finder. "His North Pole." He thought as Pooh took his hands and led him to the wall.

Pooh had a small frame, but it was full to its sexual limits. Ample hips, full B-cupped breast, and slender legs and waist. The Hostage walked forward and placed his hands on Pooh's waist.

Pooh licked her lips as the Hostage closed the space between them. Although he wasn't big, he appeared strong. Easily strong enough to...

The Hostage lifted Pooh completing her thought. Pooh

Hardcore Criminals

wrapped her legs around his waist. He could feel her moisture, as he slowly slid her down over the top of his penis' head. Pooh used one hand to guide him into her, while the other hand held on to him. Pooh held on for dear life and pleasure. The Hostage wiggled his hips, as her vertical lips opened slowly to accept him. Each of them gasped/moaned as hot erotica collided with powerful black sexuality. The Hostage, once inside, pushed his full length deep into Pooh. Pooh was breathless. If asked (and she was later when she told the story to her cellmate) she'd have said she was choking. The Hostage rotated his hips with powerful intent, and slowly began bouncing Pooh atop his length. Finally after what Pooh thought to be an eternity, words sprang from her mouth.

"Shit!" She muttered, breathing hard before beginning a tirade of cursing. The Hostage stood on his tiptoes and held Pooh's hand full sized ass cheeks and he pushed deeper. Pooh's legs locked behind him. She was quivering uncontrollably. She felt the Hostage's blackness push directly against her hidden release point. Her clitoris, swollen and pulsating, gave away her secrets as it was greeted time and time again. Pooh felt thirsty and starved. She dug her nails into the Hostage's back. She couldn't let go, but she would; she promised herself. Pooh leaned her head forward and sucked the Hostage's neck in resistance. But like her two friends, it was a stroke or two too late. The Hostage let Pooh fall back into the wall for support. He turned his short strokes into long, powerful menacing strokes. The Hostage began grunting before and after each thrust. Sweat made his brown skin shine. Pooh began felt a tingling, generating from her small ass. Then the feeling soon overtook her entire body. The erupting orgasm moved

SexPressions

around her whole body. By now Evelyn and Dina had gained control of themselves, and had begun watching the show. The captive Hostage verses the small Pooh. The Hostage's muscles rippled under his skin as he continued pushing deeper into Pooh. Her tingling became moans accompanied by trembling.

"Please... pah pah please." She begged/demanded.

The Hostage soon began to tremble. The orgasm had been building in his loins and he meant to have it released, but not until he defeated his last captor. Pooh bit her lips as a sensation of flying swept over her. Pooh's body locked around the Hostage and she clung to him while powerful waves of pleasure washed over her. Pooh panted softly as the Hostage continued to push. She seemed to lose control of herself. She told her eyes to open and her fingers moved. She commanded her tongue to moisten her lips and her eyes opened. And the only person she had to blame was their Hostage. Her Hostage. Pooh let the electric sensation run over her, as the Hostage grunted in her ear. She felt him grow terribly hard before giving in. The Hostage's knees buckled and his entire body shuddered. The Hostage slowly pumped sexual release into Pooh. Soon his strength was drained and he slowly lowered Pooh to the floor. His muscular sculpted chest heaved. A tight smile grew across his face. The Hostage reached to remove his blindfold to survey his work.

"Touch it and I'll kill you!" It was Dina. "You fine and all, but this is business."

The Hostage could feel the pistol in close vicinity to

his head. No need to be a hero.

"Tie him back up!" Dina said to Evelyn, who was still naked.

The Hostage shook his head in defeat.

"Had to give it a try." He thought to himself. "Even if it didn't work."

MY TWO WIVES

    Before I begin, I believe I should tell you how I came to live with Suzy and Sara. I'd bought a condominium downtown, and due to my constant traveling, I decided to sublet. No point in paying full price for a place I was only staying in half the time. Seeing as how I really wasn't pressed for the money, it didn't really matter who my roommates were. I just decided on the first person who met the criteria, which I made into a short list. First the person should be tidy. Secondly, the person should have a job and lastly, the person should have *a job and be tidy.* I didn't think that I was asking for too much. So when the doorman called and told me I had a visitor; I hoped this would be what, or who I was looking for. I quickly gave the place a good last minute look over and moved to answer the door. I even had my salesman's pitch ready. First, I'd talk about the great view of the Sear's Tower, then the finer points of the building. I really wanted to put my best foot forward. I made sure the place was presentable, and then I gave myself a last minute inspection. I wore a pair of heavily starched khaki pants, with a white linen shirt, and a pair of shined Kenneth Cole shoes and matching belt. An unsuspecting knock jolted me from my impromptu inspection. I quickly made my way across the living room to the door, before the second knock ended. The first sight I was greeted with was the back of a tall, beautiful, black Amazon woman. I tried to gain my composure before she turned around. The woman was calling to someone down the hall, her friend I assumed (really I hoped she wasn't calling a man), and hadn't taken noticed of me. She turned, expecting the door to be closed and was surprised to find me gawking at her.

"Hi. I'm Sara West." Her smile was intoxicating. "This is the place for rent, right?" She asked, half expecting a negative response.

My mind told me to quickly answer before she believed I was deaf, blind, or plain ole' dumb.
"Breasts!" I blurted, ushering her in, trying to act as if I didn't notice the slip. She emitted the cutest giggle softly to herself, before saving me from having to explain.

"Don't worry about it. As hard as I work to look like this, I'm glad somebody notices them."

She gave her breast a small upward mock adjustment and walked in. Sara was sexuality in motion. She had a sassy caramel complexion. I sized her at close to six feet; two or three inches tall, giving her an easy five or six inches over me. And that was not including her heels. If her intent was to intimidate me, then she'd accomplished her mission. Her breasts were large, without being overwhelming. She had two thick lips that seemed to pucker automatically. Her dress was slightly provocative. Her conservative blouse and skirt allowed more than enough of her body to peek out and tempt me into more than I'd care to share now. As I watched her go by, I wondered what made me wish I hadn't been wearing pants that didn't highlight my unexpected

My Two Wives

erection. I would've let her stay for free had she asked. But before I could propose, a soft sugary voice, snapped me back from my world wind wedding and honeymoon.

"Well this is a nice building." A very voluptuous, conservatively dressed, dark skinned woman said. Her sex appeal came from a sense of cute innocence. A friendliness, that gave one a warm hugs, drifted from her smile. She had the appeal of a virgin. "*Quietly Sexy*" is the term I'd like to use to describe her.

"Thank You." I answered doubly ashamed of the new stiffness between my legs. I showed her in, quickly trying to suppress my sexual thoughts with mental mood killing snapshots. I allowed them to look around. The place would do a better job of convincing them than I could. Plus it would be hard to convince them that the drooling and staring would end once they moved in. And although I'd already decided they could stay if they liked the place, I still gave them my sales pitch. "I'm Gabriel Harris." I started, using what I hoped was my million-dollar smile. I started in with finer points when Suzy; the sweet looking of the two, asked about the price. Staring dumb- founded into her innocent face, I realized I hadn't settled on a price. And just as I decided on a course of action, Sara stepped in.

"Let's negotiate over wine and dinner." she said, smile out shining mine.

"Okay." I agreed, still assuming I had the upper hand.

Smiles were then exchanged between the two women, and after a very brief conference dinner of Mexican take-out

SexPressions

and tequila, we began our talks. Well it was more like, they talked and I listened in a goofy erotic state of amazement. The two women executed a very well performed (although later I learned they just had a knack for togetherness) speech. They told me about their jobs; Suzy was a photographer and Sara was District Manager of something-or-other. They told me how they were best friends from birth, literally.

"We were actually switched in the hospital." Sara began. She walked; or at least I believed she did, as she continued. The story's delivery had the feeling of one that had been told and retold countless times.

"And after the switch was discovered, our folks just kept in touch." Suzy finished before delicately placing rice in her mouth; past her tender lips. It was at that moment, that I realized my erection had been replaced with a soft throbbing and warm stickiness on my thigh. I also noticed two other things while I sat there staring. First; my virgin-for-too-long-to-like-it ass was sitting across from my two new, very sexy; very beautiful roommates, with a fresh cum stain in my pants; and second, I just blurted out the first price my slightly-tipsy brain, but very drunk lips could pronounce.

"We can't stay here for free." Suzy said, giggling herself into a sweet jiggily frenzy, reassured me. Sara muffled a laugh under a shot of the Mexican ambition remover.

"Hell, and here I thought I was gonna' have to suck his dick for him to say half."

My Two Wives

That sent them into an even bigger wiggily, jiggily laughing orgasm. As for me, my erection had returned in full force. Using the bottle as cover, I excused myself and went to change.

"I think he came in his pants." Suzy whispered loudly to Sara, and they both erupted into sexually enhanced, tequila induced laughing frenzy. After I returned in a pair of jeans and an old college shirt, we continued our evening without a hitch. We got closer, more acquainted, with one another. I told them my reasons for wanting to sublet. They smiled, asking a few questions. I talked, they listened. Both women had moved from the table clearing the food and grabbing another bottle of tequila.

"So what do you do?" Suzy asked, sitting on the over sized love seat, tucking her legs beneath her.

"I'm in sales." I said, or believed I did.

Maybe I should have warned my new roommates that I'm not much of a drinker. And since I'm not much of a drinker, can't trust my memory when it comes to my beliefs, I believe I saw them having sex later that night, but that's a story for another time.

"I sale air-filtration systems." I continued, my speech becoming more slurred and sluggish with each word. I do remember them nodding their heads as if they were following the conversation. I also remember them laughing. I just can't remember if it was with me, or at me. Actually a lot about that night has been erased from memory. I do know that it was on that first night that I met the two women

SexPressions

who would take my virginity; and that was the same night I fell in love with them. It was also the same night I decide I would marry them both.

I guess I should clear a few things up about me and my being a virgin. I'm technically not a virgin. I had sex on my prom night and then again in college with a sexy, yet ugly; drunk freshman. "What can I say, she was desperate." It's not that I'm ugly; I'm a nerd. So my lack of fashion sense and little money easily turned women off. Now add in my shyness to that and you have the makings for a lot of lonely nights. And other than the occasional magazine, I haven't seen a human naked outside of my dreams in a very long time. Without the "burden" of a relationship, I concentrated all my energy into my career; which required me to travel eight months out of the year. So even if I wanted to, I couldn't start a relationship. Plus I was earning a boat-load of money.

Now it was Sara who jumped-started the conversation about the other aspect of my *'virginity'*.

"Are you gay?" She asked, although it sounded more like an accusation.

My back was to her so the slight frown that grew across my face was hidden. I had just returned from a trip and as was our new routine, Sara helped me unpack and quizzed me about my travels. Only this time she never got around to doing that.

"What makes you ask that?" I said turning to face her with my arms crossed.

My Two Wives

"Well the fact that you stand like a fag." She shot. "You dress like you're gay, and we have been living here for five months and you haven't even tried to fuck either one of us."

"Ya'll my girls. I don't want to fuck that up." I answered.

"Could've fooled us."

She stood up from my bed and moved around the room. Sara had been lying across my bed wearing a pair of tight shorts that hugged her nearly perfect ass and showed off her long toned legs. She wore a cut-up mid-riff shirt that showcased the coat of sweat that covered her abdomen from her work-out; *Tae-Bo*. I wanted to yell that I was by no means a homosexual. But my erection drained blood from the thinking side of my brain. Then I reacted in a manner that almost justified her outrageous statement.

"See!" Sara said, pointing her finger and erupting in laughter, "only fags roll their eyes like that."

"Yo' crazy ass," I said, shaking my head, and returned to unpacking.

"No, I'm for real." She placed her head in her hand. "We never hear you talk about women. It would be different if you were ugly. So we just assumed you were gay."

Again I rolled my eyes (I really should stop that) and thought about what people said about assuming. The direction of this conversation was already planned, so I

SexPressions

decided to stay the course.

"So I guess this is the part where I ask how I can prove I'm not gay and you saying by fucking you; right?"

Sara looked across the space of the room, giving me a matter-of-fact look.

"No." The answer was so simple and short that I believed her. "I just don't understand how you don't have a woman. And I think you would fuck me doggy style, just to prove me wrong. So if you're not gay, then what is it?"

I hunched my shoulders and mumbled and incoherent answer. The truth was that it had been so long since I had sex that I was intimidated by women. Not to mention having two beautiful desirable women living with me was overwhelming. Sara studied my face for a brief moment, turned the idea over in her head, and dropped the subject. Or so I thought.

"So tell me about L.A."

It was another few months before the topic of me and either of them having sex came up. Suzy was the one who brought it up, but not as you'd think. It, like most things, sort of just happened. Like Sara, Suzy and I also developed a routine of our own. We'd lie in my bed, dressed of course, and watch kung fu movies. Sometime we would fall asleep before the end. And nights like this particular one, we drank and talked. Usually the movie was one we'd both seen, so it was more for background noise.

My Two Wives

"I wonder what that must feel like." She said, pulling her knees to her chest.

"What what's like?" I said, stuffing my mouth full of popcorn. "Chopping a man with your hand?"

"No. To love somebody enough to kill for them."

"OOOOkay" I answered, moving my eyes back and forth. "What brought that up?"

"Just wanna be loved, I guess." She said, at almost a whisper. "And not that, *'You're a sister'* or that *'friend'* love. Ya' know?"

I shook my head *yes*. I guess there was nothing wrong with wanting real love. She lifted the popcorn bowl, nestled her head in my chest, and then placed the bowl on my stomach.

"Do you think I'm ugly?" She asked, as I pondered the upside of being in love to the point I'd devote part of my life to learning a new kung fu style so that I could avenge someone's death.

"Naw, Sue, you're far from ugly." I said, still shoveling hands of popcorn into my mouth (no wonder I'm not having any sex, right?) And before I could say anything stupid, I felt her lips press against my cheek. Delighted shock froze me and I turned to look at her. Suzy brushed the side of my face with her hand and kissed me softly on the lips. Now a regular man would've kissed her back. A normal man would've already had sex by now, but not me. Not

SexPressions

Gabriel Harris. I looked her square in the face and ruined the moment. Still pressing her lips against mine, she looked into my eyes apologetically.

"That's right, you're gay." She said, embarrassed for the both of us. "It's either that or married, right?"

Just then tears began to flow from the soft brown eyes that just nearly seduced me. I placed her head on my chest and listened while she cried.

"I'm sorry." I whispered, sometime later.

"For what?" Her voice came from between sobs.

"Everything." I stroked the sides of her face. Soon the sounds of her sleeping, lullabied me to sleep as well.

The next day was when my entire life changed. When I woke, Suzy wasn't in the bed. I gathered my bearings (still dressed, damn!) and went to find her. Maybe I could take her to lunch. Just to show her even single straight men were good. I walked from my room to the kitchen, which was just down the hall. All I found was a pot of coffee, a few doughnuts, and a note taped to the refrigerator. I fixed myself a cup of coffee, grabbed a glazed doughnut, and read the note. Seeing that it was addressed to Sara; I read it fast.

Ra-Ra, (Suzy's nickname for Sara)

We're going to have to go shopping another day. I got that photo shoot I was hoping for and I have to get equipment and look at the place. I'll see you and Gab

My Two Wives

tonite. Tell him I want to watch that movie so don't take it back.

Suzy

P.S.

Oh yeah girl, you were right. He's working with something!!!!!

I scanned the letter a few more times, and smiled. At least I was *'working with something'*. Now I just had to get something to work on. I decided to find out what Sara thought I was working with. And that's when for the first time that morning I heard soft humming. Both Suzy and Sara sang, so humming was nothing new around the apartment. I quickly moved across the kitchen and living room to the room she and Suzy shared while I was out of town. I planned on surprising her.

"What' cha doing in here?" I said as I flung the door open.

I stood froze, mouth open and coffee cup feeling like a bucket of mud. Sara lay on her bed, naked except for her socks, legs open. Her eyes were closed. One hand was between her legs, working a small white vibrator inside of her neatly trimmed vagina, while her other hand, twisted and tugged, at a small chain that connected the gold rings that pierced through her nipples. Sara's body was far more beautiful than I thought. It was brown and neatly flawless; I felt my penis begin to throb. Her humming sounded to me how the Siren's Song must have sounded to so many sailors. I was hypnotized. She rotated her hips, as she worked the small sex toy. Her humming soon morphed into moans. Her breasts were large, round and blemish free. The small rings seemed to melt into nipples. I felt my lips form curse words. I'm not sure how long I was watching before she opened her eyes but when she did, she saw me stroking myself. She smiled; the effects of her actions leaving a dreamy look in her eyes. She pushed her knees apart forcing her vagina to blossom into a sexual smile of its own. She slowly moved her lips to form commands; I stood there unsure if they were for me. Until she stopped long enough to wave me closer. My body trembled with each step that covered the small space, before collapsing at the foot of the bed.

"Please?" She said, using my lips and voice. I crawled on the bed and locked eyes with Sara.

"Don't be scared." Her body told mine.

I placed my head between her thighs; her warmth encasing my entire face. I steadied my gaze against hers. Sara closed her eyes and slowly removed the vibrator; her liquid sex coated the white pleasure device. She brushed my face with her hands, slowly moving me to her vagina. My eyes began to tear, as I approach her plump labia and just as my tongue moved past my lips, I felt the tears beginning to march down my cheeks.

"To the Death of a virgin!" My body toasted, as my tongue parted her vaginal opening and I tastes her sexual wine.

I heard Sara exhale loudly, nearly whistling. She allowed me to kiss and lick hungrily, before guiding me. Teaching me. Saving me. My tongue moved across her

My Two Wives

clitoris, sending her moans to rest in the cups of my curled toes. She moved slowly beneath my eager tongue. Her flavor was sexually robust, like dark Tuscan wine. I finally moved my hand to touch her; hold her in place. Moans flowed, broken and jumbled, around my working tongue.

"There you go." Sara coached, "Just like that."

She traced light directions on my neck; first small circles for my tongue to mimic. Then backward and forth, side to side and flicking movements. Each one, my tongue quickly obeyed and repeated. She tossed a leg over my shoulders, locking her ankles and raised her pelvis to meet my full tongue. I licked at her juices like a man dying of thirst, because I was. This was a rebirth to me. I no longer was the old, stupid Gabriel Harris. I was Gabriel Harris, the knowing. I knew I could pleasure a woman. I knew how *sexy* truly tasted. And I finally knew what it felt like to lay next to, and between, a woman. I soon found myself experimenting with my movements. I used just the tip of my tongue; she moaned sharply. I used a soft sucking; she howled. I used my teeth; she corrected me with rough passion. I kissed Sara's clitoris softly, hating myself for never having this experience before.

"Damn!" My nipples said, as they became stiff and sensitive. I giggle as my orgasm began to grow in strength. Sara's pants grew in harshness and tempo, which forced her hips to grind more roughly against my face. I listen as the word 'yes' explode from her mouth like a warning. I felt my tongue quicken, but I couldn't; no wouldn't; stop. Sara's trembling thighs massaged my face as they tightened. She grabbed the back of my head, forcing me to stop my

SexPressions

breathing as I continued licking. My nose was filled with her wet smell. A sticky, throbbing wetness oozed against her leg, just as Sara tossed her rib cage into the air, pushed down on my head, and howled. I guess she came. I prayed she had. I didn't want to ask. I only wanted to lay between her legs and keep licking and kissing. She trembled and shook, slowly rotating her hips. She held onto my held, scooted away from me until she was upright against the head board. Her eyelids sagged nearly shut. A dreamy pleased look masked her thoughts.

"Can we do that again?" I wondered aloud, resting my head in my hands, smiling at Sara as if she were a movie star and I were some star-struck teenager.

"Whenever! Later." She spat, chest heaving heavy and labored. "But let me rest. First time you ate a woman out?"

"Yes!" I said. I began kissing her on the leg just under her left knee. She swatted my efforts, telling me not to be greedy. I smiled; happy I was no longer a virgin. I kissed her vagina again, watching her jump and giggle, then slithered from her sex space. I watched her the entire time, never dropping my gaze, until I cleared the threshold. I stood in the living room, moving my tongue across my upper lip and enjoyed the feel of her wetness, drying stickily on my cheeks. I floated back to my room and replayed the entire scenario until sleep re-took me.

Like I said, that was the day I was changed. That was the day I met the new me. The *'pussy-getting'* me. I'm not sure how long I was sleep but the sound of Sara's voice pulled me from my slumber.

My Two Wives

"Yeah Gurl..." she laughed, "... he right here."

I felt myself smiling.

"Well he has potential... wanna talk to him?" I felt her move on the bed, unaware of how, close she was to me. "Here, it's Suzy!" She handed the phone receiver to me.

"So you eating pussy now?" Suzy said, a trace of jealousy mixed in her happiness. "So when do I get some?" She laughed softly, partly whispering.

"When will you be home?" I said, basking in my new oral glory.

"Tonight. So don't let Ra-Ra tire you out." Her laugh was innocent. As if she was embarrassed to be talking in such a way. It drove me crazy instantly.

"I lah..." she started as Sara snatched the phone from my grip and moved quickly out of my range.

I sat up in my bed, wondered what the rest of her statement could've been. Was she telling me she loved me? It sounded that way. But it could've been anything. The suspense was killing me. I had to talk to her now. I bolted from my bed; head and dick throbbing with anticipation. I was met by Sara in the small tight space of the hallway. She smiled at me wickedly. The way a cat would at a plump goldfish inside of a shallow bowl.

'I knoooww a seee-cret!" She said, singing the taunt at me, blocking my way.

SexPressions

"What did Sue say?"

"Pull ya dick out. Lemme see it." She answered, not paying attention to what I said.

"C'mon Sara, what did she say?"

Sara moaned and began pulling my t-shirt up and away from my waist line. I became stuck with delight and sexual fear. I've never done this before, I wanted to say. I tried to say it, anyway.

"How bad do you want to know what Suzy said?"

"Very."

Sara began kissing my not-so chiseled stomach, pushing me toward soft giggles. "Whh.. Aaa aat diddd shheee say?" Sara pushed my jogging pants lower, exposing the nakedness beneath. She used the most tender touch I could remember. Pulling the bundle of my pants from my ankles, she kissed me gently above my pubic hair.

"She (moaning pause)... said (another moaning pause)... that (moaning slurp) she..." Sara planted kissed lower with each word; smile growing with each word.

"You sure you want to hear this?"

'Yes!" I answered not really sure of what I was answering.

Sara kissed me on the head of my penis. Her lips were

My Two Wives

warm just as warm as her vagina. She moved her hands ticklishly up along my legs. With one hand, her left, she gently guided my leg on her shoulder; with the other hand, her right, she gently guided my throbbing penis into her mouth.

"Shit! Damn!" I, then her, cursed.

Her tongue was wide, warm and wet. She palmed my ass, steadying me. My eyelids eased shut, while my eyeballs rolled toward the rear of my skull. I wanted to cry from the glorious feeling. Sara moved her head now, firmly pushing me against the suddenly cool wall, with her hand. I heard her moan; mouth full of my very inexperienced sex. I became lost in the warm feeling. I tried to ball a section of the wall into my fist. I needed to run; to escape. I held Sara by the head, gently, and shifted my weight. I began growing harder inside of her warm mouth; toes curling beneath me. She began making loud slurping sounds as she moved her mouth along and around my shaft. I felt warm and cool at the same time. She started stroking the bottom half of my penis as she sucked on the top. I felt lightheaded. An erotic vertigo overcame me. My heart rate increased. This was nothing new. I was having an orgasm. Sara was the only change. She was the new thing; the added ingredient.

Sara removed me from her mouth and used both her hands to stroke me. Each hand worked in opposition to the other, in a tight, twisting piston-like motion. My teeth and gums began to tingle. I told myself to move, to react, to not just stand here and take it. But I was at her mercy. She licked the opening of my penis, then re-inserted me back into her mouth. She worked my balls, lightly massaging them. The fine pubic hairs acted as 'feelers', sending electric messages throughout my body. Sara grabbed my *ass* cheeks again and roughly manipulated them. As my orgasm neared eruption, her fingers neared my anus. She slowly sucked and added pressure against my rear opening. I stood on my tip toes, unsure if I should enjoy such an intrusion. I did, and I liked it a little more when she pushed the tip inside. I could no longer contain myself. Sara didn't stop sucking *as* hot cum shot from me. My body twitched and convulsed, causing me to topple to my nearly unsupported side. She smiled *as* she kissed the very sensitive head of my still throbbing penis.

"So what did Suzy say?" I asked, breathing hard. I brought my other leg to the ground, allowing her to stand before me.

"Oh that! She said she'll tell you when she gets home."

With that, she turned and walked away leaving me standing naked from the waist down with a half erect penis.

"I love you, too!" I whispered to both Sara and Suzy.

I spent the rest of that day to myself. Sara showered and left for the day, not returning until later that night. Suzy on the other hand got home tired, yet somehow still excited about the days events. She told me how the location for the photo shoot had to be changed four times.

"Damn Model!" That was her reason for the day's mishap. "For instance, if those *damn models* were on time, I

My Two Wives

could have gotten the shots I wanted" or " I can't believe those *damn models* get paid so much." I sat and marveled at how she became a different person when she talked about photography. Her shyness and innocence were nonexistent. She became a new, powerful woman.

"What are you looking at ?" She asked, stopping her story.

"You!" She blushed at my quick answer. "You're different when you talk about your work."

"You think so?" She placed her hands on her hips and tossed her head to one side. She seemed to hang on to my every word. "So is that why you're looking like that?"
Then before I could answer, she bolted from the room, yelling for me not to move.

"Okay", I thought. Where was I going? I lay in my bed, beneath a blanket, naked as day one. I didn't really have a clue why she'd left the room and as long as she came back I didn't care. So imagine my sexual surprise when she sprang into the room like *S.W.A.T.* with her camera to her eye.

"Smile!" She yelled, causing me to jump.

"C'mon Sue, I ain't got on any clothes."

"Good. We'll tend to that later." She winked and returned the camera to her eye.
Suzy began yelling commands for me to pose. I was slow to react.
Hey, like I said, I was new to all this, but after a

SexPressions

minute or two, I warmed up to the idea. I pulled the blanket to my neck and feigned embarrassment, then allowed the camera and Suzy to take control. She moved around the room; flash bulb and smile competing for the title of brightest in the room. Each pose moved the blanket across my hidden nakedness. My erection returned, powerful and brilliant between my legs. After a few more shots, Suzy began changing film rolls.

"Okay get rid of the blanket."

I must have been moving too slow, because before I could react, she snatched the blanket.

"Damn Models!" She said, tossing the blanket to the floor. I was shocked. Pre-cum ran from the head of my penis and down my think shaft.

Suzy told me to pose as if I were trying to turn her on.

"Spread ya' legs some... now put your arms behind your head. Your instincts will take over after that."

And they did. I began-moving naked around the bed, each pose pushing me closer toward the edge. Until finally I found myself inches away from the camera. My chest was heaving, nipples hard and straight. I felt as if I was on fire. I couldn't remember the man I was just twenty-four hours ago. I was her man; their man; Sara's and Suzy's.

I lifted my hand to her face and moved in to kiss her.

"What about Sara?"

My Two Wives

"I love her as well."

Suzy collapsed into my arm and kissed me. Her embrace and kiss were filled with passion. Where Sara was lustful and erotic, Suzy was pure love and passion. Our lips touched briefly, before our eyes locked. I pulled Suzy to the bed and slowly began undressing her. We became a tandem. We had to allow for some fumbling with buttons and bra straps, but we got our act together. Suzy laid on me, her shyness returning with a sexual sheen. I ran my eyes and hands over her body slowly. Her breasts were a comfortable fit in my palms. I moved my fingers slowly over them; squeezing soft moans from her. I kissed her on her neck, just below her chin. She gasped and grabbed the back of my head. She slowly pressed her eager vagina against me in a slow grind. My penis throbbed and tingled.

"Say it again." She whispered words full of emotion.

"I love you!" I sang softly.

She collapsed onto me and kissed me hard. Our tongues moved roughly around each other; happily playful. And with only a brief warning our sexes met. My penis head moved between her wet labia; timid and unsure. Suzy stared into my eyes, and then shifted her weight. Her tight opening welcomed me deep inside of her. Her mouth fell open and she sat straight up over me. She rocked her hips, side to side, moving me further into her. Her vaginal walls were warm and plush against my shaft. 1 bit my lip and looked away. I placed my hands against her abdomen, thumbs close to her clitoris. She pumped and rotated her hips against and around my thickness. I was overwhelmed. I couldn't control my

SexPressions

body. I tried moving, but was rebuked as my penis was sensitive and new. Suzy's movements were sporadic. She bounced softly atop of me, and then only moved her pelvis, then an altogether different side-to-side motion. Her breasts mesmerized me. She balanced herself against my chest and rocked violently. Suddenly a feeling of floating and warm electricity; and even fear swept through me. It felt like had just wet the bed and passed gas.

"AAAHHhh!" She said, as hot sperm shot inside of her. I was paralyzed and unsure. She smiled and continued moving. The feeling was incredible. It was as if someone was poking a nerve ending; only it was between my legs. My entire body panicked, celebrated, and then panicked in celebration. Soon afterwards, Suzy fell off of me gasping for air. She told me not to touch her. She even thanked me, for what I'm not sure. That night, Suzy moved into my room and slept there permanently. She taught me how to make love to her. Then she allowed Sara to teach us how to fuck. And even that's a story for later.

Well a few months had gone by and the three of us were doing our 'thang'. No arguing or jealousy; just a happy threesome. I was living the dream life, or so I thought. Hell, I didn't know any better. I was still traveling; coming and going. Well I arrived home looking forward to continuing the routines I'd started; Sara and unpacking; Suzy and kung-fu movies. Oh yeah, and sex. But as soon as I walked through the door I knew something was wrong.

"Why ya'll sitting in the dark?" I asked, turning the living room light on.

My Two Wives

They both sat on the sofa holding sheets of paper. Another sat crumbled on the table.

"What's wrong? Why are you both crying?"

Each sat puffy eyed and silent. I could hardly contain my disgust. The look on my face must have been effective enough, because Suzy spoke first, which was an omen in and of it self. Sara was the spokeswoman for them. Hell, she even took up for me. So to have Suzy talking first told me shit had just hit the fan.

"We have to move." She said, sobs distorting each word.

"And why is that?" I asked, hunger and confusion, mixed throughout my response.

"Because you're being sued, because of us." Sara spoke up this time.

"Ya'll not making any sense. Start at the beginning."

Sara handed me the crumpled sheet of paper from the table. And while I read it, she told me how they had been hiding notices from the Condominium Organization about subleasing and leading a life that was.....

"Immoral and Dangerous." Sara said, using childish mocking voice. She also told me how she even confronted the building manager, who didn't take kindly to a six foot plus black woman threatening her about the situation.

SexPressions

"I'm sorry Gabe." Sara apologized, "I know I was outta' line, but that bitch made me so mad. I'll move out if it will help."

The last part sent Suzy into another crying outburst. All the crying was making my head hurt now.

"First of all, no one tells me how I should live." I nearly began yelling. "Secondly, they can't make me move anywhere. They at least have to show some sort compensation. I have an iron-clad contract that allows me to do as I please, as long as I don't remodel. Plus I have a cut-throat realty lawyer that I play golf with who'll eat them for breakfast."

I stood and yanked on my collar. Something one of the salesmen in L.A. told me about. I turned and walked to the kitchen to fix myself a stiff a drink, reassuring them I'd clear everything up on the following Monday. With that dilemma behind me, I assumed my hero work was done. I heard Sara and Suzy whispering behind me. I pictured them nudging each other. I really must give this "assuming" thing up.

"You tell him." Suzy said.

"No, You tell him." Sara returned.

They alternated in that manner for a few exchanges. I held the glass tightly against the counter, hoping they would soon resolve the argument, when finally Sara dropped the childish act.

My Two Wives

"Suzy is pregnant!" She said, in an *'I'm telling manner'*.

"And so are you." Suzy shot back, both moving toward me now.

I didn't feel the glass leave my hand, nor did I feel the small cuts.

"Ya'll pregnant?" I asked, shock slowly embracing me.

"But we'll get abortions if..." It was Sara.

"No one is killing my babies!" I yelled, scaring the three of us. "So don't even think about that shit!"

My anger turned my skin red. Both of them flinched; then stared at me. I'd never screamed at them.

"What will we do?" Suzy asked.

"We don't have a lot of room. See I should just move." Sara said, "And ya'll can stay here."

"We're a family." I said. "The three of us; and if we're having babies, then so be it." I stood in my kitchen, drinking tequila from the bottle. "I'll just buy a house." I resolved after a few seconds. Not really sure if I believed myself. "Yeah, I'll buy a house and we'll live there."

The two of them stared at me; relief and some confusion sitting on their faces. My head was swimming with random thoughts. The upper most of them being I was going to be a father. I tilted the bottle high in the air allowing the tequila to flow down my throat.

"Hell, we'll even get married." I said, stumbling toward my room, not sure which of them I was addressing. I moved past them. They both stood in her own *'what-the-fuckness'*. I splashed, drunk onto my bed. Sleep came fast.

When I woke the next morning, the three of us lay, naked, body parts tangled against and around each other. We never talked about that night in detail. I sold the condo with no problem. I got a large enough compensation large enough to purchase a big house.

Well that was a year ago...

Gabriel was cut off by the sound of keys turning and women talking. Two women stepped into the large kitchen, both talking quickly, words full of excitement. Gabriel smiled at his two sons; Gabriel Jr. and Samuel or Buddy to his mother, Sara. He was still amazed at how the two women he'd met and fell in love with still made his heart pound.

"Hey baby." The shorter of the two women said, kissing him on the cheek. "How was 'Father and Sons' day?

"I was telling the boys how I met you and Sara. And what made me wanna do this."

Gabriel held his fiancée's trembling hand and removed a small box from his pocket. He kneeled before her, causing her to become teary-eyed.

My Two Wives

"Suzy Louise Marshall, will you marry me?"

She stood next to her best friend, shaking uncontrollably. Her squeaky response sent chills through everyone in the room.

"Ya'll make a beautiful couple." Sara said, holding her son in a close maternal embrace. She turned her back to the small celebration. She didn't want them to see her tears. She pushed jealousy from her thoughts. This was Gabe and Suzy. If anyone deserved to get married, they did. But it still hurt. Always a bridesmaid, she thought.

Sara moved toward the phone. She couldn't stand to look at Suzy, her new husband or the ring. Her tears ran more freely now.

Gabriel kissed Suzy again then whispered into her ear. After a brief moment to ponder the words, she shook her head. She reached into his pocket and removed another small box, and tapped her friend on the shoulder.

Sara didn't believe she'd ever been angry with Suzy, but she knew what anger was, and for that she was ashamed, "But the bitch doesn't have to rub it in." she thought. Sara turned to face her closest and dearest friend in the world; anger fueling her actions.

"What Suzy!" She nearly yelled, expecting to be face-to-face with her friend. What she found instead was Suzy and Gabriel on their knees. Suzy held a ring similar to hers, with a different stone.

SexPressions

"Sara Marie Carter, will you marry us?"

Her heart sank. She tried to protect her son as, she felt her knees buckle. Suzy reached to brace her friend, while Gabriel reached for the baby. Sara slumped to the floor and fell into Suzy's embrace.

"We've shared everything our whole life. Can we share a husband?" Suzy asked, tears marring her make-up.

"Yes!" Sara cried, "Yes, yes, yes."

ROOM SERVICE

We step from the elevator, our laughter shaking the halls of the hotel. It had been a good idea to take a small getaway, since we haven't had any real time to be together; alone anyway. But we've quickly caught up for lost time. We had dinner and from then on, we couldn't seem to keep our hands to ourselves. After working ourselves into frenzy, we left the club early. We fondle each other as we stumble toward our door. I maneuver myself behind you. I pull you to me, kiss the back of your neck as I caressed your breast. You were braless and your nipples press against the front of your dress, tickling my palm. You snuggle back into me, pressing your soft ass against my pulsating manhood. You add a slight wiggle as we arrive at our hotel room. As I search for the key, you place your hands on the door as if you're assuming the position. Still kissing your neck, I use one hand to massage your sex kitten. You lean your head back, moaning your approval.

"Where the hell is the key?" My body yells at my hands. I can hardly wait. "We'll have to do it in the hall." I think to myself. And as if reading my mind, you pull your dress high on your thighs.

"Right here! Let's do it right now." You whisper.

SexPressions

Eager to please, I release the tiger contained in my pants. I glance around the hallway; half hoping that someone would add to the excitement and walk out of their room. I rub the head of my member against your moist hole, to announce my arrival. I quiver as shockwaves of pleasure shoot from over my sensitive spot. You begin rotating your hips, adding wet friction. I finally enter you just as my knees buckle from ecstasy. With slow, tender motion, I stroke upward and into you. Your warm walls manipulate my already sensitive shaft. With each stroke, I feel a rush to both of my heads. I reach under and massage your engorged clit. I start to increase my tempo, ignoring the urge to explode. My moans whisper against your neck. I'm not sure if I can hold off any longer. I begin growing inside of you. My shaft presses against your tightening walls.

"Shit!" My body screams. I bite and suck on my bottom lip and hold on to your hips. You feel my weakness. Reaching behind, you begin to massage my sack. Your touch ambushes my senses. And now all I want to do was to keep fighting. But you and my body have other plans.

Bending at the waist, creating an even more exciting pressure, you attack my penis with smooth, yet aggressive movements. My body betrays my mind, with a powerful orgasm. I shake violently as you continue rotating your hips. I'm paralyzed with pleasure. Your body urges the last drops from me and I oblige. I begin to tingle. You continue stroking and rotating until finally reaching orgasm. Your warm juices coat my stomach. Regaining the ability to move, I join you with soft, steady pumps.

Spent and excited, my hands return to my pocket and

Room Service

search for the key. I feel the edges of the key when the door flies open, startling us both. A polite-looking gentleman, stands looking at us holding an ice bucket. I glance at the door for the first time, and notice that we're in front of the wrong door. We apologize and quickly turn to walk away.

"Maybe next time I can do it outside of your room." The guy says from behind us.

We smile back in unison.

"Maybe!" I answer back, as we locate our room and walk inside. "Maybe..."

THE BITCH AND THE BEST FRIEND

Damon couldn't stand Stacy. And he didn't see why Lee put up with her shit. She was a stuck-up, high-yellow bitch. Damon couldn't believe she was standing at his door, demanding he tell on his friend.

"You can check if you want, but he ain't here." Damon said, as she pushed past him into the apartment. "What a bitch." Damon thought to himself.

Lee would have to do something about this and soon. Friend or not. Damon watched as Stacy stormed through the house with the force of a hurricane. Lee called earlier warning him ahead of time. He was infamous for disappearing, and as usual, he used Damon as an alibi. Her search turning up nothing, Stacy turned to Damon.

"I know you know where he is!" She spat, lips curved in anger.
"The nerve of this bitch," Damon thought to himself. Who the hell did she think she was? Damon thought of how she bullied Lee. "I ain't Lee," he mumbled to himself.

"I ain't telling you!" Damon returned. Damn right

SexPressions

Damon knew that Lee was over to Angie's house, but he wasn't telling her that. It was grimy that Lee was fucking one of her friends but Stacy knew her friend was a hoe when she brought her man around. Birds of a feather. Damon stood his ground. He stared at Stacy determined not to budge. Even if he was the tricking kind of dude; he wouldn't tell Stacy where to find water if her head was on fire. Damon placed his hand down the front of his pants and rubbed just over his pubic hair. He couldn't believe that his best friend was one of *those* dudes. One of those dudes who was too busy fucking around, that he couldn't bring the dick home. And for a second he pitied Stacy. She was thick as hell with sexy lips and she had to put up with terrible dick. Then he looked at her and the feeling past. Damon thought about the shit she pulled at the club two weeks back. She showed her ass that night, storming out the place like she was a little girl. As good as she looked in her body hugging gray dress. That night her breast nearly popped out. All Lee did was grin and apologize.

"My fault D'," He said as they walked back to the car. It was clear then that all she needed was some good dick. Damon thought about how he would have fucked her in the parking lot bent over the hood of the car, Busting a nut on her dress for good *fucking* measure.

Stacy stared at Damon and held her temper. She knew Lee had been by here and Damon was standing in front of her lying. She also knew he was an asshole from the moment she met him. Stacy had never really gotten along with dark skinned men. Damon was no different. He acted as if his dark skin and his looks gave him the right to treat women the way he did. Stacy believed he hadn't had any

The Bitch and the Best Friend

good pussy in a long time, if ever. She knew as soon he got a woman- a good woman- who didn't take his shit he would be okay. Right now he was working on getting his black face smacked.

"Oohh I can't stand you!" Stacy huffed.

She didn't have time to argue with Damon. She was horny and in a hurry. If nothing else Lee could eat the hell out of some pussy. She knew Lee was somewhere fucking around. Probably laughing at how he had her on a wild goose chase. So putting up with this fool wasn't on her schedule. The fool didn't even have enough manners to put on a shirt. Walking around with out his shirt, trying to show off his body. This was why she couldn't stand him. Every chance he got he tried to show his body. She thought about the time she had to curse him out for not closing the door when he used the bath room at her house. All she could do was scream when she saw his long black dick.

"You nasty muthafucka," she spat that night, "Close the damn door." He just stood there and shook his penis taunting her.

"Close this, Bitch!"

That was the first time he called her a bitch. Lee didn't get mad about that either. Lee was a punk. Stacy always thought was scared of Damon. She didn't care. She was no one's bitch. Even if the sound of the word made her nipples hard and her vagina twitch and become moist. She just stood staring at him, fighting the throbbing deep with in her clitoris. It had been two long weeks since she had her

SexPressions

legs held in the air; dick forcing her to yell and stutter. If only Lee was fucking her properly she wouldn't have to deal with this fool. Stacy stared at Damon and crossed her arms. "Grow the fuck up" she snapped.

"I can't stand yo' yella' ass. "Damon sneered. "Don't be mad at me because Lee ain't fucking you right!" He hoped he'd hurt her feelings. But without missing a beat, Stacy shot right back at him.

"You probably ain't no better!"

"…or you standing here because you know I'm better. I see how you be looking at me," Damon said moving closer. "You are always staring at my dick, because you know I will fuck the shit outta you." Damon grinned.

"Boy Please." Stacy said a flimsy reply. "You wouldn't know what to do with this pussy and all this ass."

They stared at each other. The challenge was made. Damon's sex grew in his pants. It was the erection of a pissed-off man. He knew this was what she needed. And finally Damon thought, "Fuck it." He pulled Stacy to him. He lifted her shirt up over her head and kissed her exposed breast. Stacy wore no bra, not surprising to Damon. Her nipples grew red as Damon sucked roughly on them.

Shock gripped Stacy in the form of Damon's roughness. How dare this nigga. She had wanted to smack him. To scratch his smooth dark skin till he bled, but her pussy wouldn't let her. She tossed her hands around his neck foolishly telling herself she was fighting him off. She

The Bitch and the Best Friend

thought if later it came to light or they got caught she could say she was trying to push him off or choke him at least. Truthfully she pulled her slim body against his thick carved frame. She wrapped her hands around his body and dug her nails into his skin. Horny or not, Stacy wasn't going to just give him the pussy.

Damon hoisted her small-framed body into his arms and carried her into the living room. She began scratching him now. He liked the pain. It reminded him how much of a bitch she was. Now he could be as rough as he wanted. His dick was hard now, very hard. He planned to fuck her out of spite. ***Doggy style***, he thought with a grin that would've shamed the devil. ***Doggy style*** like the bitch she was. He fingered her until she was wet. Quickly undressing, Damon flipped Stacy over on all fours. He glanced down and had to give her credit. She did have a nice ass. He grabbed handfuls of her butt. His jet-black skin looked even darker against hers. Stacy moaned as Damon kneaded her soft ass. He snuggled in close and brushed her swollen labia with his stiffness. Damon smacked her hard on the cheeks(really wishing it were her face) and slid his dick into her. She was warm and tight.

"Lee was a fucking dummy." He thought to himself. Damon wasted no time. He stroked with a smooth black force, always adding an extra pop of meanness at the end.

"Take this dick!" He grunted. He grabbed her by the shoulders. She moaned louder, close to screaming, as he rammed nine inches of sexual disdain into her honey spot.

"Fuck me, nigga, fuck me. Fuck me you punk

SexPressions

muthafucka!" Stacy ordered, looking back over her shoulder.
    She leaned down onto her elbows and added pressure to Damon's strokes. Damon soon worked up a sweat. He continued to stroke as hard as he could. Smacking her hard on the ass, Stacy reached back, rubbing his balls against her clitoris. Damon was right; Lee wasn't fucking her right. So she would take matters into her own hands. Damon groaned as Stacy fondled his balls into her. Damon wet two fingers and began fingering her asshole. Stacy shot up on all fours.

    "Damn." She screamed to herself. Her toes spread and she felt the bottom of her stomach drop, like she was riding a rollercoaster. A big dick rollercoaster. "You ain't doing shit, You punk muthafucka," Stacy yelled lying to herself. She added punk bitch at the end speaking strictly bout her self. A soft moan turned to a lustful yell as she felt herself reaching climax. Damon felt her muscles tighten around him. Stacy screamed his name. The name Lee called him when they hung out.

    "Yes D-money. Fuck Lee's BITCH!" She taunted, from deep inside her sex. The word sounded slutfully nice coming from her own lips. She truly was a bitch. She was close to cumming and signaled the arrival with growing yells. Damon was close too. He pumped with fierce desire. He pounded deeper into her as she came with a shudder and scream. Damon jerked and pulled out, shooting hot hateful sperm across her back.

    "Bitch!" He spat through clenched teeth.

    "Punk muthafucka," Stacy panted back over her shoulder.

The Bitch and the Best Friend

Damon sat back and looked at his best friend's girlfriend's naked red, well-fucked ass. "Damn she looked good." He thought.

Damon went off to the bathroom returning with a warm towel. Without a word being said, she wiped herself, dressed and left.

"At least the bitch could've said thanks."

Damon plopped on the sofa and listened to his dick hum with delight. All he needed now was a cigar. The phone rang. It was Lee.

"Did Stacy stop thru' there?" He quizzed.

"Man, I ain't seen that crazy broad!" Damon said, lying with a grin. "Dude for real tho, you need to leave her crazy ass alone." He had always known Lee was slacking with the macking and now he had confirmed it. He also wanted to grabbed his best friend and tell him to man up to the bitch. He just lied. They had been friends since they both learned to color in the lines back at Miss Tangy's daycare. "Naw Dawg I ain't seen her at all. But if she come through I will hold ya' down. One." He listened for the response before ending the call. "Those two deserve each other," he thought. Damon hung up the phone and went to the shower. He had to wash the smell of the bitch off.

Meanwhile down in her car, Stacy dialed the number into her cell phone quickly. She opened and closed her legs trying to relieve her throbbing pussy. She really wanted to

SexPressions

go back into the house and get all the dick she could. She kind of felt guilty, but not really. She *really* needed to be fucked. A woman answered on the third ring, no doubt using the caller I.D. to screen the call.

"Angie?" Stacy asked excited, her body still throbbing from the sex she just had. "Guuurrrlll, I told you he could fuck!" She reported to her best friend. "You can send Lee's tired ass home now."

Stacy hung up the phone and smiled. Maybe she would get Damon to be her fuck buddy. Lee wasn't fucking her right anyway.

LATE NIGHT STOP OVER

Clark glanced down at his watch and cursed himself for not taking the earlier flight. He looked around the empty terminal, realizing how much he hated small town airports. What he hated more than that was having his nine-inch blackness hard as it was, with no one to help him ease the tension. Right now, he would even go as far as paying for it, but where would a brother find that kind of action in an empty airport terminal. It wasn't as if he could go to the vending machine, press B4 and a hot cup of pussy comes pouring out.

Clark placed his headphones over his ears and allowed the sweet voice of Jill Scott to soothe his savage beast. Halfway through Track 6, Clark was removed from his personal concert by a tap on the shoulder. Ms. Scott was close to singing him to an orgasm, so why would the fates choose this moment to break his heart. Clark pried his eyes open and began to focus on a pair of well-shaped, skirt-covered thighs that stood before him. He forced a smile across his lips and slowly looked up. Smooth ivory thighs became shapely hips. The hips were crowned by a small waist, which held a torso decorated with a set of lovely, round, perky breast. Clark continued his scan, as a pair of pouty lips formed a question.

SexPressions

"Do you have the time?" A cute-enough red headed woman asked. Clark fumbled with his watch.

"Two thirty sex." He answered, not really noticing the Freudian slip. The woman giggled at the miscue and thanked him. She started to walk away, thought better of it, turned back and took the seat next to Clark. Her smell was sweet. Clark inhaled her essence in deeply and fought back the resurgence of his erection. The woman began talking, drawing Clark deeper into a zone.

"Hello, I'm Debbie Peters." Offering Clark her delicate hand.

"I'm Clark Cross." He took her hand and became mesmerized by the softness of her touch-skin.

And before he could stop himself, Clark kissed her hand. Debbie brushed his face with her free hand. A tingle skipped its way down her body. Debbie felt a warm wetness spread between her legs. The thought of sex with a black man made her feel hot and unsettled. She looked around the airport. Although it wasn't full, it was by no means empty now. Her devilish smile whispered to Clark. No words were spoken between them, but a plan was brewing. He stood, unconsciously adjusting his pants to give his steadily growing nature room to expand. Clark quickly moved across the terminal with Debbie in tow. He smiled, thanking God for sending him a pussy-vending machine. He really didn't care where the place was to be, just as long as he could touch her again. Clark pushed through the restroom door and quickly locked it. He lifted her onto the counter. Debbie ran her hands through her short flame-shaded hair. Clark

Late Night Stop Over

kneeled down between her thighs. The area was smooth and gentle against his goateed face. Debbie rested her legs on Clark's shoulders and wiggled her dampen bikini panties down. He smiled up at her. Clark couldn't remember being this excited. Her inner thighs grew warmer with each brush of his beard. Clark slowly kissed up and down each thigh. Debbie sucked in a long breath, leaned forward and kissed Clark's neatly shaved brown head. Tiny beads of sweat formed. He smelled of a musk aftershave and power.

Sexual power!

Clark moved higher up her left thigh. He soon found her ivory sweetness. Clark placed his hands under her tight ass Clark and pulled her slightly toward him, introducing his tongue to her puffiness. And She was a true redhead. A "Fire bush" beauty.

Debbie inhaled and then exhaled harshly. His tongue was wide and rough and eager. Debbie tried to mimic the movement of his tongue with her own. Clark's tongue welcomed her clitoris like a large sofa. Debbie wondered between small tremors, if his tongue was this good, this educated, this well equipped, then what about the rest of him; the best of him. Clark rolled her ass cheeks in his large palms. Debbie was near insanity. She balled Clark's shirt in her hands and pulled him and his tongue deeper. With each brush of his tongue, Clark brought her closer. Debbie bit down on her lips as Clark used the full length of his tongue and tossed her over the edge.

"Geronimo!" Her body yelled.

SexPressions

Debbie fell back into the mirror as Clark licked wave after creamy wave of her orgasm. Clark glanced up at the results of his tongue's work. The sweet cream of Debbie's release coated his cheeks, lips and goatee. He watched her quiver from the aftershocks of her powerful orgasm. Before she could recover, Clark pulled her from the counter and turned her around. His erection throbbed painfully to be released. To be freed. To be heard. Debbie's green eyes screamed at Clark from the mirror's reflection.

"Now!" Those eyes yelled.

Clark watched his African sex slowly disappear into Debbie's alabaster warmth. Slow, soft, half strokes soon gave way to fast, forceful, full strokes. Clark grunted to Debbie's moans. Debbie fit tightly around his shaft. Debbie's ass cheeks sipped at the brownness of Clark's hands, giving them the appearance of coffee with too much cream. Debbie used the mirror as leverage and pushed back into Clark's thundering determination. And she knew his he was close. His penis pushed her walls to their limits. He grew with each stab. Clark gained momentum pushing aroused blackness deeper into Debbie's white-hot lust. A sweet dizziness rushed over Debbie just as she felt Clark cum with an explosive finale. His/Her each of their sex organs continued to throb as he pulled his length from her. After a few minutes of kissing recovery, they dressed and headed back into the terminal. They both went in separate directions.

Clark soon boarded his plane, his body tired from spontaneous sex and air travel. He felt like a convenient man ho'. The Kwiki Dick. The stewardess gave her safety

Late Night Stop Over

briefing, pointing out exits and the use of the air mask. Clark placed his headphones over his ears and tried to reconcile with the soulful love of Jill Scott's voice. He'd no sooner drifted into a track number nine sleep, when he was snatched from his slumber by the polite voice of a stranger.

"The pilot would like to see you." The stewardess whispered.

Bewildered, Clark smiled, more politely than he felt, and staggered to the cockpit. The stewardess knocked twice before poking her head through the cockpit door. She ushered Clark in, muffling a small giggle. The area was dark and cramped, but more spacious than Clark had envisioned a cockpit would be. Sitting in the pilot's chair was a lovely brown-toned woman. She smiled at Clark from behind a politely outstretched hand.

"I'm Dina Jones and I'll be your pilot for this flight." She started, her smile never wilting. "My co-pilot tells me you have the perfect remedy for jetlag."

And Before Clark could answer, the co-pilot turned and stood, red hair peeking from under her hat. Clark felt like a cartoon character whose eyes shoot from their face. "What the hell," his dick thought. Debbie smiled back and gave a wink to Clark. He nodded his head in agreement, as the pilot told him to lock the door.

DALE'S PASSION

Dale smiled as he read the poem again. He liked how Dawn turned actions into words, especially when those actions were his. He thought about each line and how he felt when the actual event had happened. Dawn was sexual without sex. Her touch was sexual, even when it was applied casually, and her poetry exuded that sexuality.

Dale lay naked under the thin cotton sheets and scanned the poem again. He could still smell the scent of last night's sex on the pillows. Dale's penis slowly grew warm and stiff against his inner thigh. He scanned the page again, his hand slipping below the surface of the sheets, brain transmitting each word to his fingertips. Dale closed his eyes, allowing Dawn's poetic self to work through him.

Dawn stood in the doorway, watching Dale's activity. She was still damp from her shower. The coolness of the apartment made her nipples sit erect from her copper-toned breast. Dawn braced herself against the doorframe, as she watched Dale slowly expose himself. Each stroke inched the thin sheet further away from his body; down passed his powerfully-toned chest, his sculpted abdomen, and his muscular tattooed arms. Dawn watched as Dale moaned, flinging the sheet away from his naked body. His ebony sex

SexPressions

muscle, towered over his body, as Dale wrestled with himself. Dawn tiptoed slowly toward the bed, scared to break Dale's sexual trance with her presence. With each step her body threatened to reveal her movements. Dawn's inner thigh taunted her still sensitive clitoris. She wanted to move faster; had to move faster, but couldn't muster the strength. Her mouth watered as she remembered the taste of Dale's sex. She stood him. Her body naked and near orgasmic relief. Dawn could no longer stand not having Dale inside of her. She watched as her hand reached out to Dale's rock hard penis.

Dale's body began to tingle. He tried to wait for Dawn to return from the shower, but her poem made him impatient with horniness. Dale let his early morning stiffness move between his hands. He cursed Dawn for staying in the shower so long. Although her poem stated otherwise, he didn't think his performance was worth praise. Refreshed from a good night's sleep, Dale wanted to give her real reason for poetry.

"C'mon baby!" Dale silently pleaded, as his loins began to boil with hot liquid sex. Dale's impatience soon ate away at him. He needed Dawn. And if she wouldn't come to him, he'd go to her. Dale opened his eyes just as Dawn's hand closed over the head of his penis. He jumped slightly, surprised at her proximity. Her skin was cool and damp from the shower. Dale shivered as Dawn tried to mimic the movements of his hands. He could feel her hand trembling as she moved over him. He held onto her thighs trying to steady her. The aroma of Dawn's clean sweet sex danced lightly across Dale's tongue. A soft breath rushed from Dawn lips as she guided herself down onto Dale's early

Dale's Passion

morning stiffness.

"Good morning!" The warmth of Dawn's womb whispered to Dale.

Dale lifted his pelvis, inviting Dawn further onto him, she wiggled each throbbing inch slowly inside of her, until she thought Dale's girth would push his way through her. Her body shuddered, as she used her hips and pelvis, along with Dale, to dig deeper into her. Each thrust powered Dawn's sexual locomotive and soon she was a run-away *freak*train. She fell forward onto Dale. Dawn reached under Dale's arms and held onto his shoulders. Her large breast steadied her as she pushed and pulled herself to ecstasy. Dale rolled Dawn's still cool ass cheeks in his hands. He fought the mounting orgasm. He felt Dawn tremble, as she tried to roll them into a ball. Light-headedness enveloped Dawn as her muscles locked in place. She felt a warm liquid rush ooze down her thighs. Soft tears rolled from her eyes as she tried to hold her and Dale as still as possible. Dale wiggled under her, making the task impossible. She felt him hold her to his chest as he rolled himself on top of her. Dawn's orgasmically-locked body fought Dale's attempt to move her limbs. Numb, Dawn watched as Dale placed one of her legs around his waist, while straddling the other leg.

The delicate pressure and tender friction was more than Dawn could take. Again Dawn's brain ordered sexual paralysis. Dawn felt soft grunts against her breast and felt Dale's body began to tremble. She watched as each powerfully smooth thrust defined Dale's muscular frame. Dawn reached her hands out to touch his chest. She slowly ran her hands over his torso. She watched as Dale bit down

SexPressions

on his lip, orgasm pushing blood to his already oversized sexual head. All at once, Dawn's senses assaulted her. She hadn't noticed how quiet the room was. The sounds she and Dale made boomed against her ears. Her body tingled with frightening **_sextricity_**. The smell of their sex delightfully attacked her nose. Her tongue tingled from the taste of the last night's flavors. The only sense that failed her now was her sight. Everything went black, and a rebel orgasm attacked the gates of her vagina. The last thought Dawn had was of Dale's entire body going stiff, as he slowed himself. Dawn felt Dale's warmth collapse softly onto her.

Dawn could hear Dale's voice, as she lay in a dream-like, semi-conscious state.

"Yes Ma'am. I'll have her call as soon as she feel's strong enough."

Dawn sank back into the blackness, body stiff from sex. When she awoke she searched for Dale's presence. Just the thought of his touch made her smile. Her hands searched the still warm mattress. She opened her eyes, trying to confirm what her mind already knew. Dawn fought off sluggish, sex-induced sleep. She sat up in bed looking again this time finding only a sheet of paper.

Dawn fought the feeling of sleep as she focused on the words. First she read Dale's note explaining his absence. He'd left to go shopping for lunch and dinner. Then Dawn flipped the paper over and read what turned out to be a poem.

Dawn, fully awake, scanned the paper as Dale's voice

Dale's Passion

spoke the words for her.

She read the poem three times. Each time she closed her eyes afterward and allowed Dale's voice to guide her to ecstasy.

A Simple Dinner Date

Even I had to blush. It wasn't everyday a woman flirted with me as well as my wife. At first we thought the saleswoman was just being friendly. When you're selling high-valued homes and properties, being friendly goes with the job. The price of a few of the homes didn't make flirting so far-fetched. Hell, a blow job should come with the closing. So to watch my wife squirm while a sexy woman flirted with her made house shopping fun. Not to mention, she was Spanish.

I decided to let my wife take the lead on this. She was the tougher of the two of us when it came to money. If it were possible to stuff all our money in her large D-cup bra she would. This time she was putty in this woman's hands.

"Mizz Anna Gomez." Her accent was thick and musical. She was a little taller than my wife, that's before the heels she wore pushed her even higher. Her hair was long, black and gorgeous. She wore it tied up tightly and allowed it to dangle past her shoulders. When she spoke it was hard not to notice her lips. Her make up was light, but her lips still seemed red and

SexPressions

exotic. She had thick legs that seemed trapped in a black skirt that stopped at her knees. Her ass looked perfect. I tried not to get caught looking at her lovely ass. I wanted to see if I could notice her panty lines. Not seeing one drove me and my thoughts crazy. I wondered what type of panties she wore. She seemed like a thong or bikini woman. That's if she was wearing panties at all. Her white blouse was low cut, but not low enough to take away from her being a professional. It only added to my imagination. The closest I ever came to having sex with a Spanish woman was the time I beat my dick to porn about Mexican women. Damn Ms. Gomez was sexy. My dick throbbed from the introduction.

My wife was no slouch either. She was heavier than Ms. Gomez. Where she was slender my wife was thick and muscular. My wife's ass was rounder and fuller. Her legs were long and defined. When she walked into a room, her body commanded attention. She had lost close to eighty pounds since we started our consultation firm. Who would have known people would pay so much for us to tell them how to run their business? What I found the sexiest about my wife was her assertiveness. She wasn't a prude but she liked to be chased.

There was something about my wife that brought out the fire in Ms. Gomez. She either really wanted to sell this house or fuck my wife. It was hard to tell which. Anna would move in close to tell my wife about each room's highlights. How the foyer had perfect lighting for that special off-to-work kiss effect.

A Simple Dinner Date

How the living room's ceilings were high and the fireplace made for a very romantic evening, about how sexy breakfast would be in the kitchen with the nook. She showed us the bathroom with the large marble standing shower and the large deep soaking tub. I didn't need her to tell me about the sex that could be had in that. She whispered something to my wife that caused both of them to look at me, laugh and fan themselves. All the time her accent peeking out at those times that were sexually charged. We exchanged cards and told her we would contact her with our decision. I wonder if she knew how full of shit we were. I think she knew the house was sold before we left. I knew it was sold after my wife still smiled when the price was mentioned. We could afford it now, but damn, like I said, it's best to flirt when you say things like two hundred fifty thousand dollars.

It took us a couple of days to get back to the real estate firm. During those days all we thought about was Anna and that accent, those lovely legs and the way she talked with her delicate hands. We would lay in bed those nights lying to ourselves. We tried talking about business but we arrived at the same thing.

"Damn that woman was sexy." That's what my wife said as she sat on my dick slowly rocking her hips. The more she said it, the further she drove my dick inside her, until finally her clitoris brushed against my stomach. That was the first night my wife used her limited Spanish.

SexPressions

She grabbed my head and called me *"Papi Chulo"*. She screamed *"ayi"* when she came. I just screamed. It was the sexiest thing I had ever heard. The second night we ate Mexican and Brazilian. I told my wife that they spoke Portuguese in Brazil. It didn't matter to her. All she could say was, "Damn she was sexy." As if her sex appeal was a magic trick. She really was sexy.

"I wonder what her pussy tastes like." she said that night.

"When did you become so interested in pussy and how it tastes?" I asked, shock filling my dick with hot blood.

"Since always, Judy ate my pussy at our reception." My wife said in an "I've been around manner."

I didn't know if I should be angry or excited. I had to settle on both. Judy sucked my dick that night as well. Ms. Gomez didn't call us until a few days after we called her.

"So you like the Morgan Estate?" Her voice caressed the sides of my face through the phone speaker. It was easy to see the effect wasn't wasted on my wife.

"Yeah we really enjoyed the viewing as well." I said, trying my best to sound as if I wasn't about to explode with hot sperm down my leg.

A Simple Dinner Date

"We would like you to celebrate with us." My wife said, "Please don't say no."

She giggled softly. "Ms. Gibson, I'm flattered, but my job…"

"Please it's only dinner." My wife said, cutting her off.

"Okay, I'll come."

"And call me Janet."

"Okay, Janet. I'll come. It's to celebrate right?"

"Right."

That was it, a simple dinner date.

I have to admit, my wife is a good cook. She didn't try anything crazy, or out of the way. She baked whiting with lemon pepper, garlic, and a slice of lime over wild rice. She tossed a salad crowned with vegetables, a few boiled eggs, and cheese. For dessert, she stopped at the bakery and bought a Dutch apple pie and ice cream. Pie for after dinner, and ice cream for after that. I had never seen my wife so nervous. If I had known this would have happened, I would have introduced her to a sexy Latin woman sooner. My wife had taken control of the entire night. She told me to shave, both heads, and my face.

SexPressions

"Wear that cologne that makes my pussy quiver." She whispered as I stepped into the shower. She picked out my outfit; starched gray slacks and a white shirt. She told me that outfit always makes her want to fuck in public places. I'm no fool. I showered and did as I was told. By the time I was dressed my wife had put on what I thought to be the sexist dress she owned. It was orange with thin straps that barely held the dress up. Her beautiful cleavage was exposed by the low cut front. She wore a body spray that was made with glitter that added a shimmer to her breast. The dress fit just tight enough to require her to wear either a g-string, which is usually orange as well, or no panties at all. She wore a matching pair of open toe shoes that tied around her calves.

"Damn baby. You look good enough to eat." I whispered as I pulled her close.

"I hope she thinks so, too." She kissed me on the lips and wiggled out of my embrace. "We have to save some for later."

I believe women truly speak another language than men. They understand each other a lot better. I'm very impatient, yet my wife didn't see anything wrong with Ms. Gomez being late.

"Anticipation is sexy." She told me as we sat hugged up on the couch listening to music. "Plus why can't a woman just wanna chill with her husband." She paused then turned to face me. "You *are* okay with this?"

A Simple Dinner Date

I shook my head "yes". Why wouldn't I be? If I wasn't, I damn sure wasn't going to say anything. Not tonight anyway. I kissed her softly on the lips, moved my hand over her breast, and then kissed her neck.

"We have to save some for later." I said winking at her.

Just then the door bell rang interrupting our petting session. My wife took a deep breath, stood up, fixed her clothes and moved to the door. I took a while longer. It's not very easy hiding the bulge of a thick nine inch erection.

I heard the two women greeting each other with a hint of excitement. By the time I reached the door they were hugging, and all I could see of Ms. Gomez was her arms and head. I didn't get a chance to take a deep breath; I should have. My wife had taken her jacket and was still blocking my view. When I finally saw her I had to remind myself to close my mouth and stop gawking. She was stunning. She wore a white shirt that hugged her delicious body. The hem stopped a thumb's width from her knees with splits on both sides. A white silk top that was but just enough to expose her lovely caramel cleavage with showing her bra. One good laugh and a breast would pop free. I decided to be very funny the entire night. I didn't know how much of a foot fetish I had until I saw her open toe shoes along side of my wife's. Each woman's polish matched her outfit. Twenty very delicious looking toes. I looked to the heavens and thank the Lord for whatever reward I was receiving.

SexPressions

"Welcome Ms. Gomez," I said, trying to return my voice to its natural tone.

"Anna. Please no need to be so business-like."

"Okay, Anna, welcome to our home."
Janet and I exchanged smiles and winks. We gave her the grand tour before dinner. We offered wine, but somehow it didn't feel right.

"Do you have any vodka? Or Rum? I love rum." Anna said smiling and breaking the ice that had began to form.

"Anna You my kinda people," Janet said pulling her toward our small bar. Drinks were poured, drank and poured again. After that things went smoothly. Dinner went well. We ate and talked. The conversation was light and free. The women did most of the talking. I just sat and let my imagination go unbridled. I just basked in their presence; their very sexy; very dick-stiffening presence. Janet told Anna about our company and the success we were now enjoying.

"It turns me on to be able to boss white folks around, and then take their money," Janet said, smiling across the table.

"What else turns you on," Anna asked, no longer being polite. Janet raised her eyebrow, nodded her head and replied, "Maybe we'll find out."

A Simple Dinner Date

Drinks were refreshed and the conversation's heat rose from there. Anna told us more about her. We found out she was from Puerto Rico.

"I'm from Falardo," she said. At first it was easy to see that she was talking to us, but when she spoke about Puerto Rico she spoke to Janet and Janet alone. Her words were sexually hypnotic.

"I used to walk to the beach," her words slurred into her accent. Beach sounded like 'beash'. "I would lay in the warm water and dream," she slowly closed her eyes and internally hugged herself. "The water was blue as a jewel. The sun's warmth brushed against my skin." The more she talked, the harder my dick grew. She told us about losing her virginity near the beach.

"I never had a man touch me like him. His name was Dimar." When she said it, she put an emphasis on the last part and softly rolled the 'r'. "I remember lying naked beneath some trees, young and scared. His head between my legs and the sun kissing my little *titas*,"

By then Janet and I had moved closer and began softly rubbing each other beneath the table.

"Dimar slowly moved up my body with kisses. He kissed my mouth with fire." Janet had slowly begun stroking her hand along my throbbing shaft.

SexPressions

" *Esta nocho nostros los vamos a matar,*" Dimar said through Anna. I didn't know what any of that meant, but it made my wife gasp. Her pussy pulsated and gushed on my fingers.

"*Yo soy todo tu yo,*" Anna whispered from her long ago.

"*Yo soy todo tu ya,*" Dimar whispered softly in her ear.

"He pushed two fingers into my little *chocha* and I nearly screamed. Then he licked his fingers and told me it tasted like sugar." Janet slipped two fingers to her pussy, rubbed her clitoris, and brought them up to my mouth.

"Mmmmm, sweet baby," was my only response.

"When I finally saw his dick I bite into his shoulder. He felt so big between my thighs. And when he put it in…" she drifted off with that. Anna's words became sweet and syrupy.

Janet just listened and nodded her head. She rocked back and forth on my fingers humming.

"He kissed me on my mouth, but not like the boys I knew. This was a man's kiss," Anna said. She had begun moving her fingers over her exposed breast and arms. Janet devoured each word then acted them out on my fingers and with her hands. When Anna said her lover stroke was deep, Janet pulled my hand as far

A Simple Dinner Date

as it would reach. I wiggled my fingers against her inner pleasures forcing a moan to trickle from her lips. Anna whispered about the heat of her body and instantly my wife's vaginal temperature soared. Anna spoke and Janet obeyed. Finally they both gave in to the moment. Anna's hand disappeared beneath the table. Her eyes closed just before mine. Janet pushed my chair backward, pulled my stiff dick free of my pants and took it in her warm mouth in one swallow.

"Damn," I cursed as the warm roughness punked me out. Janet greedily slurped and sucked on my dick. Her moans bounced off my balls and fell between my legs. I could barely hear Anna over Janet's efforts. I grabbed two handfuls of her hair and held on for my sexual life. I slowly lifted my eyelids to watch Anna please herself. I thought I had dreamt the entire episode when I didn't see her. Then I heard soft Spanish whispering and sexual moaning to my left.

"Esta mama tienetremendo culo," Anna moaned moving her hands over Janet's body. She pressed her pelvis against Janet's ass. Janet swayed and rocked between us. Anna eased Janet's dress higher revealing her orange g-string, and caressing her lovely round ass. My dick began to slowly swell as I watched the sexy Puerto Rican woman kiss and lick my wife's beautiful ebony ass cheeks. Janet gripped the base of my shaft and tried to steady herself against Anna's mouth. She moaned, slurped loudly then stuffed me back into her mouth. Anna squatted behind her, spread her cheeks apart and eased her tongue up and down along Janet's sexual crease. Soft Spanish flew,

accompanied by slurps and moans. Anna looked at me, slowly slid two manicured fingers into Janet and slowly finger-fucked her. I took it as a cue and followed suit. I slowly eased to my feet and began pumping into my wife's mouth. Jealousy motored my hips as I became determined to outwork Anna. Janet ripped open my pants and forced her hand down the back of my boxers and dug her nails into my ass cheeks. I sneered, keeping my eyes on Anna. Janet moved a hand to my stomach, raked her nails over my belly, and then pushed herself free of my dick.

"I want that dick in my pussy." She panted.

Janet crawled on the table and lay on her back. "I wanna lick that pussy too," she stared at Anna. Janet pulled her arms out of the thin straps freeing her breast and pushed the dress over her stomach, while Anna pulled her dress over her head revealing her curvaceous body. Anna crawled on the table and slowly lowered herself over Janet's face. I watched Janet kissed her clitoris before I put my dick in place. Anna sat back, bracing herself against Janet's breast and rocked. The sight was beautiful; my wife's lovely chocolate blending into Anna's sensual caramel. If a picture is worth a thousand words; this was a fucking book. I blinked twice, grabbed my dick and guided myself into Janet. I had planned on starting slow. But the pace had already been set. I had to catch up. I pumped with a smooth fury.

"Hell Yeah, Baby," I growled, "Like that sweet Puerto Rican pussy don't cha"?

A Simple Dinner Date

Janet smacked Anna on her ass and sucked loudly on her clitoris, forcing Anna to fall forward. She leaned her head to the side and sucked on Janet's swollen clitoris. I moved my hands to Anna's waist and truly began fucking my wife. Our sex was wet and noisy; the women licking, slurping, and smacking with the sound of my thighs smacking against my wife's ass. My dick began to buzz. Normally I would stop; savor my orgasm, but now I didn't care. I continued pumping and Janet screamed, "My pussy is on fire." She dug her nails into Anna's soft ass. "Fuck me, Baby!"

Anna licked Janet's clit and my shaft as I pumped. Janet's moans grew wild and harsh. Anna sat back, teased her clitoris, and did a slow grind against Janet's face. Janet grabbed her breast by the nipples. Her pussy clenched tightly then pulsated. Every muscle in her body locked, unlocked, and then locked again. Anna fell forward again and sucked tenderly on Janet's quivering clitoris.

"I'm cumin'," I couldn't help it. My ass cheek tightened involuntarily. I bit my lip and kept pumping, Janet's pussy massaging my pistoning shaft.

"Get that pussy." She growled from beneath Anna. I had no choice. A rough growl escaped my clenched jaw as a feeling of light headedness overcame me and gob after gob of electric ebony liquid shot from my body.

SexPressions

"I *Papi Chulo.*" Anna whispered as I continued pumping. I slowly slid from Janet's vagina and plopped into a chair. I should have been spent. Normally I would have been, but the sight of Anna lapping at our sexual mixture, energized me. I stood and kicked my pants from around my ankles, pulled my shirt off. I stroked Anna's hair before slipping my dick against her lips, then into her mouth. Anna moved her mouth around the head of my penis, and then slid her tongue along my thick veined length. Anna kissed and licked my dick, all the time looking up at me.

"I want you to fuck me," she kissed. Anna crawled from over Janet and from the table. She kissed me hard on the mouth, slipping her tongue in my mouth. Our tongues danced before she pushed away and bent over the table. I grabbed her waist, and then guided myself into her.

"Paaahhpppeee," she gasped.

I looked at my wife and started working. Anna's plush wetness welcomed my rigid flesh. I pulled her back to me and pushed deep into her.

"Yeah, Mami," I growled.

"I papi mas duro," she spat, then "Mi chocha es moja."

I didn't know what it meant but it fired me up. I started pounding my dick further. Anna moaned and

A Simple Dinner Date

yelled in spangles. Janet who had been slowly rubbing her swollen labia, wiggled beneath Anna's face. She held Anna's head in place while I pumped and stroked pushing her out of place. My force powered Anna's tongue movements. She panted and screamed. Anna placed a hand on Janet's breast and tried to stave me off with the other.

"Papi, mas duro," she moaned. I became driven and the foreign taunts were the sexual fuel. I opened my stance, giving me a more stable base, grabbed her ass and stroked. I tried to watch Janet, but between the sweat and the exciting sensation; I couldn't. Anna continued licking, moaning and verbally prodding.

"Fuck her baby," Janet moaned, "fuck that good pussy." I listened and obeyed. I reached forward grabbing Anna's hair, pulled back and rammed forward. Anna squealed and slapped the table. I felt her pussy wall constrict around my blackness. Her moans became quick and choppy. Janet knocked my hands away and pulled Anna's skilled tongue back to its original place and job. Anna repeated her Spanish taunt pulling me further inside of her. Every muscle in my body burned and tingled; all but my dick. It was numb and heavy with my impending orgasm. I couldn't hold it off any longer. Anna stood on her tip toes, pushed upward and squealed. She bit her lip and tried to scurry away from me. I grabbed her waist and denied her sexual parole. I copied her stance and stood on my tip toes, pushing my thickness in a downward angle and went for broke. My grunts became primal and furious. An electric growling

SexPressions

began deep within me. I smacked Anna's loving bouncing ass. I never in my life wanted to be rid of an orgasm more than I did now. My head swam within a syrupy heat just as my body ejected hot life. I pulled my scorching dick from Anna and pumped my girth. Hot white globs splashed against her ass and back. I couldn't help it. I always wanted to do that porno shit. I kissed Anna's raised cheek and plopped, again exhausted, into my chair. I could hear soft kissing and moaning as I drifted off to sleep. I want to say I woke up a couple of times to my wife or Anna sucking my dick. I just wanted to sleep. That was six months ago.

Dr. Graham pressed stop on the small recorder. This was his third session with the Gibsons. He was happy they were finally getting down to the source of the problem. It's a shame when a young couple fall prey to the stress and pressure of marriage. When they add another person, a dominating sexual presence and then things get scary. Mrs. Gibson had filed for divorce a month ago. She cited her husband's infidelity as a problem. This was to be the first in many tales. Dr. Graham could see Mr. Gibson wanted to save his marriage. He was just a victim to his desires.

NEW IN TOWN

"Need any help?" The sweet voice sang to rob from the hallway. Rob poked his head out the door to see who the voice belonged to.

"I could use some help unpacking!" rob blurted, catching himself from scaring off the thick Samaritan. She was a sexy reddish brown (or caramel) toned sister. She wore a pair of gray *"State U"* sweat pants and a tight blue t-shirt, or better yet the shirt was wearing her. Her breast hung unsupported, but not snagging, and she had a smile that made a man just say, "Yes".

"Well let me finish and I'll be right over." She said, turning slow, giving Rob a long look at her ass. Rob brought the last box up from the truck. Damn he hated moving. Next time he promised he'd hire movers. He looked around his cluttered new apartment and decided the first order of business would be a cold beer. He headed toward the kitchen when a soft knock on the door slowed his movement.

"It's open!" He yelled back over his shoulder, turning toward the door.

"Well I'm back to help!" His sexy Samaritan neighbor

SexPressions

said easing around the door. She had traded her sweats and tee for a pair of tight shorts. She had work-out legs that looked like they were carved from marble.

"Well what's first?" She quizzed, placing her hands on her hips before looking around at the clutter.

"Well I was about to take a brew break." Rob said, turning just as his penis noticed their neighbor's scent. "Want one?"

"Sure."

Rob disappeared into the kitchen and returned with two cold bottles of *"Red Stripe"* beer. His neighbor was standing in the middle of the living room looking around at the job ahead of them. Her back was to Rob. He approached her, standing too close, accidentally on purpose. She turned into him and was close. "Kissing close." Rob thought. She had the smell of roses and he could taste her smell on his tongue.

"I'm Sandra. All my fre…....I mean, friends call me Sandi."

"Well Sandra, I mean Sandi, I'm Robert. But please call me Rob." He replied hoping he was now one of her fre…. *friends*.

They finished unpacking and sat on the couch talking. Not really paying the other's words much attention. Sandra stared at Rob's arms and chest. She'd had two small orgasms thinking about *those* arms being wrapped around her. She

New in Town

imagined resting her head on *that* chest, teasing *those* nipples with her tongue, and how she would lightly scratch *that* chest once he was inside her.

"I bet he can fuck." She thought and smiled to herself. She was brown. The real kind of brown. The color of jazz music. Sandra shook as orgasm number three snuck up on her.

"Can I ask you a question?" Rob asked, not waiting for a response. "Peaches or Kiwi?"
"Peaches or kiwi, what?"

"Which do you taste like: peaches or kiwi?"

Sandra blushed. "I've never tasted myself, but you're welcome to find out."

She leaned back against the sofa's arm and spread her legs. Rob licked his lips and crawled over to her. He kissed her on her mouth. She shivered as he lay atop of her. Not missing a beat, Rob slid her shirt over her head exposing her heaving breast. Her nipples were erect and red. Rob moved lower. Planting kisses and licks as he went along. He ran his tongue around her nipples, while his soft touch entertained her tight welcome mat. Sandra wrapped her legs around him and slowly pressed against him. She moaned without hearing herself. Her body was on fire. Rob switched breasts adding a small bite to the teasing. He was hard. Rob could feel her moving her hips beneath him. He wanted to let go.

"Not now." Her body whispered to his.
"Not now."

SexPressions

Rob moved lower, leaving a trail of kisses. He unbuttoned her shorts and pulled her free of them. She was panty less underneath, and she was clean-shaven. Rob grinned before kissing and licking at her sweet surface. The taste of peaches exploded onto his tongue. Rob teased the small sex pit. She was hot, wet, and sweet. She moved her hips faster as Rob continued licking. *Oh's* and *Ah's* eased from her lips. Sandra gripped the back of Rob's bald head, holding him in place. It wasn't his chest, but it would do for now. Her body jerked, and then shuddered. Rob began humming, sending soft vibrations through her twat. Her juices flowed thick and sweet. Rob invaded her hole with his finger, still licking and sucking her pearl. Now the small flame that had ignited Sandra's lust became an out of control fire. Her body tingled. She sat up and reached for Rob's shirt. She had to see him. She had to have his chest against her. She snatched at his shirt, sending buttons flying every which way. Underneath the torn shirt, was a brown slab of rock-hard granite. Each nipple pierced. Sandra grinned and rubbed her hands over the smoothness.

"Please say there's more." She quizzed.

Rob stood over her and removed his pants.

"Hell no!" He said, pulling his underwear off. His length stood out from his body in its thick glory. Sandra cursed under her breath and swallowed hard, as Rob lifted her up. Sandra wrapped her legs around his naked body. He felt like one large sex muscle, pulsating between her legs. Rob leaned her against the wall. Stilling hold her legs and ass he moved inside of her. Rob gasped as her tight walls engulfed him. He pushed in to the tilt. His total girth and

New in Town

length pushed against her walls. Rob slowly rotated his hips, instead of pumping. Sandra felt him inside of her large and still growing with passion. She pushed from the wall and clung to him. She rode wave after wave. He throbbed inside of her. Sandra felt him weaken, and she placed a foot on the floor and swayed with Rob's movement. Rob squeezed her thighs. He was torn; torn between wanting to cum and wanting to keep going; to stay inside of her. Sandra helped him decide.

"I wanna be on top." She whispered in his ear. She had to have him; had to feel him release inside of her; had to have *that* chest and *those* arms.

Rob let her down gingerly and lay on the carpeted floor. Sandra stalked over him and squatted down on him. He felt even larger inside of her. His black rod stretched her and pressed against her pearl. Sandra placed her hands on his chest. *That* chest. *Her* chest. Sandra worked only her pelvis and hips. She dug into him. Sandra lay completely down on his chest and licked the golden rings in his nipples. Her mouth and teeth engaged in sexual playtime. Rob's body tightened. He couldn't hold back, he didn't want to hold on. His dick stiffened and erupted in her. Rob muffled a soft growl of defeat and pleasure. Sandra kept riding and holding on to *that* chest. *Her* chest. Sandra's eyes slammed shut and she pushed away from him.

"Here I cum Baby." She said, rolling his nipples in her fingertips. Rob grabbed her ass as she tightened around him. A warm wet rush drenched them. Sandra was spent. She collapsed forward onto his chest. *That* chest. Her chest. She kissed, scratched and rubbed lightly on *their* chest and fell into a deep slumber.

Rob could hear Sandra sleeping on him. He smiled and thought to himself, *"If this was the type of people who lived here, he was going to love Chicago."*

THE SECRETS

"Okay my eyes are shut!" I yell sitting up on the bed. You went shopping and had something that just couldn't wait until later.

"Okay. Open them!" You say from the foot of the bed. Instantly my jaw drops. You're wearing a satin, two-piece pants set. Red as a fire engine. The top is open and your breasts are semi-exposed. Now I'm awake.

"Weeelll? What do you think? You ask spinning around. "Speechless, huh? Well what about this?" You pull the panties down slightly, displaying you red pubic hair.

"How'd you do that?" I ask crawling toward you with my hand outstretched.

"No touching." You say, slapping my hand away playfully. "That's not all. I have some more stuff to show you. Close your eyes, I'll be right back."

I quickly close my eyes again. The sight of you in all red with fire hair between your legs sends my manhood throbbing. My mind envisions softly petting it. "Not yet Killer! Not yet." Minutes pass and you yell for me to keep

SexPressions

my eyes shut. I snap them tighter. I'm eager for what will happen next. You tell me to open my eyes, I do so while holding my breath. My member pushes against the thin sheets covering my body giving way to my nakedness. When I open my eyes, I see you standing on the side of the bed wearing a long white gown, and get the first soft scent that whispers to my nose of a sweet fragrance. There's a split running down the left side of your gown showing off your leg.

"I'm impressed!" My member says through my lips.

You smile, pulling the split open. Now the pubic hair is white as snow. Once again you spin and move away from me. The suspense threatens me as you tell me there are more to come. My mind is set ablaze with amazement. Colors run through my head. Yellow? Green? Blue? I torture myself thinking of what could be next. All kinds of combinations of colors dance through my thoughts. Once again I'm told to close my eyes. I never had them shut as tight as I do now. The sight of your passion spot, in those colors, has me craving you. I can't take it. And the look on your face, told me you knew what you were doing to my mind.

You tell me to open my eyes. This time cinnamon dances across my nose. A few throbs from my manhood signal my approval. When I finally open my eyes, I nearly have an orgasm. You stand over me wearing a gold silk teddy, which fell just at the top of your thighs. Your skin was lightly dusted with a golden sheen. And when you exposed you vagina again to me, your pubic hair was golden. A tear of joy ran down my face. I held back a

The Secrets

powerful orgasm. And just then I realized there was more to this than just the fashion show. Once again you slide away from me gliding from me. Just out my reach.

"Choose one!" You smile.

Red, white, or gold? The first two pictures join the last. What a terrible tease you are. But my dick chooses for me.

"Gold." I mumble. Holding my throbbing length tightly in my hands.

"Okay. But put this on first." You say tossing me a gold blindfold. And now I can't hold back. A light eruption takes place. You look unconcerned and hand me a hand towel.
"You're not getting off that easy." You smirk at me.

I place the blindfold over my eyes and lay back. First I feel the sheets being snatched from the bed. Then I feel a soft, wet sensation against my nipples. It's not your tongue. *Damn this blindfold.* The object moves across my chest. It's vibrating softly and it calls to my body. You lean in close to my ear.

Whispering, "Now I'm going to show you the secrets of gold."

My body screams "Yes."

I feel you hovering over my body. Your kiss is soft and golden. And again I taste cinnamon. A light film coats my

SexPressions

lips. My body tingles and quivers from your touch. The small, wet object still moves across my chest. It taunts my erect nipples. And now I feel your tongue against them. I close my eyes and try to vision you on top of me. The gold satin draped across you like shiny skin. Your hands move across my body concealing the object. *The Golden Tongue.*

You move your hand down to my life rod. The Golden Tongue assaults my erotic nerves. Your kisses land softly there, leaving a light film. Using the Golden Tongue, you run it along the length of my shaft. You cup of your hands around the base. The Golden Tongue stirs my juices. I become fully erect. Leaving the Golden Tongue on my sack, you use your other hand to stroke my shaft. My body stiffens and then goes numb. I rub your back with one hand and your breast with the other. You brush my hands away.

"Keep those to yourself"

Your stroking hand returns to my rod, concentrating on the head. I pulsate in your palm. You move the Golden Tongue between my legs and trace my black star. I shake and tremble, before trying to squirm away from you and that sexual torture device. But I can't escape, yet I can't stay. And I can't see or say. Whatever the "Golden" secrets are, they're safe with me. You feel me nearing close to an orgasm. You grin as you change the pace of your strokes. You move The Golden Tongue down my thighs.

"Shhhiiiittah!" I scream.

I'm overtaken by my arousal. I jerk harshly. But nothing happens. I just lay gripped by a tingling feeling in

The Secrets

my loins. No eruption. No life comes forth.

"It works!" You giggle in victory.

Still erect and tingling, my dick now belongs to you. You continue to stroke. I continue to pulsate and throb in your palm. I can't believe the sensation. I should've exploded and shot love cream. But I didn't. And only you know why. After what seems like hours you end the torture. You kiss me on my cheek. You remove the blindfold. Every inch of me radiates golden electricity. I'm paralyzed.

You remove the teddy. Standing in front of me exposed to the world. Your skin is still dusted gold and your treasure box is still golden. Damp; but still golden. You lay on top of me. I kiss you on your neck. The cinnamon taste leaps onto my tongue. It's warm and inviting. I roll you over, eager to taste your golden treasures. I trail kisses and licks across your body. I try to taste every golden inch of you. I lick your breast. The golden dust warms my tongue as I circle each nipple. I can't get enough of you. I move down to your belly. A small pool of dust is gathered at your belly button. I lap at it, like a sex puppy, trying to lick it all. Still unable to hold you, I move lower. I pause as I gaze at your golden love mane. Then I dive in, the taste of the gold dust and your creaminess is more than I'm ready for. I lap up your heat. I kiss and lick, hoping that I can know your secrets by tasting you. A golden soft moan leaves you lips. You wrap your legs around my neck, pulling me closer, deeper into you with my tongue. Time stops, speeds up and then slows to a crawl. Your body vibrates. You release your lock, push me away and leap from the bed.

SexPressions

"Not yet! I still have other tings to show you!" You say, dust covering you only in a few places. "But sip this wine and I'll be back."

You leave the room and me alone. Now I sit and wonder. How can you change the colors so fast? What was that golden dust? What was that toy you used? And how did you stop my orgasm. I lay back and wonder. After a few sips and more wondering, I drift off to sleep. You wake me, after what feels like hours, but I know can only be minutes. You're smiling and wearing a robe.

"Go shower, and when you get back, I'll show you the Pearl Secrets!"

You allow the robe to drop to the floor, revealing the white gown underneath. I bolt from the bed and into the shower. I still have questions and the only way to learn is by being taught. While I shower, I still wonder about the last few minutes. The changes, the toy, and the sensation of an orgasm that wasn't. How good it all felt. As I wash away the dust I smile to myself. I am truly in for a long day. I get out of the shower and towel off. It won't be the first time I've worked overtime today. I enter the bedroom. You're lying on the bed, drinking wine. You smile at me, looking better than I remember; the white satin against your skin. Cream covered ecstasy. You hand me a glass of wine and pat the bed next to you as an invitation. I slide into the bed. We hug. You smell good enough to eat. Your skin is soft and smooth under the slick material. I pull you close. I run my fingers along and across your stomach. I feel a small tremor run through your body. I kiss you softly about your face. My lips touch against your forehead; your cheeks, your chin, and

The Secrets

finally your lips. Your skin tastes sweet. I lick and wonder how sweet the rest of you must taste. You sit up and roll me over on my stomach. You straddle my back. You lean down and kiss my neck. Now it's my turn to have tremors. I feel your sex against my back. You run your hands along the edges of my sides, exposing my ticklishness. You slide down and kiss between my shoulders. I hum softly at how good that feels. I'm engulfed in your passion. Your white kisses have me swimming. You rub my shoulders. You move down my back. Firmly squeezing my buttocks, placing kisses on each cheek and then you move further down my legs. You run your tongue down my legs and my inner thigh. My ecstasy calls out to you.

"Take me or allow me to take you!" It begs for an answer.

You crawl of me. I feel your breast. Your nipples tickle my back. Your hands whisper to my emotions. Your soft voice grabs my body and guides me down the path of our newness. I roll over on my back. I reach out to you; to hold you; to see you; to be with you. I touch your thighs, as if for the first time. I inch the gown up your body, removing your white skin, exposing us to each other; slowing removing our knowledge. I finally pull the gown over your head. We sit up, you on me; brand new in our virginity; in our rebirth; the new us. For the fist time I see you again. I kiss you. Your skin teaches me. My hands learn from the touch of you. I place your breast in my mouth. I lick away at your innocence. I feel growing warmer. You hold my head closer to your bosom. Our bodies call to each other, and we reply. You guide me into you. Your freshness holds my manhood within you. We move together. I lay back still holding your

SexPressions

breast. You place your hands on my chest to steady yourself. I grow deeper and higher into you. Move my hips from side to side, while you rock slowly back and forth. Eager we tease each other's other spots. For the first time I notice the string of pearls. They were on the bed next to us, but now you have them in your hands. You roll them across my chest. The pearls feel warm and inviting. Placing the entire string in your left hand you rub my nipples until they harden under your touch. I arch my back in pleasure, inching deeper and further still inside of your pearly sex. I try to scream in pleasure. You slowly rise off of me and smile. You move to my stomach, kissing its sweat glazed surface. The area tingles from the memory of your lips. You kiss my chest, stopping to allow your tongue to dance with my nipples, and then you kiss me on the lips. You fondle my manhood, using the pearls to enhance your touch. I melt from your white heat. You lay next to me, one leg over mine, leaving my sex to wish for your touch. You slowly drag the pearls across my body. With your free hand you touch me tenderly. With your eyes you make love to my thoughts. I'm powerless yet in control; soft and firm; ready and yet still unprepared. I moan to myself and you smile. You teased and tortured me. You lay your head on my chest. We hold each other. Kissing and trading touches. Soon we're off to sleep in each others arms. When I wake you're not in the bed. After a quick search of the house, I find you in the kitchen. You're wearing the red suit and holding a glass of water.

"Drink this, it's about to get hot. Very hot!" I take the glass from your hand. I pause not knowing if I should finish the glass or sip from it. You're standing in front of me, hands on your hips, breast staring from out of inside of your top. I lift the glass to drink and you're on me fast. You start licking

The Secrets

my neck. You run your hands up my legs. I stand naked and unable to resist. You back me against the refrigerator and start kissing down my chest. You take your hands and tend to my still sleeping sex member. Using one hand, you fondle my balls while the other strokes my entire length. By now you've worn your way to my navel. Your tongue darts in my small crevices, lighting a small flame. I cringe and try to brace myself. Using your tongue, you draw circles on my stomach. My sex is fully awake now. The small fire you ignited has now engulfed the rest of my body. You make your way to my stiff manhood. You kiss the head roughly. You gaze up at me and your eyes are now ablaze with passion. I exhale and grab the side of the refrigerator. You slowly run your tongue down the length of my shaft. I feel the fire inside of you. I answer; my body answers; and my passion answers. Finally you take me into your mouth. Using your hand to stroke, you suck softly on my manhood.

"Daaammmmnnn!" I moan.

You use your hand to twist at the base of my shaft, while you slowly move me in and out of your mouth. I'm in heaven. I try to back away from you but the refrigerator gives me nowhere to run. It is cool against my back and you are warm against my front. Before pushing me deeper into your flames, you slowly begin kissing my stomach, determined, you kiss your way to my chest. Retracing the same path you took on your way down, stopping at my nipples. You vigorously bite each one. I rub your shoulders, finally able to move. I reach for your breast, caressing each in my palms. You move higher. My neck. My ears. And then my lips. We kiss with fiery lust. I taste my own musk on your tongue. I pull you closer to me. Now I'm truly on fire.

SexPressions

Every inch of me seems to be overheated. I take your top off, revealing your breast. I kiss the area around them with hot hunger. I run my tongue over them. I run my tongue under them. Finally I reach your nipples. I can taste the hot powder on your skin. The taste adds to the fiery flavor growing within my mouth. I turn you around, and place you on the coolness of the refrigerator. I inch my way down your torso. My tongue is being set ablaze with each I drop. I stop and trace the edge of your navel. As I eagerly move down you, I creep your pants down with me. A trail of soft, thirsty kisses follows me, and just as I get to your fiery spot, I turn you around and I kiss you on the ass. Then I start my way up along your back; your spine. When I reach your neck I nibble across the base. I place my hands over yours. And not only can I taste your heat; I can feel it. Turning you around again, I follow the same trail down the front. You run your hands across my bald head. And as I near your sweet fire, I don't turn back. I can't turn back. I pull hard on your pants and they fall to the floor. Now your full blaze is in view and it calls to me. Starting at the bottom, I run my tongue across your hot lips. I want to burn within your heat. Your *Fire berry*. You place one leg on my shoulder, pulling me to you. But it's my turn to push away and do it at my own pace. I use my tongue to lick at your flames. Not to extinguish, but to fuel it. You moan and hold my head. I don't stop or slow down. I continue further into your heat. Your wet and it's time for me to put this fire out. Once again I kiss the length of your body. Kisses land on your thighs; your stomach, your sides, between your breast, and even under your arm. I kiss your neck. I take your fingers into my mouth, sucking and licking on each and every digit, one by one. I finally reach your face. I kiss your eye lids. Your nose. Your forehead. And just as I reach your lips I enter you with slow

The Secrets

force, both with my tongue and with manhood. You gasp as the heat engulfs us. You wrap your arms around me, holding on for all you're worth. For all we're worth. I stroke with fiery force. We hold hands as we move with each other. Our lust turns into a wild fire. I grab your butt and pump with determination. You grip my back and kiss my forehead. I raise my head and kiss your swollen hot breast. I move deeper into you, searching for your fire; your flame of passion. Your breathing quickens. You kiss and lick my earlobes, sending me quickly into your heat. My body stiffens as I race toward an orgasm. I'm engulfed in the heat; surrounded by the flames of your sex. I can't fight it, and I can't put the fire out. I pump deeper, faster and harder. Your firewalls hold me in place, deep inside of you, urging me to explode. To add to your fire you shift your hips as I kiss your chest. My entire body tightens and I explode. You never release me from your grip. You guide me to the floor and straddle me. You massage my black rod with your warm sex. You raise yourself over me and move your hips. Your pumps are smooth and deep; awakening me quickly. I reach up to you and hold your hips, guiding them over and onto me. Now you're on top of me. Your hot strokes are short and quick. You breathe in my ear. I slide my hand between us, and massage your clitoris. You're lost in our fire. You sit up now and rock your hips. Your body quivers and jerks. I use my thumb to apply more pressure to your pearl tongue. You snap your head back as your hot juices flow from your body. Now I pump upward into you; drawing all of lust, your heat, your fire on to me. You collapse on top of me. We lay, kissing and touching each other.

Exhausted, we rise and make our way back into the bedroom. Throughout the rest of the night we explore your

SexPressions

secrets again. Until finally we fall into each other's arms, exhausted and drained. Smiling to myself I kiss your sleeping forehead.

You can have all the secrets you want, as long as you share them with me.

THE COMPROMISE

Sherri smiled. It was rare for this type of excitement. Not only were Greg and Stony, both at her house; nether wanted to leave. Now the only problem was here she sat hotter than a 4th of July display. She was or had gotten passed horny. And here she had two of the City's best finest sitting on her sofa and she still couldn't get a decent fuck.

"What you smiling at?" Stony sneered at Sherri

"You two muthafuckas." Sherri said. "I'm hot as hell and ya'll acting like kids! Don't worry about it. I'll do it myself!"

Sherri rose from the loveseat, although at the moment she was getting no love at all, and went into the bedroom. After a few minutes of cursing and tantrum throwing, the house was filled with the sounds of a soft hum.

Stony moved first. He went to the door and peeped around the corner. What he saw was Sherri laying spread eagle on the bed. Her hands were between her large ebony thighs. Stony watched as Sherri moved the vibrator slowly over the edges of her body. He became instantly aroused. Sherri's body was smooth and dark. She rubbed the ice-blue

SexPressions

sex-toy across her breast, while his hand moved to his pants. He softly rubbed the bulge wishing he were in the room. He didn't care about or notice Greg standing next to him doing the same. Sherri opened her eyes, and acknowledged her audience, and began to perform. Moaning, she slowly inserted the toy into her pinkness. She was shaven and her juices caused her skin to glisten like a pearl. She arched her back and shrieked. Her body was trembling. She had gotten here too fast. She didn't want to cum this fast, or alone. Sherri flipped over and hid her face from the voyeurs, who stood, dicks in hand, at her bedroom door. Slowly she moved her hand-held partner to her lips. She was getting wet and couldn't wait. Sherri knew she'd dropped enough hints. The next hint would be a shoe to the head.

"Damn where ya'll at?" She screamed to herself. And just as she when she thought the two gentlemen would never help a *damsel-in-desex*, a deep voice rescued her.

"Let me help." It was Greg. He stood naked at the foot of the bed. He crawled to her, manhood dragging over the sheets. Taking the toy from her, he traced the back view of her pinkness. Greg leaned over and kissed her airborne ass cheeks. He continued to trace until her wetness was more than he could handle. He licked from her honey well and spread her legs apart slightly. Sherri grinned as she fought back the disobedient orgasm.

"One down and one to…." She felt a second pair of hands rub her back. "Stony!"

He took the toy from Greg and ran it across her back.

The Compromise

He softly kissed her side. The feel of the kiss tickled Sherri's tender flesh. She giggled in pampered **sextasy**. No way was he about to cum. Not yet anyway.

"Make them work for it." Her body advised.

Greg slipped two fingers past the doors of her vagina and moved them in and out individual of each other, while Stony manipulated the nerves in her breast. She slammed her face deeper into the sheets and yelled. Stony reached down, helping Greg, and spread her cheeks wider and out of his way.

"Fuck blondes. Big girls have more fun." Sherri's pussy screamed at her body in celebration. Sherri rotated her hips against Greg's fingers, while Stony straddled her back and added his tongue to her brown-eye. Sherri's plush body sang a sexual tune. She shivered and tingled all over. Two tongues. Two men. Too much. Sherri could no longer hold back. Stony inserted his finger just as Greg inserted his tongue. Sherri exhaled sharply, as her body gave way. She released warm sweet wetness across Greg's clean-shaven face. He licked awhile longer before letting Stony have a taste. Sherri lay on the bed trying to stop herself from shaking.

"Go ahead, Bruh. You can go first!" Stony said, turning things over to Greg.

Greg nodded and moved behind Sherri. His thick curved penis moved smoothly into Sherri's awaiting warmth. Sherri shot up on all fours. She was hardly over her first

SexPressions

orgasm and they were working her toward another. She watched in the dresser mirror with giddy sexual delight. It was as if she was watching a movie, only this time she was the lead actress. Greg moved like a powerful brown sex machine. Pumping flawlessly deeper into her erotic oil well.

"Black gold digger. Texas tea with booty!"

She watched his piston move rhythmically inside and out of her. Stony moved to the bed and slid beneath her. He sucked her breast as they dangled like large brown grapes from a vine. Her nipples were erect and stiff, pointing down into his throat.

"Ooooohhh shit" Sherri howled. "Not yet," she thought, "not yet."

Greg increased speed adding more force.

"Not yet!"

Greg began to grow slightly inside of her.

"Not yet!"

He filled her warm crevice and pressed evenly against her swollen pearl tongue. Stony sucked deeper on her breast. Greg moaned. He was close as well. He changed angles, going in from the side. Stony moved from under them and began cheering Greg on.

"Hit that ass dawg!" He roared in triumph.

The Compromise

"Yeah hit that ass dawg!" Sherri cheered to herself.

Greg obeyed and pounded himself deeper. He grasped onto her waist and pulled her back into each forward thrust. Sweat coated his body causing him to glisten. Sherri felt Greg shake hard. He quivered and twitched as his penis pumped black life into Sherri womb. Sherri lay in disbelief at her will to fight off her orgasm. It was a dream cum true. Sherri started to slump forward. Then she felt another pair of hands replace Greg's. Stony, her body warned. She'd forgotten about him. He rolled her over onto her back and opened her thighs. He held her legs toward the ceiling in a "V" shape. Stony slid himself into her soaked vagina. He wasn't as thick as Greg but he was longer. And at this point Sherri wasn't about to complain. She closed her eyes and smiled up at Stony. She held her large breast in place, as Stony started off with short strokes.

Using only the head of his dick, Stony teased her G-spot immediately. Sherri gasped and squirmed and wanted to run. Her body betrayed her as her legs locked against Stony's grip. By now, Stony had worked up to full-fucking-speed. A tear ran slowly down Sherri's face as her entire body broke with orgasmic rebellion. Driving deeper still, Stony stepped forward onto the bed with leg up. He prolonged each orgasmic wave with his ebbs and flows. Stony growled softly as he tried to fight off his impending eruption. Sherri fought off her lightheadedness and grabbed his ass. She dared him to stop. Her inner walls held and massaged his invading shaft. Stony winced loudly, and without warning exploded hard. Surprisingly Sherri still held onto him. A fourth orgasm, creeped from deep within her. She pulled Stony closer to her and began grinding up

SexPressions

into him. This eruption was closer to an aftershock.

It whispered softly to Sherri. "You go girl."

Stony collapsed onto Sherri breathing hard. Sherri drifted off to sleep. When she awoke, all that was left of the two men were their business cards and expended condoms. Sherri hugged herself, as she tried to remember why she had called the two police officers in the first place.

CONJAGAL VISIT

Sonny smiled across the small room at his wife. His hands tingled with shy nervousness as she crossed the distance to be near him. It was high school all over again; the tension of sneaking around driving his hormones to the hilt. Same feel, different chaperon.

"Are you hungry?" Sonny began, before his wife smothered his words with kisses. Sonny sat back against the empty table that made the small room seem even smaller, and pulled his wife deep within his embrace.

"We don't have much time!" Sonny's insisted, as she tore at his clothing. And with that Sonny threw caution to the wind. The urgency of his wife's movements spoke to him. *We don't have much time,* those movements repeated. Sonny answered with movements of his own. He pulled his wife's t-shirt over her head. Sonny watched as her breast fell braless from the t-shirt's soft cotton hold. Sonny realized how much he missed his wife's lovely breast. Sonny grinned. His eyes fondled the new tattoo of a peach, and according to the inscription underneath, cream.

"Nice tat!" Sonny said, tongue brushing just under his wife's delicate jaw line. "You're just becoming an all around

SexPressions

bad girl. When the cat's away huh?" Sonny's wife smiled and pushed her frantic hands deep into the front of Sonny's pants.

"I've missed you so much!" She said, not really to Sonny but to the stiff thickness that grew within her hands. Her hands trembled as the heat and density of her husband's penis grew. It had been too long, she thought as she kneeled in front of Sonny. She grabbed Sonny's penis by its thick base and slowly covered the head with her eager mouth. Sonny felt his knees buckle from the heat inside of his wife's mouth. His wife moaned, savoring the musky taste of her husband's sex. She moved her tongue slowly and softly over Sonny's quivering penis. She held Sonny in position while maneuvering her neck. Sonny felt large and unyielding. Sonny's wife stroked and sucked deep moans from Sonny's throat, each one heavier than the one before. Sonny ran his hands through her hair, replaying the nights they were together before the jail time. "No need in regretting anything now." Sonny thought, he knew this could happen when they began dating. Sonny's wife moved from her knees into a squatting position. Her vagina trembling as pre-cum slowly coated her tongue. She pushed her trembling hand into her jeans and panties. Her clitoris called to be touched. She applied firm pressure. Moans pushed past Sonny's thick blackness from his wife's mouth. Her fingers soon became covered in her sexual stickiness. Sonny cursed and pushed air from his lungs into a curt sounding whistle. His wife pulled his stone dense dick from her mouth. She moved the head across her lips like an erotic lipstick. She decided to shock the girls at lunch by saying she used "***lipdick***" when she tells them about this part of the visit. She felt an orgasm near and refused to waste the sensation on her fingers when

Conjagal Visit

her husband's nine inches were so close.

"Hurry baby!" She ordered before standing and lying across the small table. "Fuck me now."

Sonny moved behind his wife. He undid his pants and let them fall to the floor. His wife had begun working on her own clothes. She slowly pushed them toward the crest of her shapely, brown rump. Sonny's manhood throbbed and hung painfully swollen in midair. He pushed his wife's clothes down past her knees. He placed one hand on the small of her back and slowly fed himself into his wife's warmth. They both gasped from the tight fit.

"Deeper baby!" Sonny heard his wife moan. She reached behind her and grabbed her ass cheeks, spreading them further apart. Sonny opened his stance and pushed deeper into his wife. Her heat was growing with each insertion. Sonny held his wife by her waist and moved himself in and out of her with determination. The feel of orgasm stood at the depths of his sex. Sonny bit down on his lip and worked himself faster into his wife's tight brownness.

"There you go baby! Fuck me!" She cheered, pushing herself onto her tip toes. Sonny obeyed, driving himself deeper. His harsh grunts splashed against her back. His wife gripped the sides of the table and rocked back into Sonny. Harsh moans carried curse words from her mouth.

"Smack my ass!" She demanded. Lightheadedness consumed her as Sonny's hand and penis hit their marks.

SexPressions

"Don't stop... please." She panted.

Sonny smacked her ass cheeks as her body froze around his erection. A powerful orgasm ransacked his wife's body. She slowly descended onto Sonny's thick girth. Sonny felt his orgasm growing and tried urging it along with powerful thrust. A sharp pounding at the door forced Sonny to break his concentration.

"Wood!" The guard's voice boomed from the other side of the door. "Visit's over!"

"C'mon man. A few mo' seconds!" Sonny yelled, still stroking.

"Fuck that." The guard responded, "I don't care how much you paid. Now kiss ya wife and get dressed. You'll see her next week."

Shock and anger embraced Sonny.

"Sorry baby!" His wife said. Smiling and pulling her jeans up. She walked to the door attempting to fix her hair and clothes.

"Just nineteen more months and I'll be home for good."

She tapped on the door, blowing Sonny a kiss as the guard turned the key in the tumbler. Sonny stood, pants around his ankles and erection still wet from sex, and watched as his wife was escorted away to her cell.

"What a crime." Sonny thought as he pulled his pants past his thickness. "What a fucking crime."

TABLE FOR TWO

"Women are never on time." I think to myself as I glance at my watch. We decided to have lunch together, actually you decided and I agreed. But here you are, late as usual. This time I was prepared. I ordered a drink for myself and took a table on the second floor. It overlooked the main floor and had a view of the street. So if a person on the other side of the street wanted, they could look up and watch people eating without straining their necks. I took a sip from my drink and check my watch again.

"Don't worry, it still works!" You say as you slide into the seat across from me. I smile and signal for the waiter. Late, but at least you look good. Your breasts peek out from your low-cut gray cashmere sweater. The waiter arrives as you notice me caressing your breast with my eyes. I dream about licking whip cream from them and file that thought away for another time.

"So what do you want?" You ask, luring me away from my thoughts.

"Dessert!" I say, still thinking of another time." Yeah let's have dessert first."

I'm grinning now as you start reading my eyes. You nod your head and we place the order. The waiter jots down

SexPressions

our order and walks away grinning knowingly. I guess my eyes are easier to read than I thought. I reach across the table and touch your hand. The feel of your smooth silky skin alerts me to how horny I really am. I silently thank you for setting up this late date. I place your pointer finger in my mouth and slowly suck on it. You giggle as I use my tongue to trace the side of your finger. I give each finger the same seductive attention, thinking how sweet you'll taste when dessert arrives. I reach under the table and begin rubbing your thighs. I love the way you feel beneath the satin hose that covers your softness. The further along I go, the more and more I realize you didn't wear panties. We share a smile as the waiter and my discovery both arrive.

"Dessert and champagne for the lovers." The waiter declares, placing the bowls of creamy sweetness in front of us. He sip bubbly until the waiter is out of sight. When he's gone I tell you to sit on the table.

"I have cream, now I need something to go with it." I say, raising one eyebrow.

Without a second thought you sit across the table and lay back. Inching your skirt high up, I expose your *Devil's freak cake*. I take a spoon and coat your inner thighs with ice cream. Small soft moans slip away from your lips, as the heat from your thigh clashes with the coolness of the ice cream. Starting at the trail that starts below your knee I kiss, lick, and suck the ice cream from your chocolate thighs. You seize my head and squeeze, holding back the moans that have welled up in your throat. You squirm underneath me, just as I finish the last of the ice cream. I pull you closer to me, diving tongue first into your chocolate filling. Still holding my head, you rotate your hips to the music of my

Table for Two

tongue. You whisper a curse loudly into the air. The restaurant's main floor has started to fill with the lunch-time crowd. If any of the diners look up they'll have a view of our sexual lunch date.

Teasing your black pearl tongue, I reach up to caress your heaving breast. I lick at your sweetness, bringing you closer to that special moment. Tracing your clit's circumference, I quickly bring you nearer to the brink.

"Not yet baby... Wait for the main course."

I stand and look at the half-finished dish I've prepared. My black nature anxiously presses against my pants. I release it from the thin material of my trousers. You reach down and help me place myself into you. You stroke and caress each and every pulsating inch before guiding my length inside of you. Now it's my turn to moan. Your thighs are cool and warm. I lean down over you, raising your legs up slightly and begin slowly stroking. I release your breast and place one in my mouth. I mock your nipples with my tongue. Your inner heat envelops me as I drive deeper into further into you. I rise slightly, adding easy force and powerful leverage. Your body responds immediately. Gripping my shaft, you pant hard. Your body begs me for more. Stroking with my full length, I feel you quiver and twitch.

"Yes!" Your body screams through your mouth. You grab my ass, pulling me deeper, harder, and faster into you. Until finally you give way to a full erotic spasm. I continue to pump as your sweet syrup warms my body. I stroke until your eruptions turn to small sexual tremors. I slowly pull

SexPressions

out. Once again I eye the beautiful dish laid out before me. I sit down and began kissing and licking at your juices, bringing you quickly to another orgasm.

We gather ourselves, just as the waiter returns. We order a small lunch and enjoy our time together. The waiter presents the check and pours more champagne into our empty glasses. The waiter smiles and informs us that the bill was taken care of by another couple. The waiter's smile grows into a grin and he slides a note to me.

"They say they thoroughly enjoyed the show!" He walks away, giggling to himself. We exchange a knowing glance.

"Read it!" You urge with your eyes.

I open the note, read it twice, and laugh.

"Well?" You ask.

"They want us to have dessert with them!" I say, telling you only half of what the note reads. I figure I'd save the rest for later.

GLEN'S GUEST ROOM

Glen looked directly at James and shook his head. He always found himself on the short end of a few favors, so anytime James told him not to worry, he knew to worry that much more.

"So explain this to me again." Glen said, turning his attention back to his partially groomed beard.

"All you have to do is keep Missy's girls company." James said crossing his arms and he leaned against the bathroom doorway. "The only thing worse than a cock-blocking friend; is two."

Glen chuckled softly in agreement, thinking about the countless third and fourth wheels that made things hard for him. Glen had to admit, when James was right he was right.

"How do they look?" Glen asked. He decided to get to the *important* questions first. "And how much will it cost you?"

"Cost me?" James thought better of it. "Aight, I got'cha. Here you go." He nearly flung the picture at Glen, who now knew he'd been set up from the beginning. The

SexPressions

picture was of three women, dressed in various types of bathing suits. The background was of a beach; which jolted Glen's memory.

"They went on that trip to St. Croix with you and Missy?" He asked, still examining the photo.

"See, that's what I mean." James said, peeling through his billfold. Glen recognized the woman in the middle, Missy. He was with James when the two of them met, but the other two were new. They both posed so that their legs peeked from under their festive wraps. "Provocative and half hidden", is the term that Glen thought about. One wore her hair in twist, while the other decided an Afro would be suitable. Other than those differences they look similar enough to be twins, sisters at least. The last thing Glen noticed was the women didn't really smile, they sneered.
"Why do they look so mad?" He asked, handing the photo back to James.

"That's just how those hateful bitches are. So will you hold me down or what?"

Glen gave it some more thought and decided he would. Hell, if you can't help a friend in need, then why need friends?

"Have them meet you here. That way I can entertain them while you and Missy enjoy yourselves."
James' smile grew. He hadn't seen Missy in an entire month and it would be good to spend some time alone with her. He checked his watched and started toward the door.

Glen's Guest Room

"Oh yeah." He turned back toward Glen. "Is it okay if they stay here for the weekend?"

"I knew there was something to it. Yeah man, whatever."

James shook Glen's outstretched hand; happy he'd taken care of his weekend's distractions.

"I better get some ass, too." Glen yelled toward the door.
"That's all up to you. You can have them." James yelled in returned, nearly laughing.

"It's not as if I'm making either of you go." Missy didn't remember when, or how, the conversation had gone to this extreme. In her head, either they went with her to visit James, or they stayed at school; one or the other. But Bonnie and Irene had a way of turning everything into a big production number.

"So what are we supposed to do while you're getting your freak on?" Irene asked. She was the more reluctant of the two, and for Missy, she was making matters worse.

"I already told you. James' friend Glen said you guys could stay at his house for the weekend. Glen is cool enough." Missy said, still stuffing clothes into her suitcase. She would be damned if her girls would ruin her get-a-way with James. "Wait, I have a picture of him."

Missy hurdled mounds of clothing and bags to her large bureau. She fished through the top drawer until she found the pictures James had sent her. There was one of him

SexPressions

and Glen, with the customary "hook-up" request written on the back. She hadn't given it any thought until right now. She held the picture up and cursed herself for not talking to the passenger that day. Although she did love James, Glen was worthy of at least lusting over. He was tough looking. His complexion was a hard working brown with the body to prove. He looked like when he smacked an ass, you felt it; even though he wasn't a big man. But she had chosen James, who proved to be more than able.

"Like I said, 'he's cool."

Missy handed the picture to Bonnie, the closer of the two girls. Her reaction was instant and positive.

"This is *him?*" She sprang from the bed and held the picture out as if it were of her favorite star. "Guurrll, *he's fione!* See Bitch, you've been holding out on us."

Irene smiled, not really knowing why, but if Bonnie, who also was very picky when it came to men, acted that way, he must be something.

"Lemme see that!" She said, nearly having to fight with Bonnie. "He has real potential." She tried to downplay the fact that her back was growing tense and her feet itched from the ideas that ran through her mind.

"Maybe we can *slave* him. The three women howled with laughter. Bonnie and Irene has begun practicing Domination and seized any chance to turn a man into a sniveling slave.

Glen's Guest Room

"Naw Gurl." Missy said, snatching the picture from Irene. "I don't know if Glen get down like that. Actually I think he's a church-going man."

"Hell, they're the biggest freaks." Bonnie laughed.

" I always thought all those police officers were sex fiends!" Irene said. She eased the picture from Missy's grasp and stared at her new sex slave candidate.

"Well I guess you can never tell. But he is always talking about what happen at church. He seems cool to me." Missy added the last part to ward of the frown that was planting itself on her friend's faces. "Plus he doesn't mind spending money. He has a nice house too. Ya'll gonna have a good time."

Bonnie and Irene exchanged glances, and then hunched their shoulders. It wasn't as if they had anything else to do. Finals were over and there were a few days until the next semester began. Missy looked at the friends slowly talk themselves into going. Neither of them could pass up the chance to allow a good-looking man to spend money on them.

"I'm leaving at six, so be ready." She ordered as they began leaving her room, "And I want ya'll to be nice. Glen is cool people and I may marry James. I don't want him thinking my friends are hood rats."

"But we are." Bonnie said, laughing her way into the hallway. Missy smiled and shook her head. She felt better knowing that the women would have some type of fun. Also

SexPressions

she didn't want Glen getting in her way. The last time she visited, he had the *Third-Wheel syndrome*. No matter how good he looked, when it came to sex, Missy was a one-man woman. Let Irene and Bonnie keep him busy the entire weekend, she had plans of her own.

"What are friends for?" She thought as she held up the red nightie she had bought just for this weekend.

Glen had nearly forgotten about Missy's friends coming for the weekend, so when James called to remind him he thought about telling his friend he couldn't do it. But "a promise was a promise, and "How bad could it be anyway?" He asked himself. That was earlier. Now he stood in front of the two women and had already thought of other things he could be doing. Having a root canal or getting kicked in the nuts came to mind. They hadn't been at his house twenty minutes and they were already grounding into his patience. They were complaining about the trip and being hungry, Glen truly didn't want to spend the entire weekend with a pair of drama queens.

"Dawg, tell Missy to talk to them before I snap." He said as he pulled James, who assured him that he would relay the message, into the kitchen.

"You better, or you and Missy are going to have enough people to play Spades and Bid all weekend."

Irene hugged Missy, embarrassed about the earlier incident. But it *had* been a long ride and they didn't get anything to eat along the way. "Shit", she thought, "who doesn't get cranky when they haven't eaten?"

Glen's Guest Room

But she and Bonnie had promised to make the best of it. They had gotten Glen to open up and calm down. Damn, he was fine. He had promised to take them clubbing, then maybe to church, which sent both Bonnie and her into eye-rolling fits.

"We'll have fun girl, and don't do anything I wouldn't do." Irene joked.

"Shiiitt, I'm trying to hurt somebody tonight; and tomorrow night too." Missy said as she broke their embrace. "Be nice to Glen, he means well."

"I think he's just mean, but we're cool. I got'cha. Now go have fun with James."

Glen pushed his plate away from him and exhaled. He had outdone himself this time. Dinner was light, yet filling; Chicken scampi with salad and homemade pie. He didn't make the pie himself, but no need in telling them that. His two-house guests had stuffed themselves with food, and drink, and were starting to get comfortable.

"So how come you don't have a woman living in this house with you." Irene asked, "The way you cook, I'd marry you tomorrow."

Glen blushed and thanked her. "Not ready to settle down yet." he said.

"That means you still wanna run the streets." Bonnie cut-in.

"Yeah, that too. Can't run the streets if I have a family

SexPressions

at home, right? And I still have a little ho' in me. Can't turn a ho' into a husband, no matter how good he cooks." He smiled at Irene. "So do I give ya'll the grand tour or just the plain 'ole tour?"

"What's the difference?" Bonnie said, nipples tingling from the fullness in her belly. Good food made her horny. Really, sitting across from a sexy man who can cook good food, made her horny.

"Well one, I tell you where everything is and the other, I show you. And since you've already seen this floor, the basement is next."

His house was larger than it looked. There were three levels in all; two on the upper floor and one on the main floor next to the kitchen. His living room was also his den and was home to a wide-screen television, a stereo and all the other modern gadgets that went along with them. He neglected to tell them he also owned his own video cameras and video editing equipment. That was on what Glen called a *freak-to-know* basis.

"So what do you do for fun?" Irene asked. She had to admit, he had style. Every room had its own color scheme. The kind of place she would imagine a woman living in. Maybe you can turn a ho' into a husband, Irene thought to herself. Glen flicked a light switch and gave a one-word response. "This."

The basement's shadows were erased by brightness. The basement's stairwell was spiral. Directly across from the staircase was a large mirrored bar, with a built-in fish tank,

Glen's Guest Room

where a lone shark cut through the water looking for prey. To the left of the stair well was a wooden floor, lined with a mirrored wall. A large pool table with red felt sat a few feet past that.

"It's like a club down here." Irene said, surveying the room. "What's in there?" She pointed toward two doors next to the bar. Both doors were nondescript, which made them stand out in the house.

"Those? Well one is the laundry room and the other one is my guest room, the real play room." Glen smirked and turned toward the pool table.

He found that the women weren't as bad as James had made them out to be. The three of them had talked over dinner and they were cooler than he led on.

"The real playroom?" Both women asked, nearly at the same time.

"So really what's in there?" Irene asked blocking his way.

"Don't worry about it. Maybe I'll show ya'll tomorrow." Glen stepped past her and moved toward the bar. "Let me make ya'll a drink, turn on some music and if you want we can play some pool. I would bet but I don't want to get hustled." Glen said the last part mockingly. He'd been in and out of almost every pool hall since he was seven. It was safe to say to say he knew his way around a pool table.

Bonnie winked at Irene; a smile winking across her

SexPressions

lips like a cat burglar.

"Okay let's play for shots." She looked from Irene to Glen. They both hunched their shoulders and agreed.

"I'll get the vodka and put on some music. He moved toward the bar, unaware of the two women silently celebrating behind him.

Glen should have known better. If you watched for a hustle it was easy to spot. Plus they were still in college. Guys must try to use pool to hustle women out of pussy all the time. Had he known he would have saved them all some trouble. But the chase was always better. He'd easily beat both women who by now were giddy from the alcohol. They both removed their sweaters and stood in their t-shirts and jeans; which seemed just tight enough to highlight their bodies. Irene, the one with the Afro in the picture, had large round breast that made it hard to look into her beautiful brown eyes. While Bonnie removed her sweater. The twist which she wore in the photo, now wore her hair down in a flat ironed style, had breasts that were a smaller sexy C-cup that sat up full and inviting. They both appeared to be size sixteen's; only Bonnie's legs were longer. Each had thick lips with the right color of lipstick. Very *kissable*, is the thought that came to Glen's head. Irene accented her warm face with a piercing in her left eyebrow. Both owned an ass to kill for. Just like Glen like them thick, round and sitting high; also very kissable. It soon became easy to tell them apart in other ways as well. Irene was chatty and out-going. Where Bonnie was the quiet one, although that didn't make her very quiet, just more quiet than Irene. She listened intently, asking questions, which kept Glen *(distracted)*

Glen's Guest Room

talking. That's how he knew he was being hustled. He won the majority of the games but he was also a lot more intoxicated than they were.

"Not only were they sexy", he said to himself, "they were slick as hell." Another thing he noticed was that their balls were disappearing from the table when they weren't taking a shot. "Soon they wouldn't have to cheat", he thought, "I'm drunk."

"So what will we play for now?" Irene asked, as Glen sank the eight ball, forcing her and Bonnie to take another drink.

"Ya'll pick." Glen said, far past tipsy. He had been a lot more drunk than this before. He couldn't drive, but he could fuck and that's what mattered.

Bonnie eased next to Glen, while Irene leaned over the table.

"How about we play for that." Bonnie said, smiling and pointing toward the playroom door.

"I think I'm being hustled." He smiled now. It didn't matter now. If they wanted to see what was in his guest room, then he would play along. He just hoped they wouldn't chicken out. His dick had gotten too hard for to many more games. "Okay what's the bet?"

"Slavery." Irene said, moving around the table and next to Glen, sandwiching him between her and Bonnie. Glen repeated the word softly, contemplating the idea.

SexPressions

"So you mean..."

"We mean, if you win, we'll be your sex slaves." Irene started.

"And you can do what ever." Bonnie finished.

"And what if I lose?" Glen tried to gather his composure now.

"You get to be ours for the weekend." Bonnie said guiding his face closer to hers with her slender finger. "And you have to show us what's in your guest room."

"Okay rack' em." His dick roared, hard between his legs. "The best two out of three games." Glen clapped his hands and refreshed everyone's glass.

He had made the shot close to a million times. It was-had to be-the easiest shot in pool. He had just sank the 7-ball and used "english" to set up his next shot. The cue ball came to rest slowly behind the 8-ball, which now sat on the lip of the right corner pocket. He used what he knew to be proper force. The shot would make itself. All he had to do was set the cue ball in motion.

"Aight, move back from the table, sexy lady." He said to Irene. He was surprised they didn't try anything funny. No showing of breast. No whispering sweet nothings in his ear. Nothing. "I would've cheated," he thought to himself, "but after this shot I won't have to." He had easily won the first game. As a matter of fact he had walked the table.

Glen's Guest Room

"Easy does it," he coached himself. He moved the cue stick through his powered fingers with shark like ease.

"Too easy," he whispered to the table although meaning it for the ladies. He pushed the cue stick forward and instantly knew something was wrong. "Damn!"
Both Irene and Bonnie moved from there seats as the cue ball moved too fast. The cue ball rushed along the table's padded sides. Glen prayed that the ball would slow down, or that he had struck the ball in the wrong place, causing it to miss its mark. Neither of those things happened. The cue crashed into the 8-ball with a loud cracking sound, then bounced high above the table. The trio of players watched the ball descend and hoped that it would go their way.

"Go in!" Bonnie and Irene's inner voices yelled.

"Get back!" Glen's psyche ordered.

The ball landed on the table with a slow back spin, falling into the pocket after a slow pausing briefly.

"Scratch!" Irene yelled.

Glen nearly broke his stick in disgust. "No thang," he told himself, "I'll just whoop they ass this next game. How can I lose on my own table. I'm playing for pussy." Glen thought more about the wager and *knew* he couldn't really lose.

"I'll rack'em," Glen said, grabbing the triangle from the wall. He felt the ladies' eyes on him the entire time. "I can't lose."

SexPressions

"Men are so predictable," Irene thought to herself, as she stood next to Bonnie smiling. She watched him place the balls neatly into the rack systematically. Like that mattered it really mattered how the balls were arranged, as long as the 8-ball was I the middle. But men-no slaves- acted as if it mattered. They were either showing off or trying some trickery. Then the sudden loss of blood pressure going from their heads to their dicks, caused them to make a fatal mistake by racking them too tight. Irene's ex-boyfriend was a pool shark from Chicago, who told her a few secrets.

"If they rack them tight, which they prolly gonna do, then hit this ball here," Rick Money said in her memory, sounding in her head as if he were standing behind her. They had spent close to four hours practicing the shot. Eight out of ten times the eight ball found a pocket, usually a side pocket. First she believe it was luck, but physics and ratios don't lie. She leaned over the table and focused on the shot. Nothing else mattered. Not Bonnie sipping slowly from her glass. Not Glen, leaning forward supporting himself on his pool stick. Nothing, but the shot.

"Remember Re', its all one motion," she heard Rick telling her. The cue ball moved from its spot with a muted thud and smashed into the formation of balls, with a loud snap. Three balls; the seven, the twelve, and the fifteen, all fell quickly. But those didn't matter. What did matter was the eight ball. It rolled from the back rail and careened off with an awkward spin. Glen slowly began shaking his head in denial. Bonnie held her glass tightly; she knew. She had seen Irene do it far too many times to believe it was luck. She never doubted the outcome. The eight ball rolled slowly to the corner pocket on Irene's left, as if it were guided.

Glen's Guest Room

"Game, slave!" Irene yelled, leaning over the corner of the table. She looked sinister in the shadows. "Any last request?"

"Yeah, all I ask is that it's recorded." Glen raised his right eyebrow.

"Okay. Now get clean I hate to the stench of men." Irene said as she walked over to Bonnie and kissed her full on the mouth. "Also turn your phones off. We hated to be disturbed."

Glen stood in the shower cleaning himself slowly. He used the soap the women had brought with them. It had been sometime since he had a *Dominate*. And seeing as how he never had two, he wanted this to be just right. He enjoyed being with aggressive women and having a *dominant* was the next natural step. He dried himself and put on the pair of cotton pajamas the women had picked out for him. He sprayed a mist of *FUBU's Plush* cologne over his chest and went back to the basement. He hoped to see the ladies, but he found the basement empty.

"Keep them waiting, right?" He whispered to the empty basement already. Glen moved to the bar and poured himself another drink. The shower had cleared his head some, so he needed his buzz to return. He unlocked the guest room door and leaned over the bar. This would be fun, he told himself.

Bonnie stood at the top of the stairs dressed in her tight black latex shorts, thigh high boots and matching bra; sexually fuming. She couldn't believe the disrespect of this

SexPressions

one. She motioned for Irene to walk softly as she came down the stairs. Then she motioned for her to look across the basement to the bar. Irene, dressed in a red latex bustie and mini-skirt and tall red stiletto heels, gripped her red leather paddle with angst. . She stormed across the small area, starting her swing at the base of the stairs and ending it across Glen slightly drunk ass cheeks.

"What the fuck!" Glen howled, dropping the glass on the bar. He turned to face who had just assaulted him. "Ya'll done went crazy."

"Silence, slave!" Irene snapped. "You've already broken rules. So anything else that comes from your mouth will only fuel my anger."

"Who told you to wear clothing?" Bonnie yelled, snatching at the top of his pajamas, nearly ripping them from his body.

"And where are our glasses? Didn't you think we would want something to drink?"

Glen stood, stiff and motionless. First he was angry, being caught off guard. But as the ladies shot question after question, Glen's mood changed slipped into fearful arousal.

"Please accept my apologies." He said, bowing his head. "I'll try to act accordingly." Bonnie and Irene shared glances.

"So you've been trained?" Irene said, crossing her arms.

Glen's Guest Room

"Well I still believe you should be punished." Bonnie spat.

Her boots elevated her to a clear four higher inches than Glen. She moved in close and stared down at him. She liked the feeling, but he loved it. Bonnie lifted her foot and slowly pressed the toe of her boot into Glen foot. A grimace flashed across his face before returning to a blank, emotionless gaze. She leaned forward, adding more pressure, and kissed Glen on the forehead, drawing a scowl from Irene.

"Couldn't help it." Her smile replied.

"So Ms. Irene," Glen started, before Irene swung across his face. Glen fought the instinct to rub the stinging sensation that buzzed through the left side of his face. He moved his mouth to speak, then thought better of it.

"You will address me as Madame Thorn," she pointed her paddle toward Bonnie, "and she is Madame Vine."
Glen nodded his head then repeated the names.

"Now what were you going to ask me slave?" Madame Thorn hissed softly before biting Glen roughly on his earlobe. She felt a new excitement begin to rush through her. She had never had a slave who was already trained.

"I just wanted to know if you like what you see."

And for the first time, Madame Thorn and Madame Vine gave Glen a real look. They had to admit he was quite the specimen. The women slowly circled him, admiring what they saw. Madame Vine smacked him sharply on his ass cheeks, causing his already stiff penis to jump and bob. Pre-cum dripped from the thick veining length of Glen's brownness. His face was still blank but the inner-Glen smiled from ear to ear.

"These bitches think they can break me." He laughed to himself.

"So where will be begin?" Madame Vine asked, looking around the basement, "I guess we should start where it was settled." She walked over to the pool table and eased atop of it, allowing her feet to swing. She motioned for Glen to come closer. He looked from her to Madame Thorn, and then was ushered with swat on his rear.

"Get over there, dammit!" Madame Thorn spat." See what she wants."

Glen nodded his head, stepped from his tattered pants and walked to the table. Both women swallowed hard at the sight of his full healthy dick. Their breast heaved and pushed their nipples against their shiny latex bras. Madame Thorn exhaled softly and mockingly fanned herself behind Glen.

"Whew!" Her vagina breathed as her labia pushed her thighs apart softly.

Glen stopped in front on Madame Vine. He bit down on the inside of his cheek. She looked even more titillating under the light of the pool table. She looked like some mixed a mixture of smooth caramel and a shiny-black form of chocolate. "More like licorice." Glen's dick whispered.

Glen's Guest Room

Inner-Glen nodded in agreement.

"Yes Ma'am." Glen said, as he stared just below her chin at her delicate neck.

"My boots are dirty. Clean them with your tongue." She ordered.

Glen extended his tongue past his lips and moved it slowly over the wet looking latex. A soft moan rolled from his mouth as he covered her boot with his tongue and a few forbidden kisses. Madame Vine bit her lips as the pressure of Glen's tongue moved across her latex skin. Glen moved his tongue over her toe and ankle causing her to swallow a giggle.

"Can't let a slave know you're enjoying it." She thought. Madame Vine peered between her legs and watched Glen wipe her left boot with his tongue. She could never get enough of the sight of a man-slave kneeling before her. She held a black leather, riding crop and slowly moved it across Glen's head. Her vagina hummed as the strong feeling of his tongue transmitted signals to her sexual epicenter. She couldn't see his dick, but knew it was hard. Madame Vine wondered if the rest Glen's touch was as strong his tongue. It must be, she told herself. She was new to the *'Domination'* game and all she had were weak men; body, brain and spirit. It was new to have someone like Glen be submissive. Madame Vine shuddered at the thought of when she and Madame Thorn would turn him loose. Glen slowly moved his tongue across the last part of her right boot, ending his task.

SexPressions

"Okay, now hers. And slave do be more gentle." Madame Vine said, swinging her leg so that she would be completely on the table. "Her feet are more tender than mine."

Glen nodded in understanding. He began to turn to face where Madame Thorn was standing. She placed her paddle atop of his head and put her foot on the pool table, giving Glen and Madame Vine a view of her pierced and shaved pussy. "If you do a good job I may let you watch me masturbate." She whispered to him, "Okay? Now get to work."

Glen suppressed his smile. He licked his lips before puckering them. Madame Thorn's shoes were open-toed, so would have the pleasure of cleaning her feet as well. He placed his tongue where her toes met the shoe. He circled each toe slower than he did with Madame Vine. The sight of Madame ' s Vine vagina caused a shiver to run through him. Glen couldn't wait until he could taste her. Really both of the women made his mouth water. When he reached her big toe, he sucked softly then kissed it. Madame Thorn tapped him lightly on the head in admonishment; secretly hoping the wetness she felt wouldn't ooze down her leg. She didn't know how her slaves maintain such control. She even admired them for the control. Like this one here, his penis was rock hard and all she could think about was how it would feel inside of her. While he never wavered.

Glen kissed the top of Madame Thorn's raised foot. He covered her entire foot with soft brushes of his tongue. He felt her shiver and moan. They were new to this, he could tell. Her pussy oozed with disciplined sexy juices. They

Glen's Guest Room

were in trouble and didn't know it. Glen moved his attention the thin straps, slowly and carefully tracing each with his tongue. He moved closer to the smell of her sex. She smelled like roses and vanilla. He finished with the first shoe/foot and kneeled defiantly facing her vagina.

"Newbie!" His dick announced to the rest of his body. His inner self snickered at them and he wondered how long it would take to break them.

He watched as Madame Thorn placed her foot on the floor and raised the other. Then she nodded for him to continue. He gave this foot the very same *sexcruciating* treatment as the other. She leaned forward and taunted him with the smell of her aroused vagina. Again the inner-Glen smiled. He pressed his tongue over her shoes and feet. She enjoyed the pleasure. She curled her toes of the foot on the floor. She shot a look at Madame Vine, and they both knew. She believed the slave knew as well. They could not break him. But she would have fun trying. Her laugh was powerful and loud against his ears. She liked the sound of it. He decided to see how far he could go. He moved his tongue over her shoe again, then up and slowly traced her ankle. Madame Thorn shivered, and then stuck him harshly on his arm. He withdrew his tongue from her skin with a slight flicker.

"I see you want to be a bad boy." She started, planting her foot on the floor, "Okay have it your way." She motioned for Madame Vine to get up from the table.

"Lay down." She ordered Glen. Using her paddle, she forced his arms and legs apart. "Don't move!"

SexPressions

She walked away leaving Glen under the watchful eye of Madame Vine. She looked down at him the way a scientist may look at an experimental specimen. Madame Thorn returned just as she made her second rotation around the table. Madame Thorn walked around to where Glen's head. She placed a bag on the floor and disappeared from his upside down vision. When she returned to his vision, she held a blindfold. She frowned upside down at him, and then covered his eyes, leaving him with the use of his other senses. Glen shifted slightly, drawing a quick swat across his groin. "To small to be a paddle." He thought.

"Didn't she tell you to not move?"

It was Madame Vine from the right side of the table. He inhaled deeply, but quietly. Rose and Vanilla. Madame Thorn was still above his head. The next sense of his to help was hearing. The sound of Velcro, ripped through the stillness. Glen then felt wide, comfortable restraints, tightening around his right wrist. Then the feeling of tension being applied to the rope or cable pulling him to more snug against the table. Next he felt a restraint being tightened around his left ankle. Glen's ass puckered and blood-flooded sex sexual veins. Maybe these two wouldn't disappoint. Glen would let them have their fun, for now anyway. He lay against the felt's plush ness and relaxed while his other foot and wrist were restrained and tightened against each other. "Now the fun begins." He thought. Glen heard the sound of clothes being removed roughly. The he heard the sounds of both women climbing atop of the table. He quizzed himself on if he should be defiant. Inner Glen told him "No, lick whatever they present you."

Glen's Guest Room

He felt the closeness of one of the women over his face and round his head. It was the scent he really desired. Wild berries and cream; Madame Vine's scent. He saw the bottle of body lotion while they unpacked and again while he showered. He stole quick whiffs of the bottles and catalogued their names and exotic combinations. Glen breathed in her heat and extended his tongue. Her moans told him to continue. Her vagina was warm, sticky and damp. He brushed his tongue along her elongated labia, not caring about the wildness of her pubic hair.

"That's it, slave." Madame Thorn said softly cheering him. Glen moved his tongue deliberately slow. He wanted to savor this moment. He parted her vaginal lips and incurred moans and long exhales with each flick of his tongue. Soon he knew which way and how to move his tongue to cause the sound he wanted. Short, quick flicks brought about rough fast pants. Long, slow licks pushed moans over her lips. Glen used his tongue to bring a mixture of sounds and feelings. As he licked, she trembled and shuddered. Vine's vaginal warmth; it was too much for her now. She collapsed forward completely covering Glen's face. Her pussy throbbed with heat. She rocked her hips and pelvis roughly over Glen's face while Madame Thorn assaulted his unyielding erection with light lashes. Glen still licked. The sounds of inner-Glen pushing him.

"You can't stop now, you're breaking her."

Madame Vine grabbed the sides of Glen's head and steadied herself.

"I just have to have him." She panted.

SexPressions

"You're worst than the slaves." Madame Thorn scolded. "Move then. And he better not be tired. "

Glen lay on the table while the women changed positions. Madame Thorn straddled him, as if they were going to "69". She wiggled over his face, moving her clitoris against his tongue. The blindfold hid the grimace that shadowed her features. His tongue was warm and fat. She sat back, positioning her throbbing vagina over his mouth. He kissed her damp, sexual lips before slowly tracing the perimeter of her clitoris and vagina. Madame Thorn shuddered and tried unsuccessfully to muffle her exiting breath. Glen's efforts were deliberate and methodical. She clenched her hands slowly, coinciding with the movements of his tongue. She suddenly felt ashamed of her outburst at Madame Vine. She now fully understood. He was masterful with his tongue. He taunted her with powerfully smooth strokes, while his penis mocked her with its erection. It didn't throb or pulsate. It didn't rebelliously pump unwanted pre-cum. It just stood, swollen and straight, from his body. Her mouth salivated with lustful hate.

"How dare he be in such control of himself?" She thought as her hips slowly rotated against her wishes. Some *dominatrixes* they were, her mind laughed, as her nipples poked forward from her concealed areola.

Madame Thorn's sexual wetness was thick and creamy. I coated his face and mouth. He lifted his head, closed his mouth around her opening and sucked gently. She cooed in pleasure. Madame Thorn adjusted her stance so the pleasure wouldn't cause her to fall. She held Glen by his

Glen's Guest Room

penis, slowly tightening her grip with each brush of his tongue. She began stroking slowly. The warmth of his sex grew more intense, as well as dense. She moved her eyes to see Madame Vine skillfully moving her finger deep into her own pleasure box. Vine stood with bowed-legs, mouth open. Vine silently trembled and shook. Madame Thorn couldn't find fault with her actions. She'd taken actions into her own hands as well. This was the sexual version of forfeiting. Finally she couldn't take it anymore. She steeled herself against her actions.

"I'm the Mistress." She thought, "No matter how well a slave performed." They were no more than that; slaves. She slowly rose for over Glen's face, her body warm and trembling. She was determined to have her way, all the way.

"Thank you, Slave." She said, crawling from atop of Glen and the table, "Now show us the room. "

Madame Thorn adjusted her clothing, unaware of he smile creeping across Glen's lips.

"Yes, Mistress."

Madame Thorn released the tension of the restraints and tugged on the rope, leading him for the table and toward the room.

"Open it." She ordered, as the three of them stood in front of the door.
Glen nodded his head and slowly turned the knob. Anticipation slowly overcame the women. Their vagina's throbbed and tingled.

SexPressions

Madame Thorn heard an old game show host's voice in her head, "What's behind door number three?" She giggled as she looked around at their different degrees of nudity.

"Here goes." Glen said, as he pushed the door open.

He moved aside and ushered he women into the room. Both women involuntarily nodded their approval. The room was surprisingly large and spacious. Madame Thorn ran her eyes over the different apparatus and gadgets. A lover's swing hung from the ceiling in the center of the room. Hand restraints hung from the ceiling on both sides of the swing. A full size bed, covered in rubber or latex sheets, lay in the left comer of the room. Next to the bed, a plastic three-drawer chest held all manners of sex toys; each held in a plastic freezer bag. Madame Vine had been moving around the room, her hands and eyes over everything.

"What's this?" she asked, pointing to a brown cylinder cushion.

"It's just a pillow. I use it for leverage." Glen answered, face still blank.

Madame Thorn cut across the room to a glass door. But before she could ask, a quick inspection answered her question.

"Why do you have a shower in here with glass doors?"

"I like to watch women get clean." His voice clear, and barely over a whisper.

Glen's Guest Room

The women slowly walked around the room, visually sampling everything.

"Also Mistress, if you notice there are two cameras hanging from those corners."

Glen pointed at two security-style cameras hanging from opposite corners. They were positioned to cover everything in the room. Each woman looked at the camera in her line of sight, quickly turned to see the other camera, and then turned back.

"Okay Slave, this is impressive." Madame Thorn said, slowly turning around in the center of the room.

"So Mistress, where would you like to start?" Glen had become confident.

Actually he was closer to cocky. Awe and amazement were easily displayed across both the women's faces. He had started calling the room the *Chamber*. Most women quivered at the very sight of all the toys and contraptions. These two were no different.

"Well I don't know about her, but my coochie is buzzing." Madame Vine started; wire ran from the back of it to a small control device. Glen raised his eyebrow; a slight smirk on his lips.

"Yes, Mistress."

"That's a butterfly." He said, with a soft chuckle, "Sort of any way.

SexPressions

Madame Thorn walked over to him and took hold of the restraints and pulled Glen behind her. She motioned for Vine to assist.

"We're going to try some of these while you watch." Thorn positioned him so that he could get a full view.

Madame Vine had already moved to the bed. She laid on the bed with her knees bent, legs up. The toy she chose had two plastic straps that completed the "butterfly" design. Glen watched her manipulate the small control, sending her head backward and her eyes rolling into her skull. Soft moans dribbled down her cheeks. Glen watched her and enjoyed the look of relief that washed over her face.

Madame Thorn stalked around Glen admiring his full nudity; the manliness of his scars on his brown skin; the symmetric design of his body, the dangling heft of his penis. She retrieved a small array of things from the bin, a bottle of oil, a string of medium sized pink beads and a slender metallic-finished vibrator. She slowly walked to the bed, turning on the balls of her feet as she went. Glen admired how her thick body barely jiggled. "I'mma kill it!" He and his dick both thought, as a dark heat slowly grew within him. He had no choice but to bide his time. His mouth watered from the memory of their scents and taste.

Madame Thorn lay on the bed and faced the opposite of vine. Their legs mirroring the others, again Glen was overcome with a feeling of them being twins. The sexual version of the equal and opposite reaction. Madame Vine moaned and tugged gently at her nipples. Soft pants pushing

Glen's Guest Room

and shoving over her tongue. Her toes curled and straightened in sporadic intervals. Thorn had coated her pubic area teasing her exposed clitoris. She twitched and purred as her large nipples grew and stood like sexual sentries over her. She gently inserted the plastic pleasure dick inside of her womb and increased the speed. Her left leg shot straight and she turned slightly, lifting herself from the mattress. The women caressed and fucked themselves; moans, pants, and purring being exchanged as if they were in an erotic debate. Thorn poured more oil over her vagina, allowing it to flow down to her anus. She removed the vibrator and slowly began working the anal pleasure beads into her brown rear hole. Vine had decreased the force of her own toy and watched Thorn in the mirror. She envied her friends cavaleric approach to sex. The only things that came that close to her asshole were tissue and panties, she still was turned on whenever she watched her. Vine's vagina throbbed powerfully as she continued to watch her best friend masturbate. She could see the slave in the reflection and knew that this was torture for him. She felt it, even if he didn't. Her eyes and ears watched and recorded Thorn's *sextivities,* her pussy begged for the slave. She slowly moved from the bed, legs and vagina quivering. Vine stood in front of Glen and stared into his eyes, before kissing roughly on the mouth.

"Come here *and fuck* me!" She ordered. Her words spread over Glen's face like sweet oil. Glen smiled and nodded his head slowly.
"As you wish." He answered.

Madame Vine unfastened one of the restraints and returned to the bed. She lay as she had and watched Glen remove the other restraint. She wasn't sure if Thorn was aware that she had left the bed and freed the slave, by now her eyes were closed and she was enthralled with her own pleasure, but Vine was sure she would like the surprise.

Glen reached into a small bag and closed something into his fist, then kneeled next to the bed and began gently kissing and licking on Madame Vine's breast and abdomen. She giggled from the feel of his hands and mouthing brushing against her body. She purred for Glen to enter her. She could no longer stand the wait, the torture, and the sexual absence.

"Please?" Her body finally spewed.

Glen stood and opened his fist, where he held a small package. Madame Vine watched as Glen slowly covered his girth with a latex sleeve. At the tip of the condom was an intricate design formed into ridges and was covered with feelers. Madame Vine expected for Glen to mount her. To straddle her so she could wrap her legs around his waist and pull him deeply into her. But she was pleasantly surprised. Glen stood on the bed between the two women. First he stared down at Madame Vine, his penis pointing straight from his body, stepped over her, then turned and faced away from her. He kneeled down, placed a pillow under the small of her. Vine lay bewildered and in awe. Glen eased forward and slowly entered her surprised vagina.

"What the fuck is this?" Her clitoris and vagina yelled.

Glen scooched forwarded and drove himself down and into the back of Madame Vine's vaginal walls. Her

Glen's Guest Room

body lifted itself toward the ceiling, waist and rib cage first. Glen slowly wound his waist, brushing his balls against her clitoris. Vine grabbed his ass cheeks. She lightly smacked his ass and instantly understood why men loved doing it. Glen grunted and pushed down. He continued half-pumping and rotating his hips. He slid his hands beneath Madame Thorn's ass and began kissing and licking her thick labia. Madame Thorn; surprised and slightly frightened, moved her hands from between her legs and caressed Glen's face.

Madame Vine gnawed at the inside of her cheek. She forced her eyes to stay open despite the feel and warmth of the pleasure. She guided Glen, gripping his dark ass cheeks, watching him fuck her and orally please Madame Thorn. She and Thorn had been part of a lot of threesomes; but never like this, never with a slave like this. *A man like this!* Vine gyrated her hips beneath him and smacked his ass again. She had never felt more in control than now. His ass cheeks were muscular. They felt thick inside of her palms. She tried to urge him to push further and with more force. But the position wouldn't allow it. It would only accommodate for the exquisite, torturous pleasure of his penis dragging against the bottom of her womb.

"Yes!" Madame Vine hissed. Then as she watched Madame Thorn, she saw it just as it began to happen.

"Oh my God! She's..."

"I'm cumming!" Madame Thorn spat. She pulled her legs closer and dug her nails into Glen's head. He fought her off and continued licking and absorbed the heat of her labia. He sucked softly and used his full tongue to lick at her clitoris. Madame Thorn mumbled a protest as her orgasm

SexPressions

swarmed her body. She trembled and tried to move away. Thorn turned her head and caught a glimpse of Glen pushing rhythmically into Vine.

Her orgasm forced her eyes shut just as Madame Vine yelled. "I can't take this shit!"

Vine pushed herself from beneath Glen, trembling and shaking, onto the floor.

"Good." Glen said to himself. He pulled the tickling condom form his penis and exchanged it quickly for a fresh one.

"Turn over." He growled. Madame Thorn shot him a queer look before, slowly rolling over on her stomach. Glen leaned forward and kissed Thorn on the small of her back. He could feel her leg trembling slightly. She laid forward, ass in the air, and breathed laboriously. Her vaginal walls slowly contracted and pulsated. Glen palmed Thorn's ass cheek with one hand and guided his blackness inside of her.

"Now talk that slave shit."

Glen pushed forward with a quick jab of his penis. Glen pushed forward with a quick jab of his penis. He grabbed a handful her hair and turned her face toward the mirror.

"Look at me *fucking* you!" he smiled, then snarled, then smiled again. Glen grabbed her by the waist and squatted behind her; still pushing himself deep into her. He rotated his hips, pulled himself slowly from her warmth, and then quickly pushed forward before she could catch her

Glen's Guest Room

breath. His strokes were full and powerful. Glen smiled and wound his waist. He felt his orgasm rising within him. Madame Thorn gasped and turned from the mirror. She smiled at Mdm. Vine just as the uncontrollable urge to pee overcame her tingling sex area. Thorn hunched her back and moaned. Vine moved behind them and massaged Thorn's clitoris and Glen's ball. She acted as if she were using Glen's own hands, assaulted her clit and held Madame Vine in place. Vine pulled Glen to her, feeling him bend briefly inside of her, before straightening himself out. Madame Thorn kissed and licked along Glen's back and shoulders. The ticklish sensation nearly caused Glen to miss a beat, but it only made him shift his sexual gears. Vine began to move faster and rougher. Her body was suddenly rebelling against itself. Her hips bounced and rotated on their own. Her nipples defied her brain's order and stiffened. Her hands tingled and refused to dig her nails into his back. She cursed and wrapped her legs around Glen, squeezing his torso in erotic revenge. Her clitoris giggled and snickered. A wave from her orgasm pushed forward. Madame Thorn cheered the entire scene. She guided Vine as if it were her dick that filled her. As if she derived some pleasure from being so close. Vine felt Thorn's hands tremble as her body quivered with after shock.

"Ooohhh shit!" The women moaned and whispered.

Vine pushed away from him allowing his manhood to slide from her womb and swung back into him, seconds later she felt hot stickiness splash against stomach. Vine swayed slowly smearing the warmth into their skin and the moment into her memory. The three of them collapsed into each other. Each woman placed her head against Glen and

SexPressions

listened to his raging heartbeat calm itself. Madame Thorn moved first. She nudged Vine, who lifted her head leaving a tiny bed of saliva trailing from Glen's chest to her lip. After helping her out of the swing, Madame Thorn unfastened Glen's restraint. He smiled with weak glee. Vine collapsed onto the small bed, followed by Thorn and Glen, who produced a large thick blanket. The three of them slept soundly, only waking to eat and further drain themselves of any sexual energy that they could muster.

Glen woke early on Sunday morning. Saturday and had come and gone with neck speed. Glen didn't remember getting in the bed. He also didn't remember setting the video camera up either. But there it stood, red light still on. And here they lay; knotted and tangled with each other. Glen felt a crusty stickiness on his face. He frowned and slid his tongue out to sample the substance.

"Ice cream." His taste bud reported.

He chuckled softly to himself, as he replayed his half naked trip to the store for more ice cream and champagne. He felt one of the women fidgeting herself into the world of the conscious.

"Morning Killer." She said, puckering her lips and kissing him on the forehead. Bonnie, he told himself. He nearly called her by her Mistress name. Inner-Glen repeated both names, Bonnie and Irene, until they felt as comfortable as the other names. Glen shook his head. He'd be sure to tell James that he had a terrible time. The taste of the lie forced a smile on his lips. The telephone's ring roared through the house. Glen knew who it was before he picked it up.

Glen's Guest Room

"Sup Jay?" Glen said; the gravel-morning voice sounding louder and full of more grogginess than Glen anticipated.

"Sup Dude?" Ya'll straight?" James asked, sounding happier than a person should at that time of the morning.

"Good sex the night before usually did that to a person." Glen thought.

"Yeah, we're good." Glen said, surveying the two women.

"Where are Bonnie and Irene?" James asked.

Glen could hear Missy talking softly in the background. She kissed James close to the receiver. Glen assumed on the cheek.

"They're right here."

"Yeah? So what happened?" James asked, moving around on his side of the phone.

"I was tied up with them the whole weekend. Nothing special." Glen answered.

Irene snuggled closer against him and kissed his chest. "But call me back and I'll tell you what happened. "

Glen placed the phone down softly. He didn't remember how they had gotten into his bed, so he decided to refresh his sexual memory.

THE GAMES

"I haven't done anything!" I say, as you giggle from behind the blind. I had an idea and wanted to test it as soon as I got home from work. And like a little kid I sat in anticipation of your arrival. No sooner had you step through the door, did I grab you. I rushed you through a shower, a quick bite to eat, and a nice rub down.

"Stop moving. So I can finish putting this on" I'm horny as hell. I'd been working overtime and for the first time this month, the weather had broke and I could come home early.

"Okay. Now that you're tied down and blindfolded, I'll explain what's going on. I have a few things here, and I want you to guess what they are. Some will be easy and others will be not so easy. Ready?"

You shake your head, *yes*. There's a growing slowly across your lips. "Save your energy." I think to myself, "You're going to need it." I leave you alone in the room so I can get the items from their hiding place. I couldn't risk you sneaking a peek and spoiling my surprise.

Walking back to the room, the sight of you laying

SexPressions

across the bed, makes me want to give up and jump on you now. But this was worth waiting for.

"Damn right it is." I smile to myself. I take out item one. I turning it on, you respond instantaneously.

"That's a vibrator!" You blurt.

"Not close." I say holding the small device. "But it is vibrating."

I slide between your legs. You shake as my breath brushes against your inner thighs. You moan and giggle. I apply the device to your sweet sex spot.

"Clippers." You sing. "Those are clippers. Ooooohhh I'm about to get shaved."

"Like that?" I ask removing hair with one swipe. Your moans tell me you approve. You raise your pelvis to meet the warm vibrating surface. You gasp for air before exhaling hard. Your pussy starts to glisten from your own wetness. My mouth waters. I can't wait until it's my turn to touch you, but the game is first. By the time I'm finished you're shaking with erotic pleasure.

"I think I'm going to like this game." You say between orgasmic short breaths. Using my hand, I brush off the new bald area. Then I lean in close and lick away the juice from your kitten. Your taste is sweet and tart. I sip from your pleasure glass. I sit up and study your body. I think of the next area to attack.

The Games

Rising from the bed, I grab item two. This time I sit at the top of the bed. I kiss you on the neck, slowly and softly. I nibble at your earlobe. You panting eases as I slowly let your sensitive treasure rest, for now anyway. Stopping at your lips, we kiss. I caress your large ebony breast. I stroke your nipples with my thumb. They become swollen as if to burst. I lean closer still and introduce my kiss to your breast, left then right. Next, I place each one in my mouth. I lick, suck, and blow on each nipple. You curse, wishing you could hold my head to you bosom.

"Time for item two." I think, as I turn it on. It is a soft humming device. Its sound is almost lost to your ears.

"What's that?"

"Guess!"

I apply the device's moving motion to the valley between your chocolate hills. You inhale hard and try to move into the fetal position. Moving the device over your breast, I trail its path with my tongue. I'm stretched over you. With my free hand I reach down and with smooth circular movements, I entice and tease your clit. It's throbbing from the shaving. I delicately insert my finger. You start to ask a question before the ability to talk is stolen from your lips. The small rubber cover on my finger has a small raised surface. I finger your hole with the small French tickler, while I tease your nipples with small circular motions from device number two.

"Stop…playing with …me and …oh shit…FUCK ME!"

SexPressions

You're screaming now. And that's what I'm waiting for. I remove the toys and flip you over. The scarves I used to tie you down, have just enough slack that I don't have to untie you. Your pussy is soaked from my torture. I disrobe and slide in behind you. Your brown ass cheeks quiver as I enter you doggy-style. I pull out and drag my blackness across your smooth skin. And just as you begin to lie forward, I slide inside of you with my fullness. I start with slow strokes. I pound you with eight and a half inches of sex. You pant with each entrance, grabbing the sheets into a ball. I use my free hand to rub your clit with my French finger. You snap back onto all fours. Your breathing becomes faster. I can feel you getting tense. You taunt me with your tightness; urging me deeper and deeper. I stroke a little faster with my finger and just as you scream and hunch your shoulders. I turn on item two. I place the small device on your ass. I trace your brown-eye. Your body is confused and stuck between gears. Without losing a stroke I attack your two holes. You scream. Your body jerks and a burst of hot liquid rushes against my stomach and swollen dick. Even with your orgasm I can't stop. I continue on my mission to please. I continue pumping and stroking. Teasing and taunting. Your entire body shakes as you're overtaken by the aftershocks of cumming.

Dropping item two, I turn you on your side. I lift your leg up slightly and keep pumping myself into you. I'm growing inside of you. Your walls press back against my shaft.

"Yeeeessss!" You whisper.

I feel you become tense. I rise slightly and enter you

The Games

with quick and powerful half strokes. You/I/We scream and moan. I'm panting now. You bite down on your lip, anticipating another eruption. I want us to cum together. Using my French finger, I slowly insert it into your brown eye. You inhale hard. You inhale harshly. I rotate my finger around the rim of your hole. My muscles become tight as a rope. I feel us both. Your walls grab my dick and hold for dear life. My determination to hold out is broken. The rush of light-headedness hits me hard and fast. We collapse into each other, kissing and petting each other I untie you. You hum and run your hand across your still wet shaved pubic region. The look on you face tells me you're satisfied.

We shower and return to bed. Quickly I fall to sleep. After a brief nap, I'm awakened by a soft humming in my ear. I snap fully awake. I can't move my arms and although I have my eyes open, the room is still dark. I feel you close to my ear. The humming fades and you whisper softly into my ear.

"It's your turn!"

I smile and lay back into the soft comfort of the bed.

And the games begin.

OLD SCHOOL LOVE

The Call

"Hello?" Sharon's voice froze Charles to his end of the receiver. Why had he called her? He knew and more importantly she knew.

"Hello?"

He wanted to speak. He had to speak, but couldn't.

"Just hang up then." The tear that stood in the corner of his eye told him. "Just hang up." Charles heard his lips whisper into the telephone. He had all the courage in the world when he listened to the Isley Brothers. But Mr. Isley and his brothers were not around, it was only him. And he was the one who should say something first, because no matter who was wrong; it was always his fault.

"I didn't mean..." he started, before Sharon's sobs cut him off He wished she wouldn't cry. Not right now anyway. Not while he wanted to talk.

SexPressions

"I was hoping you'd call." Sharon said, saving him from himself. "You were right."

"About what?" Charles asked wishing she'd just for once let him be wrong.

"About what you said earlier. Maybe we should try it your way."

Charles fought back a smile but allowed his tears to flow. "Is it okay if I come back over?" He asked, before either of them said something to spoil the moment.

"Yes! Please do." Sharon answered, her smile growing with each word. "I can change into something else, since our night was ruined."

"Don't change." Charles said beaming, "Don't change at all!"

Charles grabbed his jacket and bolted out of the door. Ron and his brothers would be proud.

The Visit

Charles stared across the table into Sharon's eyes. He thought looking into her eyes would help, but now it only made things worse. Sharon's eyes were hazel brown. Some people would describe them as cat-eyes, but Charles called them *ocean-eyes*. They were the type of eyes a person could lose themselves in. You could bask in their warmth, but Charles didn't want to bask. He wanted to talk. More importantly, he wanted to touch. Charles wanted to hold her

Old School Love

against him. Allowing his body to whisper soft apologies and tender comforting words. He wanted to listen to the sound of her heart singing to his. And just as Charles thought he'd spend the entire night staring silently at Sharon, a single thought poured through him. "Touch her and let someone else talk."

"Let's dance!" Charles said standing and moving toward the stereo.

He couldn't remember putting the CD into his jacket, but there it was. It was a special "*lover's only*" Old School mix CD he'd bought from the flea market. The DJ was young, so not all of the songs were what Charles would consider O*ld School*, but the ones that were his definition of the term, were good. Charles smiled to himself as he knew the precise track to play. Sharon was standing in the center of the living room, giving Charles a chance to reacquaint himself with how good Sharon looked in blue. Her dress was a soft powder blue. It fell just past her knees, with a split on the left side that allowed her lovely brown legs to peek out and tease a man into a frenzy. The dress fit tightly over her torso and presented Sharon's deep cleavage on a silver sexual platter and flared slightly from her ample hips at the waist. Charles' nature grew firm as he pulled Sharon close to him. She exhaled and sank further into him. He was her teddy bear. It was times like this that Charles was glad he stopped doing sit-ups. Sharon ran her hand over his belly his hands crept along her back. They swayed to the music. Sharon hummed along to the music. Once again Mr. Isley and his brothers spoke for Charles. He gave Sharon a half spin and pulled her backward, snuggly into his embrace. Sharon nestled her soft buttocks against Charles, and for the

SexPressions

first time Charles noticed Sharon wasn't wearing any underwear. He grew firmer with the discovery. Charles kissed Sharon on her neck, just below her ear, sending shivers along her spine and across her body. Sharon let her hands drift across the front of her body, while Charles attended to her neck. Sharon quickly became moist between her thighs.

She was glad that Charles had come back over. Her body begged for his touch. Charles slowly unzipped her dress exposing the smooth warmth of her back. Charles kissed the nape of her neck, drawing soft moans from Sharon's lips. Charles thought he felt the sound from deep within her. The sound excited him. He kissed her again as Mr. Isley told his woman about being at her best. Sharon turned her head, trying to get a better view of Charles and his kisses. Charles ran his hands upward toward her shoulders. He pushed her dress from her shoulders and watched as it fell quietly to the floor. Charles wrapped his arms around Sharon, pulling her deeper into him. His penis, growing stiff and long, throbbed along with the music. Charles twirled Sharon around, watching her nakedness whisk past his vision. Damn, she was lovely. No, she was *Love*. His best friend. His best love, and soon to be his wife. Charles stopped Sharon so that she faced him. Now those eyes were on him again; those *ocean eyes*. Charles was sure he'd drown. But this time Charles closed his eyes and opened his ears. Now he saw what he should do.

Charles opened his eyes again and watched his lips land gingerly between Sharon's breasts. He sucked at her womanly shape. He needed her and wanted her close. Charles placed his hand over Sharon's breast and slowly

Old School Love

closed his hands. Now he knew. With each moan drawing kiss, Charles knew. He cupped Sharon's soft ass cheeks into his palms and lowered kissed his way lower. Sharon's moans floated onto his ears. So as Ron Isley sang, Charles kissed. His face tickled the sides of Sharon's inner breast. He kissed each nipple as they heaved back and forth on Sharon's tender brown canvas.

As Charles bombarded Sharon's breast with kisses, she hummed along to the music. She couldn't imagine life without Charles. The more he kissed, the more she was glad he was hers; his mind, his body and for the moment his kiss.

Charles kissed at Sharon's belly. He could smell the sweet aroma of her sex. He didn't want to rush. He couldn't rush now. Sharon held his sweat-covered bald head, hand shaking slightly, and pulled Charles to her. His kisses weakened her with each touch of their wetness. A small orgasm began to gather from the depths within her. A tear warmed her face, as Charles lowered himself to her sexual center. Sharon was wetter than she thought. She tossed her leg over Charles' shoulder and pulled him deeper. Charles still kissed as Sharon's plump vaginal petals presented her clitoris in a pink blossom. Sharon tossed her head back, allowing a moan to ascend from her mouth. She tried saying his name, but was struck silent. Charles tongue now swept over her clitoris with a full stroke. Her sex pearl throbbed with each pass until finally, she couldn't hold off the pressure deep within her. The orgasm that struck Sharon was fierce. Her body shook. Sharon collapsed forward; although it felt as if she had erupted with orgasmic lava, her sexual volcano slowly seeped her creamy juices onto Charles' eager tongue. Sharon clung to Charles, as he continued tasting at

SexPressions

her flow. Sharon bit down on her lip and waited for the end to come, cursing its arrival. She shivered as Charles gave her vagina a final lick and kiss.

Charles stood and wrapped his arms around Sharon's naked quivering body. He kissed her tenderly on the cheek and swept her into his arms. Sharon let her head fall onto his shoulder. Charles began walking toward the bedroom, carrying Sharon tenderly in his arms.

"Aren't you forgetting something?" Sharon whispered.

Charles nodded his head in agreement. He continued to the bedroom. He placed Sharon easily on to the bed. He kissed her softly on the lips and went back to the living room. The night would be long and they would need music. Charles smiled as he thought of the other songs on the CD.

The Bedroom

Charles stood in the doorway and studied Sharon's naked body. The moonlight provided her skin with a light sheet of radiance. Charles took a breath and held it. He thought back to the first time he'd met her. She wore blue that night as well. It was then that he knew she was for him.

"You must be desperate." He could still hear her saying over the phone.

"No, just determined." Charles confessed. But if pressed he would've said it was a little of both. He left the club no sooner than she had written her number down. As he traced her body with his eyes, he thought of her. That night

Old School Love

the dress she wore was backless, giving Charles a perfectly erotic view of her neck and back. The only difference now was the tattoo.

"*Adored By Him.*" Charles whispered the words that were transcribed across her lovely shoulders. The comers of the smile that grew on Charles' face, acted as hands catching the tears that rolled from his eyes. This time Mr. Isley was obsolete. Charles walked to the small CD player sitting on the dresser. The song was the reason he'd bought the CD in the first place. He'd seen the name and thought about Sharon and that first night. He wiped his face and let the CD player slowly swallow the inspiration for the night. He pressed play and then the repeat button. The first bars of the song caused Sharon to stir from her thoughts. Sharon moaned softly, as the singer spoke for Charles. She rose to her knees, dancing slowly to the words; to the music; and to the thoughts of Charles.

Sharon barely noticed Charles' hands wrapping around her waist. His touch was warm and relaxing. Charles pulled himself to her and kissed Sharon lightly across the tattoo. She exhaled a light passion-filled breath and they began swaying in unison. Sharon and Charles both could feel his bulge growing steadily powerful in his pants. Charles suddenly felt hot and confined. He slowly moved his hands from Sharon's body to his own. He needed to be closer to Sharon; closer to her heat, to exchange touches. Charles slowly began loosening his silk tie when Sharon moved his hands and replaced them with her own. Her touch was soft and delicate. She removed the tie and kissed Charles tenderly on the lips. Charles watched her work from the reflection in the mirror across the room. He burned the vision of her features in his head; the curves of her buttocks;

SexPressions

her slender back, and the tattoo. He closed his eyes and watched her in the mirror in his mind. He watched Sharon slowly push the shirt away from his shoulders. Charles shivered as Sharon kissed him on the neck and shoulders. Charles ran his hands across the tattoo's smooth surface, before massaging Sharon's shoulders, trying to fight off the tremors that rose throughout his body. Using her tongue, Sharon coaxed Charles' nipples to rise. They stiffened as she nurtured each one with her mouth's warmth and her lips softness. Charles continued kneading at her shoulders as she moved lower, before slowly laying him back onto the bed. Charles laid back and relaxed. He was with an angel. And with that thought he closed his eyes.

Sharon deftly worked Charles' belt buckle loose. She surrounded Charles' navel with butterfly kisses. Sharon watched Charles' attempt to roll himself into a small ball, having to settle with only his feet, toes, and hands. Sharon looked on in sexual amusement, as the zipper worked itself lower, with the assistance of Charles' swaying hips, and like a trained team, Sharon pulled Charles' pants from his body. Now it was Sharon's turn to study Charles' body, and the even darkness of his complexion. She loved how his skin looked as if it were shining without looking greasy. She loved to lie on Charles' body, it was soft yet solid and firm. Plush was the word Sharon thought of when she lay on him. He was her sexual throw pillow, although he'd been the one doing the throwing. And as she stood at the foot of the bed, a tear slowly descended down her cheek.

"Of losing you!" Sharon mouthed the answer to the Charles and Artist's question.
Sharon stalked forward over Charles, tears bombarding his dark landscape. She stopped over his erect penis. She took him in her hands seriously. Charles froze for a second before relaxing with Sharon's grasp. Her palms

Old School Love

were a warm wonderful prelude to the intense heat of her mouth. Sharon slowly filled her mouth with Charles' length and girth. She used her tongue to massage and coax his manhood firmer and deeper into her mouth. She started a slow pivoting motions. Her mouth working opposite of her hand. Charles began to squirm, but was calmed by the touch of Sharon's on his belly. The belly of his she loved so much. Sharon wanted him in her; inside her most intimate places. She wanted to repair the wounds she'd made and wanted to use the intimate place that caused those wounds. As she increased her movements, so did Charles. She felt him begin to tremble, fighting the entire way.

"Let me have this!" Sharon thought, tears pooling on her enclosed hands. "Let me have you."

And as if in response, Charles shuddered with a loud powerful exhale. His entire body contracted and contorted, as Sharon pumped him for all he was worth. Charles' body was being ravaged by a chilled fire. Drained; Charles closed his eyes and replayed the entire scene again in his mind. Sharon laid on him, her man, and cried softly to sleep.

Her dreams were filled with Charles and the sight of him holding the box in his hand. Even in her dreams he was a fighter, but he could beat the tears. Because this time Sharon said, "Yes."

TO THE MAX

"I have an idea." Maxine burst with excitement.

We'd been sitting around my apartment catching up on old times. Maxine had flown in from Virginia and decided to hang out with her "ex", before leaving. But now with nothing to do, we soon drifted into the *Bored Zone*. So here she was with a bright idea.
"Anything to keep awake." I thought.

"Let's shave each other." She continued. A warm smile sprang from her thick, chocolate painted lips. My dick agreed before my mouth.

Maxine stood up from the couch and took off her shirt. Her smooth dark breasts were nestled neatly in a power pink bra. She turned and headed to the bathroom, stripping away the bra as she went.

"This would be fun." I thought, as I followed her lead. By the time I reached the bathroom, Maxine was standing in the shower. Her body called to me. It had been a long time since we'd been together, but you never forgot a body like hers. She was tall with thick chocolate thunder thighs that grew from her lovely feet into a big round ass.

SexPressions

As I stared at her I nearly ripped my boxers off. Maxine still knew how to get the full nine inches out of me. She waved me towards the shower. The warm water attacked my body as Maxine ran her soapy hand over me. I pulled one of her D-cup breast to my mouth and softly sucked on the nipple. Maxine began to moan softly.

"Not yet." She said playfully pushing me away. "Later, after we shave!"

I held back a small riot as my stiff dick brushed against her ass while she turned. I quickly, yet tenderly, washed her body savoring the sight of lather running down her flesh. We both step from the shower, clean and horny. Still wet Maxine while grabbed the razors and shaving cream. Maxine lay across the foot of the bed smiling.

"You first!" She said pulling me down to the bed. My blackness softly throbbed, as she massaged it before applying the shaving cream. I closed my eyes and gave myself to her. While one hand held my dick out of harm's way, the other made smooth, careful, circular strokes. My body tingled with each swipe of the razor blade. Maxine began slowly rotating her hand at the tip of my dick just under the head. The soft slow friction sent a bolt of erotic lightning through me. A soft breath of passion betrayed my lips. I was close and Maxine knew it. She began stroking harder and I knew I couldn't hold off any longer. Just as I was about to explode Maxine stopped. She slowly kissed her way up my body and whispered slyly in my ear. Maxine straddled me, sliding all of my nature deep into her sweet hole. My freshly shaved pubic area tingled as she slid up against me. Maxine sat up and rotated her hips. My entire

To the Max

body shivered. I held her breast in my hands, teasing her nipples with my palms. Maxine leaned back slightly and began to massage her black pearl.

"Wait for me...baa...ba...bbee." She stuttered as she felt my body began to tremble.

But I couldn't. I gripped her hips and joined her rhythm, as I pumped up into her. Maxine fell forward, clit swollen and pressed against my newly shaved skin, and rotated her hips quick and vigorously. I felt light-headed as the first wave shot through my body. I bit down as my hot cream shot into Maxine. She gasped as my warmth flowed against her inner walls. Maxine braced herself against the headboard and rotated her hips on my still throbbing dick. I moaned harshly, moving my hips to her rhythm. Maxine tossed her head back as her body slowly began to stiffen around my shaft. I reached down and massaged her clitoris with my thumb. She wiggled atop of me as the first wave drew a small roar from her mouth. She held onto my arms as the entire orgasm molested her body. Her sweet cream ran between my legs and coated my stomach. I increased the speed of my hand job. Maxine shrieked, as she became a fountain of sex juice. Finally she collapsed, exhausted, against me. We kissed and fondled each other until we fell asleep. When I woke, Maxine was gone. She left a note promising to call. I lay in the bed rubbing my shaved area grinning at the smooth feeling. With all the excitement, I never had a chance to shave her.

BETWEEN SISTERS

Carl read the note taped to the door.

"Shower and come to bed."

Carl smiled as he undressed. Times like this he was glad he had given Nicky a key. It had been a long hard day at work and he was glad she'd stopped over. She had a way of making a day like today disappear. Carl quickly moved to the bathroom to shower. The hot water soon relaxed his muscles. Washing away layers of grime, he returned to his own light complexion. Carl felt better; much better. The shower did him well. Reaching for his towel, he noticed Nicky had left him another note along with a glass of Brandy.

"Put on the blindfold that's hanging on the doorknob. Then knock."

"Blindfold?" Carl thought smiling. Now he was definitely glad Nicky had a key. He dried off and rubbed his body with musk oil. He glanced at himself in the mirror. He liked how his body was shaped. By most standards he was skinny; 5' 10" and 143 lbs.

SexPressions

"But I can fuck!" He mouthed to himself. Carl looked down at the sex unit that hung between his legs and smiled. It was skinny as well. Skinny and nine inches long with a curve. He and "J.J." had done some damage in their day.

Flexing in the mirror, he left the bathroom. The blindfold, really one of Nicky's scarves, hung on the doorknob. Carl did as he was told and knocked. Peeking through a slit at the bottom of the blindfold, Carl saw Nicky's hand take his. She guided him to the bed and laid him down on his back. She ran her hands across his legs, spreading them apart. Starting at his left knee, she kissed her way up his crotch and down the other leg. Nicky fondled him gently. Her touch was soft and nurturing. Nicky felt Carl slowly stiffen in her hand. She kissed her way up his right thigh. Nicky sucked and kissed softly on "J.J's" little friends. Carl wanted to scream. It was rare for Nicky to go down on him. He inhaled and moaned in pleasure. Using her hand, Nicky slowly stroked his penis. Adding a slight twist at the head, she began sucking softly on Carl's length. She began taking him in her mouth a little at a time, until she could nearly swallow him whole. She teased his head with her tongue.

"Ooohhh baby, you gonna make me cum." Carl warned, holding back the explosion as best he could.

Slowly pulling it from her mouth, Nicky kissed the head of Carl's rod as it cleared her lips. She crawled forward and mounted Carl. Nicky guided Carl easily into her sweetness. Nicky used her muscles to grip and squeeze Carl's rock hard nature. Carl caressed her breasts as his hands began softly tingling. Her nipples were large and

Between Sisters

thick. Carl sucked softly on each nipple. He couldn't stave off the oncoming explosion. He was ready.

"I'm finna cum!" He grunted.

"Wait for me!" Nicky urged.

She quickened her pace and force. Carl couldn't hold back for long. It hadn't felt this good in a long time. He couldn't stand it. His body jerked and he grabbed Nicky's ass. He exploded hard. Nicky didn't stop. She was breathing heavy. She sat up and began working only her hips.

"Ooohh, Ooohh shhiitt!" Nicky panted. Her moans grew deeper with each thrust. But now her voice changed. Something wasn't right. Carl reached to pull the blindfold off, but Nicky pinned his hands over his head. With a few powerful humps she came. Nicky gasped and worked her hips until Carl's stomach was coated with her stickiness. She rolled off Carl. He sat up and pulled the blindfold from his face. Carl was frozen. He should have known, how could he be so fucking stupid. To his surprise it wasn't Nicky, but her twin sister Nancy. Nancy smiled at Carl and began dressing. As she left she looked over to Carl.

"Tell Nicky I said "We're even!"

Carl sat motionless in the bed with one thought.

He wasn't telling Nicky shit.

CHAINS AND ALL

Lance smiled at the reflection in the mirror. It wasn't his chiseled body that pleased him so much, although he did take pride in the fact he'd went from chump to champ. It was the sight of Gloria sleeping the sleep of the well sexed that caused him so much joy. They'd been arguing for the last few weeks and after a night of "negotiations", they'd decided to give their relationship another chance. And as far as Lance was concerned, anything was better than the daily dose of hand to man combat. Well there was the small technicality of Lisa, but he'd deal with her soon enough. Lance didn't see the need in clearing the slate so soon; especially a slate that fit nicely in his arms.

Gloria stirred in her sleep, shifting under the thin sheet that lay across the bed. Her long brown legs peeked from beneath the sheet, reminding Lance of the light texture of her skin. Lance felt himself begin to grow firm within his boxers.

"Hell another round wouldn't hurt before breakfast." He thought, as his hand slowly moved over his morning bulge. Lance turned and began crawling onto the bed. He softly kissed Gloria's covered flame as he moved higher. She stirred beneath him, moving closer to the world of the

SexPressions

awakened. Lance moved his hand over Gloria's breast just as the sound of his front door opening then closing; drew his attention. Lance turned to look just as Lisa stepped into the bedroom doorway.

"Surprise baby!" Lisa said, hands on her hips exposing her nakedness beneath a red leather trench coat. Lance stared in disbelief, as Gloria sat up in bed next to him.

"We had a key made. I hope you're not mad." Lisa said smiling, tossing the coat from her shoulders and letting it fall to the floor.

"We?" Lance asked dumbfounded.

"Yes! *We* had a key made" Gloria's soft morning voice was accompanied by her hands moving across Lance's stomach. "We couldn't decide who should have you so we decided to share." Gloria said, kissing Lance on his ear. Stunned, Lance let his head fall into his hands.

"Relax baby." Gloria whispered as the bed sank under Lisa's added weight.

Gloria kissed Lance's neck seductively. She pulled him back against her. Lance shivered against her warmth. As much as he wanted to, Lance couldn't relax. He was both embarrassed and excited. Horny and horrified; Lance bit down on his lips as Gloria ran her tongue from the area between his shoulder blades, upward, along his neck. He lifted his head from his hands, but kept his eyes closed. He didn't want to see what was happening. It was better that way. Lance felt Gloria moving. She placed her legs on both

Chains and All

sides of him and pulled him deeper against her. Her breast welcomed the touch of his back. Lance could feel Gloria's ebony sex grow warmer; and moister. Lance exhaled as Gloria grinned slyly behind him. She let her hands work independently. Gloria wanted to scratch as well as soothe Lance. She wanted to repel him away as well as welcome him to her. Gloria loved, lusted, and longed for Lance. She also detested, despised, and disliked him. So from behind Lance's back Gloria ushered in victory and celebrated revenge-filled defeat. She bit tenderly on his neck as she roughly tweaked his nipples.

Lisa looked up at Lance. She held his morning stiffness within her trembling hands. Lisa leaned forward; kissed and licked Lance on his inner thigh. Lisa liked having Lance defenseless before her. She slowly stroked Lance's length with scornful effort.

"How could he?" She thought to herself. "How dare he?" Angry sexual excitement swelled deep within her loins. And before she would be through with him she had to have him. Have him; her own way. Lisa happily cursed the warm tear that crowded her eye, as she tasted the heat of Lance's manhood. Lisa's taste buds were greeted by the surprisingly sweet taste of Gloria's sexual residue. Lisa fought back the urge to bite down on Lance's penis as she felt herself becoming moist between her thighs. Lisa slowly fed Lance deep into her mouth. She peeked up at Lance, curtly scraping her teeth against Lance's flesh. A grimacing smile fought a soft frown on the battle field of Lance's face. He moaned loudly, opening and closing his fist. His entire body radiated with comfortable submission. Lance reached behind him to stroke Gloria's neck, while slowly pumping upward into Lisa's mouth. Lance could feel a powerful orgasm swelling deep within him.

"Not yet!" He scolded himself

Lance leaned forward, pushing Lisa from him. Lance thought of both women's taste. His mouth watered with anticipation. Gloria was sweet and creamy, while Lisa's taste was juicy with a slight tartness. Lance knew there would be no short changing them.

"Not if l can help it!" Lance thought, standing up in the bed.

Both women's eyes were on him now. And unlike them, Lance could make a decision. He smiled at Gloria. Her early morning face beaconed to him. His blackness bobbed before him in its early morning stiff brilliance. Lance kneeled before Gloria and kissed her on her right knee. He slowly moved his hands over her legs. Gloria's temperature slowly rose from sleeping warmth to newly awakened heat. Lance continued kissing Gloria's leg, slowly pulling his lips closed as if her skin were wet. Lance moved deftly across Gloria's lower body with greedy hunger. Gloria leaned back against the headboard and tossed her legs on Lance's shoulders, inviting him to her. The erotic smirk that sat on Lance's face blossomed into a full smile. Sexual thirst consumed Lance. His mouth became dry and his tongue felt swollen and Gloria presented him with sweet creamy relief Lance trailed kisses down Gloria's thigh until finding her sexual creaminess. Gloria panted softly as Lance moved his full tongue across her pearl tongue. His palate shuddered from her sweet taste. He rolled the tip of his

Chains and All

tongue around her clitoris; each movement pushing Gloria closer to the edge of ecstasy. Gloria arched her back, as Lance reached beneath her and grabbed her voluptuous ass cheeks. He kneaded her buttocks, tickling her sensitive brown exit with her own softness. Gloria crossed her ankles behind Lance's head, locking him in place. This was the Lance she wanted; the *"freaky"* Lance. This Lance she could have to herself. Gloria tried to contain the small rumblings that grew deep within her. Lance continued working her ass cheeks, taunting her orgasm with soft brownness. Gloria cursed the smile that grew on her face. She hated the passion Lance evoked. But as her orgasm neared, the real secret she and Lisa shared could wait. No need in spoiling the moment. Gloria shifted her hips upward against Lance's tongue. She felt her large breast shimmy and sway. Her nipples sat erect from her like antennae, transmitting her sexual feelings into the air. Gloria could hear Lisa soft moans float throughout the room. Lisa had been sitting on the bed pleasuring herself. The sight of Lance pleasing Gloria filled her with jealous arousal. Lisa closed her eyes with the sight of Gloria's face wrinkled in erotic defeat.

"Yes!" Lisa's lips moved mimicking Gloria's. Gloria pushed down on her thighs and tried to brace herself against her orgasm. Her body screamed as she coated Lance's face and eager tongue with her juices. Heavy moans filled her throat; each one moving faster and louder from her lips. Lance used his tongue to tug and pull at Gloria's sexual weakness. Gloria took a deep breath and fought off the light-headed feeling to talk.

"Not without you." She said pushing her words

SexPressions

around each moan. "Come to me."

Gloria pulled Lance's head, guiding him over her until they were face to face. Lance's manhood throbbed thick and full against Gloria's swollen labia. Lance slowly rotated his hip, further teasing Gloria.

"Now! Please now" Gloria panted.

Lance kissed Gloria's puckered lips and slowly worked himself into welcoming warmth. Gloria gasped as Lance slowly entered her. Gloria cursed at the second orgasm that threatened her. Lance pushed himself deep within Gloria, slowly rotating his hips and pulling himself from her. Gloria dug her nails into his back pulling him to her; urging him to her. Lance held Lisa's hand as he slowly reentered Gloria. Lance rocked back and forth before working himself into a smooth rhythmic stroke. Lance's body quickly became tense. He grunted along with Gloria's moans and Lisa's pants. His body begged for her Gloria's orgasm to join his. Sweat coated his body with a light sheen as he gained momentum. Lance's stomach muscles tightened as the pressure of his orgasm mounted. Gloria felt Lance stiffen. She grabbed his neck as her second *cumming* tore threw her body. An instant later Lance's body shuddered and hot life flowed from his shaft. Gloria held back the urge to scream as Lance continued to fill her with his length. Tremors evaded their bodies. Gloria bit down into Lance's shoulder as he slowly moved. Lance kissed Gloria's forehead softly. His penis throbbed deep within Gloria's womb. Lance watched tears slowly roll down Gloria's face. He caught one between a kiss before turning his attention to Lisa.

Chains and All

"I believe it's your turn." He said, slowly replacing Lisa's hand with his own.

Lance rose from Gloria and pulled Lisa into his arms. Where Gloria was thick and voluptuous; Lisa was slender and petite. Lance lifted Lisa in his arms and placed one of her breast in his mouth. Lisa wrapped her legs around Lance and buried her head into his shoulder. Lance sucked Lisa's B-cup breast into his mouth and used his tongue to arouse and tease her nipple.

C'mon, I need to shower." Lance whispered, allowing Lisa's vanilla-brown breast to fall from his mouth, before replacing it.

Lisa sucked harder into his shoulder and moaned her agreement. Gloria lay curled in the fetal position and toyed with her swollen clitoris.

Lance felt the beginning of a hickey being formed on his shoulder. Lisa smelled sweetly of cinnamon and apples. Lance inhaled her scent in deeply, as he sat her on the sink. The coolness of the marble beneath them pushed Lisa's nipples to become erect. Lance tenderly bit down on the one in his mouth, buffering the edge of his teeth with his lips. The smell of sex tickled Lisa's nose. Her body begged for Lance. She'd fingered herself silly with sexual anticipation. Lisa had been fighting off an orgasm since she'd received the call from Gloria last night. Their trap had been set, and now that they'd sprung it, Lisa nearly exploded. She leaned back against the mirror in anticipation. Lisa turned her head and caught a glimpse of the passion smeared across her face.

SexPressions

"I thought you were leaving him." A tiny voice within Lisa said, as Lance's mouth moved lower on her soft landscape. She pushed Lance's head tenderly toward his destination.

"I changed my mind." Her vagina whispered in response. "I just changed my mind."

Lance kneeled before Lisa. Gloria's sweet taste and aroma laced his lip and now he'd add Lisa's tart spiciness. Lance ran his eyes over Lisa and cursed to himself. Her body was flawlessly sexy. Lisa's pubic hair was wet and sticky. Lance moaned as he wiggled his tongue through her passion bush and found her creamy opening. Lisa tossed her legs over his shoulders just as Gloria had done, and she pulled Lance's tongue deeper into her slit. She held the back of Lance's neck and allowed thin moans to flow from her mouth. Lance attacked Lisa with his tongue; licking her clitoris with strong forceful movements. He held Lisa, as she tried to wiggle backward, in place. Lisa's legs wobbled as Lance's masterful tongue summoned her orgasm. Lisa watched herself in the mirror. The look on her face changed from vengeful determination to sexual defeat. Lisa panted uncontrollably. Her chest heaved with each flick of Lance's tongue. Lance moaned loudly from between her legs. Lisa's muscles froze her in place, while warm electricity rolled through her. Lance pushed his tongue fully against Lisa's black pearl, as her ebony sex juice coated his face. Lisa clenched her fist as Lance licked at the last of her orgasmic waves. Lance stood before Lisa admiring his work. Lisa held herself tightly, as if the aftershocks of the orgasm were shaking her apart. Lance kissed her cheek.

Chains and All

"Don't move." He commanded tenderly. Lisa shook her head in affirmation.

Lance quickly moved to the shower. His entire body tingled now. His manhood bobbed before him. Lance smiled while the warm water washed over his full eight and a half inch muscle. He quickly lathered and washed away the traces of the morning's sex.

"Round two!" His penis muttered as he stepped from the shower.

Lance stood behind Lisa; water dripping from his body. Lisa had just regained control of her body. She faced the mirror and smiled at the reflection of Lance standing behind her.

"You moved." Lance said, placing his hands on her hips.

Lisa turned her head to speak, but all she could muster was a slow sweep of her lips with her tongue. Lance grinned to himself He leaned forward and kissed Lisa on her neck, eliciting a soft moan from her lips. Lance's penis jumped from the touch of Lisa's body. She was still moist. Lance placed one hand on her petite cheeks and slowly began entering her. Lisa gasped as each inch began to fill her. Lisa spread her legs and pushed back against Lance. She took one last look at them in the mirror, before closing her eyes. Lisa thought of Gloria. She thought of their deal and the bond they now shared. And as her body welcomed Lance's thickness, she thought of the new lives *they'd* live.

SexPressions

"Happily ever after." Her voice sang in her mind.

Lisa moaned to the words as Lance increased his rhythm and force. Lance grunted quickly. He pushed himself deeper into Lisa. His orgasm grew quickly within his body. His teeth itched from the pressure of the impending gusher. He could hear Lisa cursing and cheering him on. Lance grabbed Lisa's shoulder with one hand and held Lisa's ass cheeks with the other. The force of his orgasm swirled behind his abs.

"Damn, I'm cumming." Lance groaned as he grasped Lisa's ass cheeks with both hands. Lance begged his orgasm to show with vigorous pumps. He shut his eyes as his eruption screamed its arrival.

Gloria watched the entire show from the doorway of the bathroom. She quivered with excited envy. It wasn't everyday that a woman could watch her man having sex with another woman. She hated admitting that it turned her on, so as Lance neared his release, Gloria neared them. And as Lance's body became stiff, Gloria stood behind him, and smacked him spitefully on his ass.

"Yeah baby!" She whispered to herself as the vibrations of Lance's orgasm ran through him.

Lisa felt Lance's life fluid splash hot inside of her womb. She moaned harshly from the thought of the first time she'd felt that. Felt him inside of her. She wondered if it felt that good to Gloria. Lance slowed himself to grind and Lisa told herself she really didn't care to know how Gloria felt. Lance slumped forward and tried to gain control of his

Chains and All

body. With Gloria's touch against his back and Lisa's body covering his front, he was torn with indecision.

"What next?" Lance thought to himself.

A blindfold and Gloria's voice gave him a small hint.

"Like I said before, relax."

Lance let Gloria, with Lisa in tow; lead him back to the bedroom. He really wasn't into being blindfolded, but now he'd swear by it. Lisa firmly fondled his tight buttocks. She saw the look in Gloria's eye. It was time to let Lance know what they knew. Gloria guided Lance to the bed and had him lay down on his back. She whispered for him to spread his arms and legs.

"What the hell?" Lance thought. *"Anything once."*

Lance complied without fuss. The excitement pushed his penis and nipples erect from his body. Lance's body became ultra-sensitive from the suspense. He could feel each woman move onto the bed; Lisa on his right; Gloria on his left. Each woman ran her hand over her perspective side of Lance. When Gloria teased his stiff penis, Lisa taunted his nipples. Lisa wet her finger and playfully pampered Lance's brown exit, while Gloria bit his nipple gingerly. Lance moaned with numbness. He closed his eyes beneath the blindfold. It was his natural reaction to pleasure this good.

"Let's get real freaky?" Lance heard Lisa whisper.

SexPressions

Lance shook his head *yes* to the suggestion, and grinned uncontrollably. He wanted to rip the blindfold from his face, but the unknown held him stiff. The expected thought of Lisa's head between Gloria's thick thighs, made him throb with wonder.

Each woman moved to opposite ends of the bed. Soft kisses assaulted Lance from top to bottom. Again Lance went numb. He barely felt the coolness of the handcuffs around his wrist and ankles. Lance throbbed with bonded rapture. And suddenly Lance felt wet heat engulf his penis. Gloria took Lance into her mouth. She softly stroked and sucked his penis. Gloria took her time. She needed to savor the moment. She knew Lance was close to exploding and didn't want to rush him. She wanted to remember the feel of Lance in her mouth. Remember his taste. So as she watched Lisa work on Lance's chest, she took note of everything. Including that goofy look of pleasure Lance held on his face. The sweet warmth of pre-cum oozed against her tongue and Gloria even recorded that in her memory.

Lisa straddled Lance. She ran her tongue over his chest; moving slowly and with revenge-filled erotic purpose. Lance twitched beneath her from the sensation. He exhaled roughly and tried to move. Lisa continued to tease Lance's chest, while Gloria slowly manipulated his stiffness. Lisa pelted Lance's chest before reaching into the pockets of her trench coat. She pulled out the items and showed them to Gloria, before returning to her task. First Lisa drew intricate designs of passion onto Lance's quivering chest. Lance couldn't hold off any longer. Gloria felt the intense heat between her palms and decided that it was time. She quickened her hand movements. Lance fought against the

Chains and All

restraints. Lisa continued with her task. Lance moaned and panted harshly at the treatment he was receiving. Gloria hurried her strokes; concentrating tension at the head of his hard shaft. Lisa finished with the first item; applied a small dab of thick cool liquid from the second item. Then placed the third item in the stickiness. Lance exploded with a violent shake and exhale. He wanted to curl himself into the fetal position, but couldn't because of the restraints. Lance trembled from wave after wave of his orgasm's aftershocks. Each woman kissed him on his cheek. Lance smiled.

"Okay. Let me out." Lance stated, eager to keep the party going. "So I can put it on ya'll".

After a few seconds of silence, Lance felt a breath in his ear.

"The key is glued to your chest." Gloria said pulling the blindfold from his eyes. "And there's a note explaining what this is really about!"

Lance sat dumbfounded in the bed. He sat that way while each woman gathered herself and her belongings and left. Lance struggled to sit up in the bed. And after a period of intense contortion, he found that he could sit up straight in the bed.

Just as Lisa said, there was a key stuck to his chest along with a note written in lipstick. Lance read the note twice and fell back into the bed cursing.

"Pregnant huh?" Lance asked aloud. "And both having twins!"

SexPressions

Lance lay still for awhile before trying to free himself.

"Dayum glue and handcuff." Lance thought to himself, as the uncontrollable urge to laugh consumed him.

THE BARITONE VOICE

It was his voice. It was a deep baritone, panty-wetting voice. All he had to do was speak and she gave him any and everything he wanted; and now she gave him her undivided attention.

"Close your eyes." He said; his voice deep, smooth and commanding. She decided that if she could pour his voice into a glass, it would be dark and taste like honey. *"Black honey"* she giggled to herself, *"that's exactly what his voice would be."* She closed her eyes and listened. If her thighs quivered from just his words, she couldn't imagine what she'd do when he touched her.

"Open your legs further." He told her. She spread her legs slightly apart, scared to move. She knew anything could send her into an uncontrollable orgasmic outburst. He whispered a command into her ear. She giggled and obeyed.

"Are you ready, Love?" He asked.

"Yes!" She ordered her body to scream. She could feel his hands drawing closer toward her. When it arrived; his touch was soft. An instant chill swept over her body. She could feel his hand moving across her back and down across

SexPressions

her ample ass cheeks.

She mumbled something about being over weight and needing to lose a few pounds. He laughed softly and that was even sexier than his words. Sweet moisture seeped from between her thighs, soaking her panties. The white cotton ones he had bought for her.

"You're not fat, Love. You're what I need." With that, her nipples began to pulsate. He moved himself in front of her. She opened her mouth hoping to taste him. He softly touched both of her hands. He exuded warmth like a sexual oven. The moisture between her thighs was now thick and creamy.

"Do you mind if I kiss your thighs?"

His voice, coated with black honey, boomed against her knees. Her lips moved but she wasn't sure if they carried words. He stood and she felt his eyes on her. She pressed hers tighter not daring to open them.

"I want you to undress and stay standing." His voiced kissed against her ears. "I'll wait while you do that. But don't keep me waiting long." Although she didn't open her eyes she knew he was aroused. Without looking, she knew that he had a bulge, thick and long, occupying the front of his pants. She undressed slowly. He liked her to do most things slowly; carefully. Her hands trembled and her knees were threatening to buckle, so she concentrated on her task. She wished he would have been the one to remove her clothing, but he had the voice and she did what the voice said.

The Baritone Voice

"When you get to your underwear, remove them very slowly." The voice demanded.

A powerful orgasm pushed against her swollen labia. She reached her underwear and started with her bra. Her breast fell from their cotton confinement, tickling themselves as they touched and brushed against each other. She placed her hands on her hips, daring her orgasm to come forward, with her touch. She tried to remove her panties with ease and sex appeal. The cotton tugged at her drenched pubic hairs causing every muscle in her body to become taut. Her toes curled, as the soft material brushed against her heat-laced thighs. A moan fled from her lips. She wanted to cum. Her body couldn't stand the sexual strain. He was punishing her for something and this was how he did it. She stood before him naked and ready to be conquered.

"Good." He said.

Now she couldn't hold it. Her orgasm swept over her with severe force. She braced herself as wave upon wave shook her body. She felt a warm syrupy fluid flow down her thigh. A tear tiptoed from her eye, as he told her it would be "Okay". She fell to the floor, begging for his touch. She hugged herself, the feel of her own body sending her deeper into orgasmic shock.

She searched for him; for his voice. He spoke softly, quieting her body. The very same voice that had sat her erotic forest ablaze, now extinguished her flames.

"I'll call you back, tomorrow, and we can do it again!"

SexPressions

She let the phone fall from her hands. He said he'd call back and she knew he would. At first he had gotten the wrong number, but as she rubbed her swollen sex, she knew he'd gotten it right the first time.

VACATION IN THE KEYS

Shawn smiled at the reflection in the dance floor's mirror. The club opened to the beach so the sunset could be seen. The sky was painted a soft coral and stretched over the Florida Keys. As she watched herself sway to the soft music, the sun began to set, turning her electric green wrap and bikini top a darker, more seductive version of itself. Shawn liked how she looked now. She'd been working out over the winter. Her stomach was flatter, accented with a jeweled belly button. Her hips were shapelier. But mainly she liked her breast and ass. Her breast no longer sagged; they sat perky and full, from her body, inviting sex-starved men and jealous sex starved women, to wonder about their authenticity.

"There all mine." Shawn thought, running her hands slowly over her breast.

Her nipples pushed against the bikini's soft velour front. She turned slightly, so she could get a better look at her ass. It was an onion-ass. Even she wanted to cry from looking at it. Shawn let her hands fall lightly over her full, ample rear. She giggled to herself thinking about the g-string she wore which didn't cover much of anything. She even wondered about the guy from the beach. Hopefully he

SexPressions

got a good look before he crashed into the hotdog stand.

"Yes, I do look good!" Her eyes said, as she stared at her reflective twin.

Shawn had become so entranced with the sight of her new body, that she hadn't noticed her hands, which were now beneath her wrap. The house band played jazz and Shawn accompanied them with her *sexaphone*. Her hand danced across her shaved sexual regions. She closed her eyes, and allowed the band and her hand, to play a private concert for her clitoris. *Masturbation in "V" minor.* Shawn felt her juices, as her g-string quickly became soaked with them. The back of her knees began to tremble, as a small orgasm rose with the tempo of the music. As the orgasm began to cause her body to tremble, contort and overheat; two other thoughts arose in the back of Shawn's head. The first was of how horny she was now. With all her concentration on working out; she didn't have time or energy, for that matter, for sex Seven months was a long time. Shawn let a finger slip under the g-string wetness, and thought devilishly about the second thing. She'd never seen herself while she was having an orgasm. She bit down firmly on her lip as the band (her hand) played her into an orgasm. Shawn opened her eyes just as the feeling of light-headedness swept over her. Her knees buckled slightly, as thick creaminess coated her hand. But as Shawn visions slowly became clearer, it wasn't only her face that looked back at her. There was also the face of a man. The mere sight of him nearly frightened her into another orgasm. The man was dark, by the look of the massive chest that peaked around Shawn's head, sculptured with muscles. Even in the mirror Shawn had to look up at him. She closed her eyes

Vacation in the Keys

again and wondered if she were dreaming. If fingering yourself made you see visions, Shawn decided she'd do it more often. As Shawn slowly opened her eyes, she half wished it were a dream, but as their eyes met in the mirror, she was glad he was still there. He placed his hands on her hips and pulled Shawn tenderly back to him. Shawn's stomach dropped as if she were on a rollercoaster. Her thighs became as warm as the inside of an oven. Shawn felt his breath on her ear and neck.

"If you had a man like me you wouldn't need your hand for that." His deep voice quietly boomed against her ear.

This time Shawn's knees buckled completely. He took her hand, still between her creamy ebony thighs, and placed them into his mouth. Shawn gasped and expelled a hushed whimper. He slowly began licking Shawn's taste from her fingers one by one. Fire raced through Shawn's body. He licked and kissed her entire hand. Shawn flinched from his touch as he ran his hand over her well-toned stomach.

"I'm Gavin and welcome to my club." He whispered." Club Testimony."

"Testimony." The word danced across Shawn's lips, as Gavin slip his hand where hers had been earlier. Shawn exhaled harshly. Gavin kissed her softly on the neck and rolled her swollen clitoris between his thumb and finger.

"And this isn't the dance floor, Lovely. This is the stage!" A second orgasm announced itself with a hushed moan.

SexPressions

The band had begun to play another selection. It was soft and sexy. Shawn continued smiling at her reflection. She wouldn't -couldn't- dare to look at Gavin. His hands, she could handle; but those eyes, Shawn knew those eyes would defeat her easily. She shivered as he worked her pearl in smooth circular motion. She told herself to breathe. Shawn let her cheeks spread on their own accord and pushed back into Gavin's crotch. Gavin wore a pair of cotton walking pants and his tremendous erection pushed upward to escape its thin soft confinement. Gavin worked his finger slowly into Shawn's wet tightness. She stood on her toes and leaned forward at the waist. She pushed back further against him drawing his length further between her cheeks. The moans Gavin had been stifling, revolted against him. He was overwhelmed by this woman. He used his free hand to massage Shawn's lovely buttocks. Her ass was well toned, but still soft and tender. Gavin heard the soft jazz melody playing in the background. He tried moving to the music, but the warm tenderness of this woman pushed him offbeat. Gavin's penis grew to its full eleven inches, but was held down by the confines of his clothing. He wanted to be free; then re-confined deeply within this woman's warmth. Shawn felt Gavin steadily growing against her. She couldn't tell the actual size, but she knew he was large. She wondered if she would be able to handle all of him. Then she knew it didn't matter; she had to take all of him. Shawn reached between her legs, finding the head of Gavin's rod. She rolled the head against her softness. By now, Gavin's two hands were full of her cheeks.

"Now!" Shawn said, as she slowly worked her g-string off.

Vacation in the Keys

Shawn braced herself against the mirror, as Gavin freed his entire girth. His blackness throbbed and pulsated in the hot air of the club. Gavin drug his massive prick, over the thin material of Shawn's wrap, pre-cum leaking from the head. Shawn begged for him, still staring through the mirror. Gavin's eyes rolled to the top of his head, unable to fight off the feeling. Shawn felt her breast swell and fall as the fire that engulfed her body, re-ignited itself. Gavin inched the green wrap over Shawn's ass. The sight left him speechless. He wanted to kiss the sweet brown round cheeks, as they wiggled at him. He had to have. Have her that very moment. Gavin smacked the cheeks curtly before guiding himself within.

Shawn gasped hard and pulled away. It was a powerfully painful pleasure that flooded through her, and she knew it was only the head. Gavin's prick curved, causing him to slide in at an awkward angle. He spread Shawn legs apart and forced her to arch her back. He wanted to have this entire woman. And he wanted her to have all of him. Gavin dipped down and slowly drove himself into Shawn's warmth. She gasped for air just as his manhood pushed against her tight, hungry sex, far into her. She wanted to yell, but her words were transformed to fetal pants. Gavin stood to his total height, driving deeper into Shawn. She stood on her tiptoes, still amazed at how she was able to consume Gavin's massiveness. She worked her inner walls against his long hot shaft. Shawn looked in the mirror just in time to see Gavin's face crumble in pleasure. She bent her knees and worked her entire pelvis. Gavin attempted to fight back, but Shawn swallowed each thrust; each pump; each inch.

SexPressions

Shawn felt Gavin begin to tremble. He fell forward and braced himself against the mirror. He was close. Now he pushed deeper into Shawn, his full entire length penetrating her. Finally Shawn couldn't take it. She slammed herself back and down onto Gavin's length. A violent orgasm shook her. This time Shawn watched her own facial expression change. Once again her knees buckled and creamy relief poured down her thigh and onto Gavin's sex. Shawn collapsed into the mirror. Gavin continued stroking. He grunted harshly and eagerly. He wanted to be done. Finally an orgasm pushed him as far as he could go. He slammed against Shawn, his body trembling with confusion. Gavin exploded as the saxophone finished its solo. Drained, Gavin slowly pumped the last of his last drops and slowly pulled himself from the depths of this pretty lady. He felt her shudder as the head came out with a quiet slurp and pop. Shawn looked tried to look at the reflections in the mirror, she was numb and barely able to see. She watched as Gavin bent down and retrieved the g-string from the floor. Shawn turned and tried to get sight of his massive sex muscle.

Gavin smiled at his new friend. He tucked himself back into his pants. Shawn stood and let the wrap fall, covering her full, lovely shape ass. Gavin took her hand and led her away. They found a quiet table with a good view of the band. They were both out of breath and throbbing for more sex. Gavin motioned for the waitress, who winked at Gavin while she took their orders.

"When does the next show start Gavin?" She asked staring devilishly at Shawn.

Vacation in the Keys

"As soon as you return with those drinks!" Shawn said, ready to try something new. Gavin smiled as the waitress disappeared and reappeared with their drinks.

"A Vodka and lime for the boss." She said placing the drinks in front of them. "And a Butter Nipple for the lady!"

Shawn winked to herself while the waitress took a seat next to her.

"Hi, I'm Angela."

Shawn's smile grew across her face. She sipped from her glass, welcoming the warm sweet comfort that flowed over her. She watched Angela's lips move, the words seemed to dance . Words dancing from her tongue. Angela was Caribbean brown. Her body was naturally sculpted. Her legs were long and they were connected to slim, shapely hips. She had full lips with exotic and hypnotic eyes. Shawn felt herself grow warm again. The band played a soft soulful tune. It was as if Angela had requested her own private number. Her words rode reach each note. Some of the words coated Shawn's ear, while the others rested against her and between her thighs. Shawn told herself it was a combination of the drink and the warm Florida air that made her warm and moist, but she knew it was the memory of Gavin's touch and the promise of Angela's passion that pushed her mercury level higher. Shawn crossed her legs, trying to suffocate the fire burning deep within her vaginal walls. She reached for her glass, hoping the ice would help extinguish the erotic flame. Her hand shook slightly as she brought the glass to her lips. A few ice chips fell into her cleavage. Shawn closed her eyes as her body sighed in relief. The ice began to melt, leaving a trail of ice-cold erotic relief. But as Shawn began to open her eyes she felt a warm sensation where the ice chips had landed. She peeked from between semi-closed eyelids, as to see Angela kissing gently on her chest. Shawn shut her eyes again and bit down on her lip. Angela's kisses followed the trail of the cool moisture that ran into Shawn's bikini top. Angela gently licked at the water, as she reached Shawn's deep cleavage. She rolled Shawn's breast in her palm, nipples pressing against the center of her hand. In the palm of her hand, pressing the center of her hand against the nipples. Shawn pushed back into cushions of the chair nearly falling over. Angela moved one hand along a trail from Shawn's breasts, to her quivering stomach to between her thighs. Shawn's thighs were still moist and sensitive from her earlier orgasm.

    Angela's manicured fingers sought out and found the right buttons on Shawn to push. Where Gavin's touch had charged her with electricity, Angela's touch had been magnetic. Attracting Shawn closer and further into an erotic field. Angela soon found spots Shawn had either forgotten about or had never known existed. Angela pried Shawn's thighs further apart with two fingers. Shawn's heart rate quickened as Angela pressed against her sexual threshold. Muffled pants escaped from Shawn's throat, as another powerful orgasm began mounting in her body. She wanted to release the rebellious relief from deep within her. She thought of Gavin. She opened her eyes and focused quickly on Gavin him, and through harsh moans she beckoned him to her. Gavin had been watching them with quiet excitement. He stood as Shawn stared at his massive sex throbbing in his clenched fist. The head was red, even for his dark complexion. Pre-cum glistened in small

Vacation in the Keys

droplets across the head. Shawn took Gavin's stiff penis into her hands and moved it toward her hungry mouth. Her lips spread effortlessly, anticipating his taste. Shawn lost track of everyone in the room. All that existed was her hunger for Gavin and his need to satisfy her. Shawn presented her tongue as an erotic "welcome mat" just as she felt a soft warmth push her thighs slowly apart. Shawn gasped and looked down to see Angela's pretty, bedroom eyes watching her as her tongue busied itself. Liquid sex coated Shawn's thighs and now Angela's face. Shawn's body trembled in sexual foul play. She felt ambushed. Angela used her tongue to slowly lick away Shawn's resistance. A soft moan announced its presence in Shawn's mouth just before she inserted Gavin's sex. She worked her tongue over Gavin's length as it throbbed deeper and wider into her mouth. Angela slid her hands under Shawn and softly caressed her ass cheeks. She worked Shawn's ass open slowly exposing her brown eye. Shawn inhaled hard and sucked Gavin's penis further into her throat. Angela's tongue and finger worked opposite of each other, pushing Shawn closer to the edge. Angela's tongue worked against Shawn's swollen clit while her experienced fingers massaged Shawn's tight hole. Shawn felt her body temperature rise. Gavin slowly worked his pelvis and Shawn mimicked his movements. Shawn sucked and licked Gavin's manhood, matching the eagerness Angela was performing on her Angela's eagerness. Angela taunted Shawn, who in turn taunted Gavin. Gavin worked his hips, driving his rock hard penis through Shawn's firm grip and into her mouth. He moaned, running his hands through her soft hair. A powerful orgasm began to organize itself deep within his loins. He could feel Shawn's excitement growing as Angela attended to her sexual center. Shawn's thighs

SexPressions

were the first to begin the rebellion. Their insides quivered against Angela's face. Next Shawn's labia joined them, throbbing open with each lick. Finally her ass surrendered to Angela. Shawn gasped and tried to concentrate on Gavin's thick penis. Angela slowly slid her finger deeper into Shawn's rear hole, pressing a hidden unknown button. Shawn buckled and succumbed to a powerful orgasm. Shawn froze allowing wave after wave to flow against Angela's expert tongue and mouth. Soon light-headedness swept through Shawn. Angela continued to kiss and lick at the sweet mess she drawn drew from Shawn.

Shawn still held Gavin's powerful manhood close to her face. Although she was exhausted, now, more than ever, she wanted Gavin to be inside of her.

Angela stood and watched Shawn try to control her breathing and the trembling that vibrated throughout her body. Angela smiled as a new thought ran through her head and tempted her thoughts. She whispered it softly into Gavin's ear; her smile growing with each hushed word. Gavin nodded in agreement. He took Shawn by the hand and pulled her to her feet.

"Maybe you'll be more comfortable on the table." He said into her ear. Shawn yelled, "Yes", through hushed sex-drained lips and as she nodded *yes*.

Gavin guided her onto the table, positioning her on all fours. Angela untied her top and the wrap from around her waist, exposing her naked beauty for all to see. Angela and Gavin stared at Shawn's curveous softness with hungry eagerness. Shawn felt their eyes on her and felt special, as if

Vacation in the Keys

everything was for her. Shawn nearly exploded from the thought of being taken sexually in front of the entire club.

Gavin moved behind Shawn, caressing her ass-cheeks slowly and softly with his eyes; then with his hands. He carefully spread her cheeks apart, then slowly guided them closed. Shawn hummed with ecstasy-filled excitement. Her body yelped with each movement. Soon she felt Gavin's penis rub across her warm rear flesh. She spread her legs slightly, calling for him to enter her. Shawn gasped harshly as Gavin's large head answered the call and pushed through her swollen labia. She thought she heard Gavin moan as well, she was right, he moaned as each inch moved deep into her.

Gavin closed his eyes and enjoyed the feeling. He continued to hold onto Shawn's ass as Angela moved her hand slowly over his stiff blackness, working it into Shawn's warmth. He felt weak. Angela used his thick length as her own sex toy. She located spots that neither Gavin nor Shawn remembered or ever knew. Gavin matched Shawn, moan-for-helpless moan. Pant for shivering pant. He slowly grew inside of Angela's hand and against Shawn's walls. Gavin's loins filled with bubbling jism. He wanted to let go, but he couldn't.

"Not now! Not first!"

Angela worked him deeper into Shawn until there was no place for her hand. Gavin began pumping slowly and softly, then faster with tender force. He felt Shawn's walls tighten around his girth. Shawn tried to fight back, but her efforts were too late. Gavin summoned her orgasm forth

SexPressions

like a sexual demon. With each thrust he touched the button that sat deep within her.

"Shawn." Gavin whispered, growing closer to the end.

Shawn pumped back into him. Angela smacked her curtly on the ass.

"Shawn." She heard him say louder. He drove deeper into her and grew stiff and straight. "Shawn!" Gavin yelled as he released.

Angela smacked her ass cheeks and rubbed them tenderly.

"Shawn!"

Shawn mouthed an answer. She fell forward as Gavin pushed farther into her, firmly pressing her button. Her orgasm quaked through her entire body. Shawn felt Gavin's hand on her shoulder as he continued pumping. Her knees wobbled as he called her name with another thrust.

"Shawn." He said going still deeper.

"Shawn." Going deeper still.

"Shawn!"

Shawn shot straight up in her chair. She looked around her office in slight confusion, before realizing where she was. No Club Testimony. No band. No Florida Keys. She had dosed off at work again. Well, at least she wouldn't fire

Vacation in the Keys

herself.

"You okay?" Her secretary Gavin asked, standing on the other side of her massive desk.

"It's these damn workouts that have me so tired." Shawn said yawning.

"Well Boss lady, maybe you should take that vacation you were thinking about. I hear the Keys are nice this time of the year."

I'll think about it." Shawn said somewhat embarrassed, before remembering Gavin had woke her up for something.

"So what can I do for you?" She asked, fixing her make-up and hair.

"Your two-thirty appointment is here."

Shawn watch as Angela stepped from her dreams and into her office. Shawn smiled as she shook the hand of the real life Angela St. Claire. Shawn sat down and listened to Angela's presentation already agreeing to do business with her and her company. While Angela spoke, Shawn thought of two things. The first was how she'd spend her days on the beaches of the Florida Keys; and the second was that she'd need new batteries for her vibrating panties.

ARIES BIRTHDAY

Aries hands shook as she read the letter again. Leave it to her sister to do something like this. Most people just baked a cake or threw a party. Not Rachelle, she threw you an orgasm. "So what do I do?" Aries asked aloud. Mainly to the letter but also to the chauffeur who stood before her.

"Well Ma'am," His voice slipped from between his lips, "I have strict orders to have you choose between these two envelopes, first!"

Then as if by magic, he presented Aries with two black envelopes. One had white lettering with the word "Scream", while the other had Golden lettering with the word "Moan". Aries looked at each envelope and pondered the choices. With Rachelle, anything was likely to happen; and usually did. Aries stared at the tall bronze-faced man and thought of the two choices he offered.

What choices these were, Aries giggled to herself. She turned from the envelopes and looked at the man standing in her doorway; slightly taller than average, shaved head with a goatee. Aries mouth watered as she thought about the sensation of her tongue slowly moving across his sculpted chest.

SexPressions

"So where do you fit into all of this?" She asked, shifting her weight from one hip to another.

A soft baritone chuckle erupted from deep within his body.

"'That's why you have to pick one of the envelopes. I'm good at both." He said.

He pulled the sides of his full lips across his face into a smile that caused the fine hairs on Aries' neck to stand erect. It had been some time since she had sex and even longer since she had good sex. Aries thought about the last time and pushed the terrible experience out of her mind. Just then an electronic chime broke her trance. Again with magical hands, the man produced a cellular telephone, seemingly from nowhere.

"Everything about this brother is smooth." Aries' now damp, sex center whispered to the rest of her body. After a brief exchange, he offered her the telephone.

"It's for you."

Excitedly puzzled, Aries took the phone into her shaking palms

"Yes. This is Aries." She said, trying not to let her excitement show. "So which one did you pick?" It was Rachelle.

"Neither of the choices has been..." Aries started before being cut off.

Aries Birthday

"Don't give me that shit." Rachelle laughed into the phone, "You playing girl. Put that fine mutha-fucker back on the phone."

Aries heard Rachelle across the digital airwaves, as she handed the phone back to the mystery man.

"Yes Ma'am...," he started. "I understand fully... No it's no problem... Sure. Thank you!" He said, as he returned the phone back to its original hiding place. He stepped toward the door. Now from across the doorway, a soft aroma greeted Aries's senses.

"You must excuse my bad manners." He said, standing temptingly close to Aries. "I'm Mister, your birthday present." He smiled. "And seeing as how you aren't able to choose, I've been ordered to give you both *Desires*."

The last word floated from his lips. Aries opened her mouth to protest, but couldn't muster the words. She watched as he presented her with his muscular arm and led her from the house to the limousine that sat in front her house. He opened the door and aided her inside the plush seat of the vehicle.

"Inside of the car, there are two CD's. Place one into the disc player. That will decide which of the *Desires* you want

After a few seconds the sounds of music filled the afternoon air.

"Ahhh, that's an excellent choice." Mister said, as he

SexPressions

closed the door.

Aries sat in the back seat of the limo and watched the gray rough city melt into plush greens of the country. When they finally stopped in front of the cabin Aries knew this would be her best birthday to date. Well this one and the time she celebrate her first birthday in her own apartment. The cabin was war and inviting on the outside.

Mister stood a few paces inside of the door watching Aries take in the entire scene. The cottage was deceptively large on the inside. Left of the entrance was a kitchen equipped with stainless steel appliances, while all the cabinets were wood. Aries was sure it was mahogany. It was the same type of wood used in most of the homes she sold; although she wasn't sure if this was real or not. A few steps from the kitchen was a breakfast nook. A large skylight allowed the sun to showcase the table's decorative center piece. In the center of the cottage was the sitting area. A large burgundy sectional faced a stone fireplace. Aries could see a large bear skin rug, head intact, sprawled out close enough to the fireplace to get toasty without being burned. A few doors finished the view. A stairwell led to a balcony that overlooked the entire cottage. The foot of the bed and its high post were visible from where Aries stood. Soft music, actually the music from the car, embraced her. She didn't notice Mister moving around behind her. The cottage had her full attention.

"I believe this is the music you selected for the first of your *Desires*."

Mister closed a cabinet door hiding the stereo back

Aries Birthday

into the cottage's decor.

"So what did I pick?" Aries asked, moving slowly about the room. She ran her hand over the smooth wood and coarse stone.

"You selected *Moans* as your first *Desire*."

There was that word again, "*Desire*." Chills frolicked playfully over Aries entire body. She hid a smile from Mister, turned her back and stared at the large pelt of the once large bear. She removed her shoes and ran her bare feet over the soft fur. Without realizing it, Aries softly moaned as the tight muscles in her feet and lower legs began to involuntarily relax.

"Exactly." Mister whispered.

He was surprisingly close. She felt his hands moving closely over her body without touching her. The music's warmth thawed Aries as the tempo of the small fire tempted her to move. She turned to face Mister. To look into his eyes, but when she looked he was across the room opening one of the doors that melted into the room.

" You're bath is ready." there are clothes that I'm sure will fit you well." He punctuated the last word with a wink; or at least Aries thought it was a wink. Aries walked toward the door realizing, for the first time, that her nipples had grown stiff and her knees were getting weak. She wondered if she fell, would Mister be there to catch her. She looked at him once again and knew instantly that he would.

SexPressions

"I'll prepare dinner while you soak. Also you may notice there isn't any lotion or oils for when you get out. Don't worry; I'll administer that when I give you your massage." Another moan escaped her Aries' mouth. She thought about the small quivering that tickled her inner thigh as her panties slowly became moist.

Aries moved inside of the dim, candle-lit room. The entire room; walls, floor, and ceiling were wood. The toilet and sink were the only items that weren't wood. The hot tub was large. Aries guessed it could hold at least six adults, who if given cause, could move freely without spilling water on the floor. Five large candles added the right amount of light, allowing the room's dark features to stand out. The taste and scent of *Ylang Ylang Muir* covered everything. Aries found herself humming and moaning uncontrollably. She then had to wonder what the "Scream" portion of the weekend would consist of. She spied a bundle of folded towels; all white, with three white Calla Lilies, one for each of her ten years. Aries did a small dance. One she secretly did when things went her way. Picking up the lilies-although she didn't know why people did I, as if you could tell the authenticity of them by their smell- Aries brought them to her nose and inhaled. The smell was pleasantly familiar. Rachelle had done her homework. Calla Lilies had always been her favorite. Aries closed her eyes and inhaled deeply. She hummed as the scent transferred into a sweet taste. When she opened her eyes she was greeted by the sight of a large mirror over the hot tub. She smiled at her sexual reflection. She stared deeply into her own eyes, as she slowly began undressing. She imagined Mister's hands tenderly searching her curves. Aries wondered about the feel of his tongue against her deprived sex. Finally removing her

Aries Birthday

panties, she stepped slowly into the water's heat. She felt knotted muscles yell in impending defeat, before dissolving. The jet streams of the water moved the hot fluid rapidly around her body. She stretched her legs, spread them apart, and rested her head on the tub's lip.

Aries found a sponge and scented soap and slowly washed away the grim of her singleness. *This was how a woman should celebrate her birthday.*

"Celebration with Desires." She whispered. Lathering her body, Aries began exploring her own female landscape. The plush roughness of the sponge tickled her breast and neck. She submerged her hand between her legs and slowly manipulated her clitoris. Her hand's circular motion created a small whirlpool between her thighs. Sweat ran down the side of her face. She felt her mouth open and listened intently for the moans that were sure to come. She felt her vocal cords tremble as the baritone sounds of her female sex escaped her body. She now felt clean and dirty. She wiped away the grit of her own inhibitions and lathered herself with sexual sassiness. Aries used the sponge and her hand to bring herself to the brink of exploding. She tempted herself until her toes began to curl, and forced her raunchy hand to stop. She bit down on her lip and calmed her sex drive. Stepping from the soapy warmth of the water extremely relaxed, Aries dried herself using one of the large terry cloth towels. A soft scent of the *Ylang Ylang* drifted from Aries' soft skin, leaving her smelling like a delicate flower. Beneath the large towels, sat a large box with a white bow. Aries smiled and wondered how many more surprises Mister had in store.

SexPressions

Aries removed the bow slowly, savoring each moment as if it were a tasty morsel. She removed the top and gently placed it to the side. Inside of the box was a pair of cornflour-blue raw, cotton pants and a large matching shirt. A pair of plush slippers accented the gift. Aries hummed to herself and slowly got dressed. Naked under the soft material, Aries nipples slowly became erect, as they nestled against the front of the shirt. She delighted in the fact that the pants hugged her size 16 waist and still embraced her size 18 hips and ass. She hummed the "Happy Birthday" song and walked from the bathroom.

The soft smells of cleanliness, self sex and flowers were smothered by sweet pastries baking in the oven and the anticipation of being touched. The frolicking smells of food alerted Aries to how hungry she really was. But the growling in her belly paled in comparison to the rumbling that rose from between her thighs. Mister appeared from the kitchen with a large pan. "Sit on the sofa," he softly commanded, motioning toward the sitting area. He had removed his shirt and was now naked from the waist up. Aries nearly fainted when realizing both of his nipples were pierced; connected by a small gold chain. She clenched her fist and held her ground until the feeling passed. She selected a soft spot on the sofa. Mister sat next to her as close as possible, without touching. And even the anticipation of the touch began to push Aries closer to the edge. She peered into the bowl to see strawberries and two cups; one with dark chocolate, the other with white chocolate.

"Lean back and put your feet on me." Mister said, a sinfully devilish grin crossing his face. Uncommon

Aries Birthday

giddiness overcame Aries, as she shifted on the sofa. She tossed her feet and lowered her legs onto Mister's lap. Aries braced her self against his touch. A soft smell of flowers tickled her nose. His hands were surprisingly warm; as was the oil. Mister slowly and firmly, moved his hands over her feet, removing the last of the pockets of stubborn tension. Aries hummed from deep within her throat. She prepared a small giggle, knowing for sure that Mister would touch a tickle spot. He slowly moved his hands over her seldom pampered feet. She closed her eyes tasting the moans-not giggles- that floated from her lips. Aries hadn't felt this relaxed in a long time, and it had been even longer since she felt this excited. She moved her knees apart hoping that would alleviate some pressure on her steadily swelling labia and clitoris. She felt Mister's touch, as he ran his hands under each pant leg; gently rubbing away tension in her calves. Aries arched her back uncontrollably and reached down to touch him. She welcomed the elongated moans that moved from her now. She slowly began to feel light headed, closer to intoxicated than dizzy.

Mister slowly retracted his touch.

"Take your clothes off so I can continue." He said.

Aries found she was erotically shocked by the demand. She ordered herself to obey him. She stood and slowly began to unbutton her shirt. Her breast revealed themselves with naive outrage as they pushed from the shirt.

"Be cool, girl." Aries warned herself, "It's your birthday!"

SexPressions

Aries slowly began easing the shirt from her body, allowing it to linger on her shoulders, before dropping it to the floor. She looked into his eyes and noticed that he had been holding his breath.

"Why shouldn't he be turned on?" Her inner voice sassed. "You look good."

Aries liked how that sounded, even if it was her own conscious. She placed her thumbs into the sides of her pants and slowly pushed the pants lower. Aries slowly turned. The everyday chore of undressing had become a new birthday wish. She looked over her shoulder at Mister, but he only watched the waist of her pants, as it dropped slowly lower. She felt the top of the pants slowly release the brown beauty of her brown, round ass. Her heart pumped hot blood through her body. Aries felt electrically charged. She turned to look at Mister, just as she released the pants. He sat erotically amazed at the sight of her naked rear. For a brief moment the mystery of him had been revealed.

"He's just a man." Her sassy voice yelled.

Mister licked his lips and returned her look. He nodded and reached behind the sofa and produced a small bottle. Horror gripped Aries as the thought of being ashy overtook her. Mister stood and assisted her to the sofa. She listened to the voice in his eyes.

"Fuck being ashy!" Those eyes said, calming her down a bit.

Aries lay face down on the sofa with her arms along

Aries Birthday

her side, and closed her eyes. She eased a moan past her lips. The soft music still played while Aries hummed along. She heard her body relaxing. The sweet smell of *Ylang Ylang* preceded the warm feeling of the body oil against her back. The thick liquid moved slowly down the groove of her spine. He slowly rubbed oil into her dry skin using a slow fanning motion. He worked the kinks out of her shoulders and upper back. He ran his hands down and along her sides. Aries' body welcomed the touch and feel of the oil. The perfumed oil evacuated the dryness in her skin bringing with it a sexual relief. Mister reapplied oil to his hands and slowly massaged her unaware ass cheeks. Aries forced air from her lungs and nearly howled. Her ass cheeks began to itch erotically as they briefly touched. Aries involuntarily arched her back as Mister continued working the oil and his hand over her back and buttocks. An orgasm began rallying deep with in her, forcing Aries to wonder how many women received this treatment. She also wondered how much this was costing Rachelle. She decided she'd ask later, when she felt the delicate pressure of Mister's kiss on her cheek, then an elongated stream of air against her unsuspecting brown eye. Aries jumped as the **sexsation** of her surprised asshole triggered a miniature avalanche of an orgasm. Aries cursed and commanded her hands and feet to uncurl.

"I'm blowing out the candle and making a wish." He said, answering Aries's unasked question. She prayed the wish would come true. Mister continued down her legs then he returned his attention to her upper body. Mister rolled Aries' arms between his palms, working his magic on those forgotten areas. Mister told Aries to roll over. She slowly flipped over and obeyed. Her breast relaxed against her body and eagerly awaited their turn to be pampered. Mister

SexPressions

dribbled warm oil between her breast and belly. He started just above each breast with slow, open palmed movements. Aries look at Mister but saw past him. She puckered her lips and dreamt quickly of the feel of Mister's lips she wasn't sure how to place her hands so she let them flop next to her and tried to melt into the sofa. Melt away from Mister's touch.

Mister slowly moved his hands, first around each breast, then using slow circular motions; he began moving closer toward her nipples. He tempted each nipple with the palms of his hands. Aries felt her heart rate quicken, each breath carried a tender moan. She felt her legs spread without her permission. The heat rising from her vagina heated her thighs as well. Mister moved his hands lower, leaving Aries' breast for later. His hand passed over her flat belly; forming small S's over and around her navel. Aries cursed passionately and pleaded with him to end her torment. Mister easily pushed his hands lower finally reaching her begging sex. He applied firm meaningful pressure onto her labia. Soon her vaginal petals opened and presented her pinkness to him. Her scent overtook the sweetness of the body oil; tempting him. Mister kneeled lower and moved his hands, one over her breast and the other over her vagina. Aries wiggled beneath his touch, emitting soft sexually musical sounds. Aries was Mister's brown piano, and he skillfully played each note and every key. Mister leaned forward and kissed her just above her navel. He slowly worked her vagina and moved his kisses higher. The top of Mister's lip brushed the underside of her breast, sending her toward the edge shivering. Aries began caressing the back of Mister's head, beaconing him higher. Mister obeyed. He kissed the crest of her breast, kissing her

Aries Birthday

nipples. He started with the left breast. He kissed her firm sensitive nipples, allowing his tongue to slip from his mouth. She turned her head as if not wanting to see what was happening. Mister softly tugged at her breast with his lips. He gently pampered each with his mouth and hand. Aries moaned and panted with force. The feel of his tongue radiated throughout her body. Mister sucked a small hicky between Aries's tender brown breasts. He gently inserted the tip of his middle finger into her puckered sex. Aries grasped before welcoming the intrusion. Her moans became rhythmic and sweet. Mister moved his kisses lower; past the roundness of her breast, over her quivering belly. He kissed the edge of her pubic hair, stopping only to enjoy the smell of her ecstasy. Mister kissed her horizontal lips flush. Aries' taste was thick and sweet. Mister slowly kissed the perimeter of her vagina. A large bulge slowly grew from her touch. Aries lifted her head to watch. She felt Mister's tongue slowly explore her. Sounds of him moaning coated her ears. She reached between her thighs and held him in place. Mister continued licking. His tongue moved slowly; daring not to leave a spot missed. Her creaminess coated his thick tongue. They both moaned as he pushed his tongue past her swollen sexual sentries. She felt lightheaded and tingled all over. Mister moved his tongue around her clitoris with diabolical ease. He placed his full tongue against her opening and sucked softly. The light pressure made Aries curse. Her heart quickened and she bit her lip. Then just as Aries believed she would explode, Mister abruptly stopped. She hadn't noticed her eyes were closed until then. Aries allowed her eyelids to move apart. She saw Mister standing over her, slowly removing his pants. He pushed his pants down freeing his sex. Aries couldn't tell if it was that she hadn't seen a penis in some time of if he truly was as large as

SexPressions

he looked. Aries' mind quizzed her eyes about the length and girth. "Dayum", was the answer her eyes reported back.

Mister slowly lowered his naked body onto the sofa and hovered over Aries. He eased himself closer to her. The sweet mixture of perfume oil and pussy greeted her taste buds. Mister moved his tongue into her mouth. The two tongues danced slowly. Aries moved her hands over his naked sculpted back. He lifted his hips so that the head of his manhood brushed against her vagina and gyrated. The friction was too much. He gasped as she moaned into his ear.

"Now." She begged.

Mister nodded in agreement. He pressed himself closer against her and slowly guided the head past her ebony sexual doors.

"Damn." Aries moaned, as Mister pushed inside of her tightness. Mister pushed deep into Aries and kissed her on the cheek. He leaned over and grabbed the forgotten bowl of fruit. He kissed her then slowly moved his hips. She tried to wrap her legs around him... tried to hold him... to contain him. She opened her mouth to gasp, but was greeted with the sweet taste of strawberry and white chocolate. Aries froze as her body attempted to accept the two sensations together. After what seemed to be an eternity she chewed the covered fruit and rotated her pelvis. Mister smiled, increased his stroke and fed her another treat. She moaned from both the taste of the sex and the feel of the fruit. Mister hovered over her, moving his thick blackness into and over her trembling spots. Aries wrapped one leg over him and pulled him

Aries Birthday

deeper into her. She dug her nails into his back. Mister continued feeding her and causing moans to leap from her mouth. Aries stroked his back as he filled the space between her lips. She began to feel a slight rumbling deep within her. She pulled Mister down to her and bit on his ear. Mister refused her body's request to go faster. He maintained a powerful, slow, and deep stroke. Her toes curled. Her body begged for the speed of him. Mister looked deeply into her eyes as he drove into her. Her moans became loud pants. Aries softly hated Mister, her body, and the good sex and she forced her eyes closed. A sudden bolt of **sextricity** hit Aries. Her body tingled and tightened around his girth. He continued to move inside of her. The small orgasmic waves didn't grow in size; but did in number. Each wave encased Aries in a deeper feeling of splendor. Mister slowed his pace, before pulling out of Aries, still hard and throbbing slightly.

Mister lay next to her on the large sectional, feeding her strawberries dipped in white chocolate. He fondled her sex and sucked on her nipples. Aries' vagina soon returned to its normal state of pre-sex quivering. She dozed into a quiet nap, with the taste of strawberries, chocolate and sex in her mouth. She was awakened by the sound of her own moans and the feeling of Mister's tongue against her throbbing clitoris. Mister used his tongue to push her closer to an orgasm. He stopped and stood over her again. He offered his hand to her. Aries placed her fingers into his palm and welcomed his strength. She rose, naked, from the sofa and allowed Mister to guide her up the stairs. Aries felt light and believed she was floating. They reached the top of the stairs and stood in an area that only housed a large bed. The bed looked enormous, like it could swallow her. Mister

SexPressions

released her hand and watched her move toward the bed. She dove onto the bed feeling like a small child. Aries lay face first on the oversized lush pillows. A sweet scent of flowers and vanilla powdered her nose. She hummed to herself as the bed's warm plush ness welcomed her full weight as he crawled over her body. His sneakingly soft kisses triggered tiny celebrations, as they landed against her neck. She wondered when she had lost control of her body. She listened as her hips, thighs, and ass obeyed Mister subtle commands to move. Mister positioned Aries with a large pillow beneath her belly, hoisting her sexy palate higher into the air. He kissed her across her unsuspecting back, concentrating on her lower back, before kissing up between her shoulder blades. Aries felt her verbal mouth pucker while her vaginal voice moaned deep inside of her.

"Please." Her vagina begged, as Mister slowly rubbed his ebony thickness against her.

Aries felt his palm become firm against her back. It was at this moment that she noticed his kisses had stopped.

"Make a wish." Mister whispered to her. And just as she began to give it some thought. Mister slowly guided himself deep inside of her. She tried to freeze *and* run. She told her body to accept *and* repel him. Her breast became warm and feigned support, while her usually trustworthy thighs went on strike.

"Mutha-fucka." Aries panted.

Mister felt like living stone as he moved smoothly inside if her. She pushed her arms out and attempted to

Aries Birthday

brace herself against the head board of the bed in escape. His strokes were LSD; long, slow and deep. He rotated his hips at the end and beginning of each movement. Aries tried to inch away from him, moving closer to the top the bed. Mister lightly patted her brown bottom, coaxing her along. Aries soon found the safety of the large head board. She looked up and saw her own eyes staring back.

"A mirror!" She heard her body yelling to warn her. But now it was too late. Aries watched as the look on his face changed slightly. His **sexpression** went from a numb happiness, to a devilish determination. He glanced at her in the mirror and winked. Aries felt and watched as Mister pushed both himself and her deeper to the edge. Mister shortened his strokes and increased his tempo. She tingled from the minute pause he offered as he pistoned inside of her. Aries began to tremble and her breathing became louder. She hated the delightful moans that poured from her mouth and quickly wondered what the *Scream* desires would be like.

Aries heard Mister pants grow stronger. She felt him grow even harder inside of her. Mister's shudder had become tense. She closed her eyes, but still peeked in time to watch him tuck his lower lip between his teeth. She felt an orgasm boiling within her and pushed back into Mister to usher its arrival. They both cursed softly. He grabbed her large ass cheeks and pushed and pulled her to him. Aries prayed their orgasm would come soon enough to save them. She felt Mister shudder violently. A surprising wave flowed quickly from him. Aries pushed backward into his still blackness as a minor form of her first explosion engulfed her. Her womb became vise-like. First she held Mister's

SexPressions

pulsating sex niggardly inside of her before finally sapping him of his strength and sexual life. He slowly gained control of himself. He marked her back with tender licks and whisper soft kisses. Aries collapsed onto the bed. She had come down with what she and Rachelle called the "Sexual Flu". She shivered uncontrollably and began sweating as if she had just run a marathon.

Mister slowly moved from the bed. Planting kisses over her newly sexed body. She hummed and tried to calm her throbbing vagina. She heard Mister's feather-like steps disappear downstairs. He soon returned with the strawberries and chocolate. He also had a large slice of boiled Jamaican rum cake. Aries lay on her back as he moved his hand slowly over her body. He fed her while repeatedly serenading her with different birthday songs. Aries snuggled deeper against his warmth. She promised herself she would tip him heavily as sleep unwittingly rocked her.

Morning Sleepy Head." Mister's deep voice bellowed. "I thought you were going to sleep forever."

I could have." Aries wanted to say.

"I'll bring you breakfast and run you a bath."

A smile awakened Aries' entire face. Music moved across the room from hidden speakers. It was a quick tempo, urban jazz sound. Although Aries liked the sound of music, the underlying darkness spoke to her wild side.

"Something's wrong!" Her instinct said. Aries moved

Aries Birthday

from the bed to the balcony and looked at Mister. He moved about beneath her; not slow, nor fast. Just with a purpose.

"So what's for breakfast?" She said bouncing toward the stairs. Thoughts of an exotically-prepared breakfast driving her every step.

Coffee, doughnuts and dick!" He said over his shoulder.

Aries descended slower down the stairs, not sure if the third choice was what she had really heard.

"But I don't smell any coffee brewing."

Her smile slowly dissolving from her face. Mister turned to face her. He wore a large white bath robe, but was naked underneath. The only things that Aries noticed was his wide sparkling grin and the thick long muscle that hung from between his legs.

"There isn't any, and I ate the last doughnut, as well."

Aries stopped a few feet away from him; heart and vagina pounding with fright.

"So really Mister, What's for breakfast?"

She tried to look tough, by placing her hands on her hips with an *"I mean it"* look to emphasize her point. The only thing she accomplished was brushing her nipples with her arms and looking silly; or at least feeling silly. Mister reached into his left pocket and removed a black envelope.

SexPressions

"Here. This goes good with the dick." He said, tossing her the envelope.

Surprisingly Aries caught it against her breast and read the word "Scream". A puzzled frown blanketed her face, as she looked from the letter to Mister and back again.

"So hurry and get cleaned up so you can have breakfast." He slowly removed his robe. "I'll be on the patio. And I hate waiting." He turned toward the door. Aries was sure his face was still covered with that grin.

"Wasn't hungry anyway." Aries thought, quickly moving toward the bathroom. She stopped at the door and pushed an ear-splitting scream from her throat.

"Now I've screamed." She said over her shoulder, mockingly.

Mister stood on the patio, naked, rubbing warm body oil over his cool brown skin. The sun would be up any second and he wanted to feel its heat against his body. A loud high pitched shriek cut through the early morning calm.

"Exactly." He said, smiling before beginning his pre-dawn exercises.

Aries walked onto the patio, still wet and sure some parts of her body were still soapy. Her timing was perfect. The sun slowly crested the horizon and the silhouette of Mister's face against its new day glory. Aries slowly absorbed the heat and looked around. The patio was a large wooden deck. A large barbeque grill sat just beneath the

Aries Birthday

kitchen window. A large table occupied a decent portion of the deck. A large bowl of cherries centered the table. A large coffee pot stood next to it like a watchtower over a prison yard. Two large duffel bags lay neatly aligned near Mister's feet. She told herself everything would be okay, but the sight of Mister and his entireness, had her body doubting the outcome. This was the first she'd really saw him uncovered. His body seemed to her to be symmetrically erotic. Everything flowed fluidly to and over everything else; as if he were built instead of born. A rap lyric Aries once heard came to mind.

"Half-man, half-amazing." Her mind's voice sang. "And he has a pretty dick!" Her body yelled.

Aries stood before him and the morning sun, naked and shivering with anticipation.

"So now what?" Aries asked. The words came out sounding more like a threat than a question. Aries' sexual side immediately wanted to take it back. She moved her lips to apologize, but was halted by Mister's approach. Now a smile grew across his face that went from delighted shock to devilish resolve. Aries felt her body cringe and begin to retreat as Mister stopped directly in front of her and spoke one word slowly.

"Breakfast." The word left the softness of his lips and stretched itself into two very long syllables.

Aries felt something surprisingly hot, press against her inner thigh as Mister placed his cool hands against her cheeks and softly kissed her on the mouth. Her nipples grew

SexPressions

defiantly away from her breast.

"He's just a man with a dick." Her nipples reported to her brain. "Yeah, like Michael Myers was just a man with a knife." Her brain responded.

Mister stepped away from Aries; the sun shining stronger now, quickly covering Aries in its golden glow. Mister grabbed one of the large duffel bags and slowly opened it. Aries froze; her mind trying to guess the diabolical things that he kept in such a bag. She felt herself breathe again as he pulled a large blanket from the bag. He walked to the table, removed the coffee pot and bowl, before tossing the blanket over the wooden expanse. Mister walked around the king sized table and stood before Aries again.

"You can eat after breakfast."

Before Aries could answer, he dropped and lifted her into the air. He placed her on the table and smiled.

"Don't move. I'll be right back."

Mister turned and walked back to the duffel bags. And no sooner than he'd walked away did Aries' stomach instigate a revolt.

'Fuck him! Get some of those cherries." Her stomach growled. "It ain't like he's yo' Daddy."

Aries watched for Mister out the corner of her eye. She spied him methodically searching through the remaining contents of the first bag.

Aries Birthday

"See." Her stomach coached, "he won't see you."

"He ain't my Daddy." She thought, turning on the table. The bowl sat on the bench just out of her finger's range. She peered over her shoulder and saw that Mister was still engrossed in his search deep within his bag. Aries inched further along the table and hooked the bowl with the tips of her fingers. The scraping sound of the bowl normally wouldn't have registered with her ears, but now the sound rioted against the deck's morning calm. Freak-filled fright powered Aries' movement. She scooped a handful of cherries into her mouth, hoping the fruity sacrifice would appease grumble the hunger god that ruled her stomach. The sweet tartness of the cherries splashed against the insides of her mouth. Aries tried to turn to sit upright. The way Mister had left her.

"I thought I told you not to move!" Mister's large voice grabbed Aries.

"He ain't yo' Daddy!" Her stomach celebrated.

"You ain't my Daddy." Aries snapped, still attempting to turn and sit upright.

Mister pressed his left palm against the small of her back and held Aries in place with little pressure. Aries heard the open hand smack before the pain and heat alerted her brain. Aries slammed her eyes shut as her vagina oozed uncontrollably with pre-cum.

"Dayum." Aries screamed, surprised at her sexually sadistic side.

SexPressions

She felt Mister move between her shocked thighs. "Even in force, he was gentle." She thought. Mister smacked Aries on her ass again, causing her to nearly choke on the cherry pits she held in her mouth. Aries tried to push her way up from the table, finally finding the effort futile. She only managed to position herself better for Mister's insertion.

Mister turned his palm, pointing his fingers toward her head and massaged her brown exit. Aries fought the numbing sensation that held her, and cursed her body for relaxing. Mister reached beneath her and roughly teased her clitoris and sensitive vaginal entrance.

"I'm glad you don't wanna listen." Mister sneered. His heart rate noticeably rising. "I like tough girls, too."

Aries closed her eyes, turning her head sideways and thought about how un-tough she felt. Aries' creamy sweetness coated his fingers.

"See, You're not so tough." Mister said, squeezing Aries ass cheeks, before pressing his thumbs further against her anal sex hole. Aries felt him ease closer to her.

"Not my ass!" Aries yelled as Mister slowly fed his ebony thickness fully inside of her wet vagina.

She slowly began to breathe a sigh of relief when Mister pushed his thumb deep inside of her last virginal opening. A scream filled with personal freedom erupted from Aries mouth. She softly pounded the thick table as he moved his thumb inside of her sphincter and slowly filled

Aries Birthday

her with his black thickness.

"Ain't so tough now, are you?"

Aries screamed again, this time from shocked pleasure. Her nipples tingled and became increasingly hard. She spat the cherry pits from her mouth, thanking her stomach for causing such a punishment. Mister removed his thumb and placed his hands on her waist, pushing and pulling himself into her. Pushing her legs out, Aries tried to feel for the safety of the deck. She felt as if she were swimming, or floating, and needed to ground herself. She peeked over her shoulder and watched the morning sun work its optical magic on his body. He appeared sexually menacing. Aries cursed herself and prayed for what Mister was doing to her with his dick. Harsh pants escaped her mouth. Never in her life had she hated the sound she made until now. Who did he think he was, treating her and her pussy this way?

"Mister!" She heard herself scream, "that's who."

Mister continued stroking; he smiled down at Aries naked ass. She had been a prissy queen the day before, but now she was stripped of her regal ness, and exposed as a regular woman. She deserved to be treated this way. Mister watched the looked of rugged pleasure cover her face, and thought all women should be treated this way. He placed his hands on her buttocks and slowly rolled upward. He pulled his thick length from her womb. Aries' sexual juices covered him; a thick vein ran along the top of Mister's shaft and became more pronounced due to sexual wetness. He pushed two of his fingers deep within Aries, and pulled them out dripping with her juices. Her sexual defeat tasted sweet against his tongue. He leaned forward and began slowly licking at both her holes. The bland taste of her asshole mixed gently with the sweet thickness of her vagina, nearly brought Mister to tears. She panted frantically as the feel of Mister's tongue confused and amazed her. Aries turned her head again to see what was going on behind her, *and in her behind*, but she convinced herself she would find out soon enough. She felt partial relief when he withdrew himself from her, but she quickly became happy with the next phase.

Aries enjoyed the feel of Mister's hand, crudely guiding her body. How he pushed her buttocks apart exposing her timid brown eye to the morning air. Doing as he pleased with her. If this was what happened when she turned thirty, she wondered what would happen when she turned forty. Aries shook off the moment and told herself to enjoy the here and now. Here was this fine specimen of a man, who right now was moving his tongue across her sexual places. Aries shuddered as an orgasm signaled its impending arrival. Mister continued partaking of Aries sexual bounty. He pushed his tongue deep into her vagina, allowing her creaminess to coat his tongue. He seemed as if he sapped away her strength with each passing of his tongue. He heard her exhale small meaningful pants. He scolded himself for briefly increasing his tongue's tempo. Inducing sexual scream was an art form. He considered each woman a blank canvas, begging for a masterpiece to be created using them. And as any artist worth their while will tell you, *"you're only as good as your last piece."* He slowly moved his tongue over her labia and up over her rear hole.

"So where's that tough girl?" He teased, sure that

Aries Birthday

Aries wouldn't scream in a room full of deaf people. "Don't go soft on me now. We're just beginning."

Mister stood again; the head of his penis brushing Aries's labia, sending shockwaves through her body. She gasped in anticipation. Mister grabbed one of the items he had retrieved from the duffel bag and ripped it open. He held his thick penis by its base and rolled the special latex condom slowly down his shaft. He spread her legs apart again.

"You ready little lady?"

Aries began to nod her head "no", when without warning Mister quickly pushed himself deep inside of her. Aries's eyes shot open and a furious howl leapt from her mouth. He slowly moved himself in and out of her. The tickly-prickliness of the condom's raised knobs massaged the unsuspecting inner walls of her vagina. It was as if Mister had taken her g-spot and divided it evenly into one million pieces. Aries tried to crawl away from his thrust, but was held in place by his hand on her shoulder. He smacked her ass again and increased his tempo from a slow stroke to a powerful deliberate pounding. She balled the blanket into a wad as her entire body either surrendered in limpness or tightened in erotic shock. She moved in rhythm with his powerful grunts as he leaned forward and kissed her between her shoulder blades. Even her rebellious breasts were reduced to a confused throbbing. Aries believed her left breast was in fact leaking. Broken syllables of curse words escaped her mouth. She was no longer hungry. She only wanted to have an orgasm, so she could quickly rest and start over.

SexPressions

Mister shifted left, then right, changing the angle to enhance the sensation. He held her by her shoulders and maneuvered her with a handful of her tender ass. He could feel her inner walls contract and vibrate. Her screams were muffled by the blanket wad she had stuffed her mouth with. Mister grinned to himself.

"Take this dick." He growled.

He pushed himself inside of her until his abdomen brushed against her buttocks then yanked himself out. She screamed and tried to escape the painful pleasure. Off in the distance, Aries heard a wolf howling. She wasn't sure if it was mocking her or cheering for Mister. She felt extremely warm and light-headed.

"C'mon dammit!" She heard herself yell, not sure if it was for her or him, although she really didn't care.

"Ahhh, there go that tough shit I like." He said, increasing the fierceness of his stroke.

"Don't just lay there, Bitch," Aries's vagina yelled. "Do something!"

Mister snatched up one of the other items from the bag. He moved it toward her anal opening and turned it on. She howled as the small vibrator tickled her rear area.

"Please." She gasped; no longer sure if she wanted him to stop or continue. Mister slowly slipped the vibrator into her ass. Aries surprisingly found her strength and pushed herself up from the table. He moved the vibrator

Aries Birthday

alternate of his strokes. Aries screamed in double pleasure. Her body panicked and quickly began manufacturing orgasms. The first took her by complete surprise. Her screams became high-pitched howls. Her voice was terribly hoarse. Her breast quivered and her stomach collapsed. She tried to fight back. She pushed her pelvis down as he came forward, but all that did was add pressure. The condom's tickler's raked quickly across her flesh. She wondered if he was near an orgasm. She prayed he was. She reached forward, gripping the table, and pulling herself forward. Finally relief found her. His thick, French-tickler cover dick was slowly removed. The small vibrator, still worked its magic, but Aries didn't care. She could hear his sexually dominant chuckle behind her.

"Not so tough, huh?" He growled, laughing his heart out. "Happy Birthday, Miss Lady."

Aries felt her vagina throbbing and convulsing. It felt as if it were dry heaving. She laid her head on the table and tried to control her breathing. She contracted her ass muscles and felt the vibrator slowly slide from her rear orifice. She wasn't sure how much something like this cost, but knew she would pay double the price, if asked. She softly mumbled the "Birthday" song to herself.

"And may the good Lord bless Mister." She hummed.

Mister slowly walked along the table surveying his work. She was sprawled out across the table spread eagle, breathing hard. He watched her body twitch in random intervals.

"She's still cumming and doesn't know it." He

SexPressions

thought.

He softly rubbed her ass, back, and shoulders. Mister allowed a pang of mercy to control him, then pushed it away. Mercy was for good girls and the wounded; she was neither. Mister listened to Aries pant and hum to herself. A wicked smile raided his face.

"No Mercy." He whispered to himself. He smacked her hard on her relaxed ass. Mister moved to the front of the table and stood before Aries.

"Breakfast time." He growled. Mister pulled the French-tickler from his dick and held in firmly. He caressed the back of Aries's head, and then lifted so that it was level with the tip of his throbbing manhood. Aries opened her eyes and mouth, instinctively. Mister slowly began feeding himself over her tongue, in quarters. Aries fought the urge to gag, as his length reached the back of her throat. "Muthafucka!" She mumbled around his wideness. She softly sucked on the head and shaft.

"He's only a man." A small voice sang inside of her head. "And men can be beat, too!"

Aries took his sex by the base and held him in place. She slowly moved her head to the rear softly raking her teeth the entire way. Mister moaned loudly. She tightened her grip and slowly rotated her head. Aries wrapped her tongue around the raised tip and sucked roughly. Mister pushed air quickly from his lungs.

"Damn!" The word escaped Mister's lips and fell

Aries Birthday

against Aries's back.

She hummed in delight and causing his penis to temporarily lose its rigidness. He held the back of her head and pushed forward with his pelvis. She feigned choking and swallowed hard. Her tongue waved across the bottom of Mister's shaft. His tight grin turned into a loose pucker, as Mister inhaled then exhaled a tight whistle. Aries sucked hard again and moved her head back in an elongated deliberate movement. Mister smacked and grabbed her ass in agreement. Aries tightened her grip on his penis. She felt his body twitch and quiver.

"He's about to give up." The small voice cheered. "Like I said girl, 'He's just a man."

Aries peeked up to admire her handy work. A blank look of confused pleasure, masked his facial landscape. Aries quickly fell in love with the taste of her sex covering his penis. She wondered if his life juices tastes as powerful as he did. She heard his moans and welcomed their arrival. He *was* just a man.

Aries felt Mister slowly become stiffer and a grin peered up at his face. This time he grinned back at her savagely. Aries felt her sassy voice retreat.

"I did my part," the voice said, "you on ya' own, girl."

Mister pulled the back of Aries's head forward and held it in place. He slowly rotated his hips and filled her mouth slowly. Aries never stopped licking or sucking. This was **her** birthday and she would be damned if she didn't

SexPressions

fuck him back. She smacked him on his ass.

"C'mon baby!" She ordered. Mister nodded and continued moving his hips. Aries grabbed his contracted ass cheeks and pulled him forward. He bit his lip and moaned in delight. Mister glanced down at Aries, who never took her eyes off him, and winked.

"So you are tough, huh?" That wink said. Aries sucked hard one last time and pushed him from her mouth.

"Fuck me again!" She growled turning over on her back.

Mister smiled and pulled Aries toward the edge of the table. He parted her labia with his thumb and forefinger and slowly fed himself into her heat. The sun was behind him and its rays softly massaged his shoulders and back. He lifted her legs and held them together by her ankles in front of him; making her already tight womb tighter. His thrusts were slow and timid, and quickly became fast and powerful. He'd forgotten how welcoming it felt to be inside of her. Aries gripped the sides of the table and bit her lip. She worked her muscles as if she were forcing out urine and massaged Mister's shaft. His movements brought him over the same spots. Aries believed he was aiming. She could barely make out the features in his face, but she could hear him panting and grunting. She was convinced he'd transformed into some sort of sexual beast. He drove into her with authority. She searched the table for the small vibrator. She could feel his impending orgasm as well as her own. But his was closer.

Aries Birthday

"Fuck me, mutha-fucka!" She snarled.

Mister tightened his grip on her ankles and obeyed. Each thrust ended with him grunting and her panting harshly. Aries took the small vibrator and turned it to its highest setting. She placed the device against her clitoris and allowed it to move across his riveting penis. He cursed. She felt him begin to tremble. She moved the vibrator toward her still twitching rear hole and pressed it against his shaft. He howled aloud and began pumping faster. She repeated her last order. His body soon turned against him. He felt his head begin to swim. His thick ebony muscle twitched sharply. His orgasm stormed his sexual gates. Sperm quickly moved from his loins and toward its only exit. He grimaced as he stroked his clenched fist down his shaft. Hot, thick, white life shot forward; surprising them both. Aries felt the hot stickiness land against her breast, stomach and finally her vagina and clitoris. Mister twitched and contorted, while he manipulated, the very sensitive head of his dick. Labored breaths moved from his lungs and out his mouth. He let his head hang and watched as Aries quickly brought herself to orgasm. Her entire body shook and her face was frozen. She moaned a curse word then held her battered sex with both hands. She couldn't believe how much her vagina twitched. She thought to herself how terribly good this had felt. She wasn't sure if she had ever felt this good, and hated that she may never get a chance to resist the offer.

Mister soon gained his composure and moved to the duffel bag. He grabbed the bag and moved toward the cottage.

SexPressions

"After you bathe, we can leave." He said, sending pangs of sadness throughout Aries. "We'll have brunch. Do some shopping, then dinner. My treat." He grinned when he spoke. She smiled and allowed the sun to wash over her. She turned over on her side and yelled her appreciation.

"Thank You, Mister Harris." Aries sang, as she took the two boxes from the doorman. "I know you're on a diet, but it's ice cream " He answered, "Moaning Mango Surprise and Screaming Scare-berry. I couldn't pick, so I got them both for you. "

"How'd you know?" Aries asked, dipping her finger into the cool solid creaminess.
"Your sister told me. And please call me Ben, Mister makes me sound old."

"Okay Ben. And thanks again." She said as she walked into her building, moving past Mr. Ben Harris. She'd often wondered what sex would be like with him. They say it's the quiet ones you have to watch out for.

BRUISED

Brenda fanned the cards she held in her hand, smiling at the uneven amount of spades she saw. She easily counted eight; three being cards in the high court and she knew a bid often was not only possible but very likely. It wasn't everyday she got to win at Spades, but when she did, she won big. Brenda peered over her cards at her partner, Joyce or as Brenda like to call her Juice, with a smile bright enough to require sunglasses.

"I got six partner!" Brenda sang. Along with her ace, king, and queen of spades, she had the ace of clubs, her only card in that suit, and the king of hearts. Brenda felt like talking a little trash; although it wasn't in her nature, she wanted to anyway. Mesha and Joani were professionals at the craft. And here they sat quietly shaking their miserable hands. The two of them had been quiet the entire night. Now that Brenda had given it some thought, Joyce had been quiet as well. It was very unusual for the Sisters of I.C.E. to be so quiet, but hell Brenda knew that a few bottles of wine, weed and music would get them talking. But right now all Brenda concerned herself with was spanking some ass in Spades.

"You hear me Juice," Brenda prodded her friend, "I got six. That's ten gurl."

SexPressions

"Hell naw!" Mesha shouted, throwing her cards down" I'm tired of this shit. Let me see yo hand." She reached across the table at Brenda and her cards.

"Stop trying to cheat." Brenda giggled, pulling her cards to her chest. "You see this shit Juice? They trying to cheat us to beat us." She began laughing festively, still not aware of the looks her friends were giving her. She also hadn't noticed that Joyce was crying softly.

"I want to see your hand too," Joyce whispered, hands tightly closing around her delicate cards," Then I want to see your back too!"

With that the tears began to flow. A befuddled look overcame Brenda and for the first time the entire night, she saw the sullen look on the faces of her three friends.

"Gurl, what ya'll talking about?"

Brenda's smile began slipping from her lips. She looked from each of her friends; finally settling on the face of Joyce. Joani had moved to comfort her but she still cried, her sobs erupting heavy and loud from her small frame.

"Juice what's wrong? What does my cards and my back have to do with this?"

"When Dexter was kicking my ass, I didn't wanna tell nobody, specially not you." Joyce began, "But I did, and you helped me leave him."

Brenda let her cards fall and listened to her closest

Bruised

and dearest mend; confused yet concerned.

"And for you to sit here and look us, *ME,* in my face with all those bruises on you, my feelings are hurt Be-Be." Joyce said, head hanging, her chin resting on her chest.

Hurt and anger rose from her and engulfed the other two women who sat across from Brenda.

"Why didn't you say you were having trouble with yo' man?" Mesha asked. "And don't even try and lie, we all saw the bruises."

"What damn bruises ya'll talking about?" Brenda felt herself begin to yell.

She dearly loved her mends, but these heffas' were beginning to get on her last good nerve.

"The ones on your back, legs, and that one on the palm of your hand." Joyce said.

She pointed at each suspected spot. She shouted at Brenda, who by now wanted to smack someone. She took a deep breath and dropped her cards, her lovely cards, and looked at her hands. Laughter suddenly erupted from her body.

"These bitches are truly crazy." She thought to herself. A large purplish bruise sat squarely within her left palm just below her pinky finger and ran nearly over to her thumb. Brenda rubbed the other locations as well. There was a bruise on her leg just below the edge of her shorts and another large (the largest of the all) bruise covered her back. She also ran her hands over a few spots her mends hadn't seen.

"Gurl, play cards. These ain't shit but hickies." Brenda couldn't contain her laughter, whisking her cards back into her hands.

She could still whoop a little ass on the table. "Hickies!" Joyce said. Half yelling, half asking.

"Yeah gurl Rudy is into that rough biting shit. And maybe I am too."

Brenda grinned to herself. She tried to bury her face into her cards. Then a thought brought her laughter back.

"What ya'll thought he jumped on me?" Brenda stopped laughing long enough to give her mends a look that said *"Bitch Please!"*

Brenda was the kind of woman people referred to as big-boned. And her new boyfriend, Rudy was mainly bone. She also grew up the last of seven children, the six before all being boys. She didn't help Joyce leave her abusive husband, she gave him a swollen eye and three broken ribs; reason to let her leave. And although she'd recently began her prissy stage, prissy for her anyway, she was still a tomboy at heart and soul. So the thought of a man, or any person for that matter, putting their hands on her was the funniest thing she could think of.

"Whew ya'll killing me." She said, tossing her cards to

Bruised

the table and raising from her chair. She thought of how good her cards were and shook her head.

"Go get the glasses and the wine." She started" I'll tell ya'll what happened." She giggled the word, *'bruises'* as Mesha and Joani ran to the kitchen.

Rudy stared around the flowers; hurt and confusion splashed across his face like terrible cologne. Most women would dance with joy if they were given a bouquet of fresh flowers from their boyfriend for no other reason than that he chose that day to flirt. Hell, Rudy would've taken a simple kiss on the cheek and pat on the ass. He'd even settle for a "whut's up" pound and thug hug from Brenda. But all he got was a shrug of the shoulders and a, albeit sexy, roll of the eyes.

"So what, you brought me flowers!" Brenda said, hands on her hips instead of where Rudy thought they should be, which was wrapped around him or his neck or even both. Brenda checked her watch. They both knew she wasn't due back for at least an hour and even that was rarely enforced. So Rudy took the hint and handed Brenda the flowers. A twinge of anger caused Rudy's lip to curl into a sneer as he quickly turned toward his car. Rudy liked Brenda, but he wasn't sure if he liked the uncertainty that came along with being with her.

"Women and their fucking games." He thought, as Brenda called to him from behind.

Rudy waved his hand in disgust, shouting a quick, "What eva!" in response.

SexPressions

"OOOOO Wweee! Is that a sexy man?" Brenda cheered to herself quietly as Rudy walked away. "Especially when he's mad." She whispered, continuing her thought.

"You better stop playing games with that man." Juices' angelic voice chided her. But the games are so fun, Brenda answered her best friend.

Brenda brought the flowers to her nose and inhaled deeply. The sweet smell of lilies and angel's breath made her knees weak. Not to mention the effect it had on her sex organs.

"Call me later. I'm cooking pasta tonight!" She shouted after her angry boyfriend, who waved his hand in sexy anger.

Brenda had lied about cooking. She hadn't planned on cooking anything more than leftovers, not before the flowers anyway. Brenda thought how all the women in the office would burst with jealousy when she walked back into the office with this bouquet of flowers. Even a few of them would be envious of her gift. Brenda smelled the flowers again, nearly bringing herself to climax. She'd wanted Rudy to put forth some effort into their relationship. Brenda knew she was being mean, and that he would soon get tired of her games, but she believed herself to be worth any trouble she put him through.

"Plus he needs to toughen up with his punk ass." She reminded her conscious' version of her best friend's voice. "Can't stand no punk ass man."

Bruised

"What do you mean, you ate already!" Brenda tried her best not to yell. It wasn't everyday that Rudy had shown up late but being late with a full belly was just too much. "I told you I was cooking."

Rudy gave her a half-hearted "my bad" shrug of his shoulders. She would have liked to say her feelings were hurt but she was a few miles past hurt. Brenda gripped the handle of the pot and slowly counted down reasons to remain calm.

"Don't trip! I'll just take some to work for lunch, Bren." Rudy moved behind her, placed his arms around her waist and attempted to hug her.

"Don't touch me!" Brenda shot, moving from between Rudy and the stove. "Go hug who ever you 'already ate' with." Brenda turned just in time to see Rudy attempt to suppress his laughter.

"What the fuck is so funny?" She thought to herself, tilting her head and turning her lips into her "umm huh" face.

"I know you ain't getting mad?" Rudy asked, unable to control his outburst. "You know I was lying. I ain't ate shit and I'm hungry like a hostage!"

"First of all, dogs get mad. I'm a Lady of I.C.E. and we get angry!" Brenda sassed, one hand on her hip and the other cutting through the air; one finger raised.

"You must be the Queen of I.C.E, how cold you been

playing me."

Rudy said, knowing he stood a good chance of starting an argument. "And for the record I told you I was going to be late."

Rudy had begun placing pasta on his plate. He only wanted to give her a taste of her own medicine; with that mission accomplished, he decided to quiet the rumbling in his very empty stomach.

"What do you mean, how cold I've been playing you?"

Rudy shook his head and sat down to the table, recited a prayer over his plate and began shoveling fork-fulls of food into his mouth. He'd decided to let Brenda play hard-to-get. Anything worth having was worth working for. Plus she could cook. Rudy reminded himself of this after the flower snub this afternoon.

"So you think I'm playing, huh?" Brenda quizzed.

It was one thing for her to play mind games, but it was something altogether different thing for Rudy to throw that in her face.

"Ain't you got yo' nerve." Joyce said, giving her friend the "that's-what-you-get" face. "I told you to stop playing games with him."

"Gone Be-Be." Mesha said, waving her hand at Joyce and turned back toward Brenda.

Bruised

It wasn't everyday that Brenda put her affairs into the street, so she didn't want to miss anything. Brenda rolled her eyes and continued her *story*.

"I know you playing!" Rudy said, occasionally looking up from his plate. He pushed his voice a few octaves higher to emphasize his point. "But it's cool. You won't scare me off so easy." Rudy covered his mouth as he spoke. He had to admit, her little act was turning him on. Normally he didn't have to work so hard, but Brenda was different. He actually liked being with her.

"You ain't still mad about this afternoon, ain't you?" Brenda grinned hoping to get a reaction out of him. "Like you the first muthafucka to bring me flowers."

Actually he was the third. But Brenda was sure her prom date, Charles, and her nephew, Melvin, don't really count. Also the time she and Joyce had sent themselves Valentine's Day roses didn't count as well. Rudy kept eating and shaking his head in affirmation.

"It don't matter what number I am. I brought you a gift and all I wanted from you was a simple 'Thank You'". He said, pushing food into one cheek.

"Will you stop eating so we can talk?" Brenda shot, pulling the plate from beneath his raised fork.

"Will you stop talking so I can eat?" Rudy retorted, hints of anger finally showing. "You act like I asked you to gimme some ass. I guess that's how you are." Rudy snatched the plate back to its original place in front of him.

SexPressions

"That's just how you are." Brenda mimic-ed Rudy, using a slightly childish voice; frowning slightly to drive home the point. Her friends erupted in laughter at her depiction of how Rudy had spoken.

"Fuck all that. Get to the hickies." Joani cut in. Marijuana smoke leaking from between her lips.

"I am. Be cool, gurl." Brenda said, regaining control.

Rudy stabbed at the food on his plate. All he wanted to do was eat, and maybe have sex. But it seemed to be Brenda had other plans.
"I'm just saying, you were the one playing games."

Rudy twisted his fork until it was past capacity and moved it to his mouth. Brenda stared across at Rudy; anger welling up deep within her. She chose her words carefully. Brenda pointed across the table at Rudy and sneered.

"No you didn't tell him 'Fuck him'. Mesha said; face beginning to become sore from all the laughing.

"Shhhiiid, yes I did!" Brenda said, joining her friends in laughing.

"So what did he say?" Joyce asked.

Rudy looked from his plate, trembling with anger. "Aight woman! You gonna start some shit." Rudy said, failing at his attempt to contain his anger.

"You heard me, Fuck You!" Brenda smiled as she

Bruised

spoke the last two words slowly.

She'd been trying to get him to give her a reaction and now she had gotten one. Rudy tossed his fork to the plate, stood up and grabbed his coat. Brenda smiled as he moved past her.

"Where are you going?" Brenda asked, her expression going from amusement to uneasiness. "I'll call you tomorrow. Sorry for being late." Rudy threw his hands up in defeat, moving toward the back door. All I wanted to do was be nice to my lady, Rudy thought as he put his coat on. The sudden sight of a plate of food flying past his head froze Rudy in place. Now it had seemed Brenda was going too far. Playing hard to get was cute, but this shit was borderline crazy. Rudy turned to face Brenda, who by now was visibly angry and standing as well.

"See, this is what I'm talking about." Rudy said picking the broken shreds of the plate from the floor. "All this isn't called for."

Rudy had begun speaking slowly. He spoke just above a whisper, but still below a normal conversational voice.

"Now, I'm going to leave. And I said I'll call you tomorrow."

Rudy stood facing Brenda, hands at his side. His breathing was slow and exaggerated. He moved past her and placed the broken plate on the counter. Brenda stalked toward him, unsure how they'd gotten this far off track, but

SexPressions

sure of only one thing. She wasn't backing down.

"You ain't going no damn where." She snarled; hand raised, finger extended, nearly touching Rudy's nose. Brenda knew she had gone too far, but she also knew she was horny. Very horny to be exact. So for the first time, she paid attention to her hormones. Anger had been replaced with sexual tension. She didn't want Rudy to leave. She wanted him to stay. Brenda wanted him to touch her and allow her to continue to be the new prissy bitch she had chosen to become. Brenda also wanted Rudy to grow a spine, which ran down between his legs and into her throbbing vagina. So she stood towering over him demanding that he stay.

"You're going to sit down and finish eating." The bully began to come out of Brenda.

The words made Brenda tingle all over. Maybe she could become a dominatrix, she thought. She liked to bully men around. It felt good and natural. And sexy, she couldn't forget it felt sexy. She did look good in black leather. She even knew a place to get a whip. Smiling, Brenda moved her finger closer; nail brushing against Rudy's nose.

Please Brenda; get your hand out of my face." Rudy said, volume slowly dropping with each word.

"I cooked so you gone eat." Brenda finished, never paying his words any attention.

"Brenda get yo dayum hand outta my face!" Rudy roared.

Bruised

The change in his voice nearly caused Brenda to jump. Her vagina quivered in surprised delighted.

"And what if I don't?" Brenda said, challenging Rudy. She had easily beaten men twice his size. Men Brenda knew were hardcore thugs. "You ain't gone do shit."

The three women hung on to their friend's every word. They had all known how overbearing Brenda could be at times. She was an intimidating person in any setting. So given Rudy's size and easy going demeanor they wondered how he stood a chance.

"So what did he do?" Joyce asked, pouring the last of the wine into her glass. Brenda smiled sheepishly before looking around the room at her friends.

"Juice remember when I told you that Rudy was a teacher?" She asked her friend, "Well I never asked what he *taught*." The last word was emphasized. Who really cares what he taught, she told herself that night. He was handsome with a job. And most importantly he was showing her some attention. So what he did for a living was a mute point, she thought to herself.

"Guurrl. Why did I have to jump bad with a martial arts instructor?"

The room erupted in laughter.

Rudy's hand moved a lot faster than Brenda thought possible. And before she knew it, Rudy had shot his right hand up, grabbed the hand that was being held before his

SexPressions

face, turned it against her arm's natural position, quickly moving Brenda off balance.

"Like this!" Brenda said, twisting Mesha's hand and arm in the same manner. "Then he put his other hand right here." She giggled, finishing the demonstration. Joyce couldn't contain her amusement. She held herself in a tight hug, before waving for Brenda to stop.

Rudy placed his left hand on Brenda's chest, just below her throat, applying force against her thumb and began walking her backward.

"See a man can't be nice nowadays!" His words flowed from his mouth behind of a small growl.

"You don't want the nice guy Rudy," He spat, moving Brenda closer to the refrigerator behind her, "You want Rudy the gangsta!"

Brenda tried struggling against Rudy's grip, to no avail.

"This nigga is crazy!" She thought to herself. "And as soon as he let me go, ooohhh...I'mma fuck the hell out of him!" She told her small group of friends.

Brenda's heart pounded rapidly behind her rib cage; sending molten hot blood down to her vagina, labia, and clitoris. Fear and Horny fought a quick battle within Brenda's body. Rudy pushed her roughly against the cool side of the refrigerator, signaling Horny's victory. Brenda immediately wished she had worn her blue silk blouse, the

Bruised

one that was too small and always came open when she moved too much, or when she wanted her breast to pop out.

"Let me go!" Brenda yelled, trying to maintain her charade of toughness.

Rudy turned Brenda's hand a few degrees more, forcing her palm upward toward his face.

"Shut the hell up!" He growled.

"Gurl, I was like 'Okay'. Just like a little punk."

Rudy held Brenda's twisted and in place and kissed her gently on the palm on her hand. Brenda felt faint as shivers ran through her entire body. Rudy moved his lips, allowing his tongue to pass over them and against Brenda's sensitive skin. Brenda exhaled partially; the sound ending in a whistle as it left her lips. He moved his hand lower and roughly fondled her breast. Brenda had begun slumping beneath the feel of his tongue.
Brenda heard herself panting. "Yo punk ass!" She scolded herself silently.

"This is the shit you like, huh?" Rudy quizzed, drawing satisfaction from the actions.

He slowly used his tongue and drew circles on her hand. By now he had pulled her breast free of her cotton bra and pinched her nipple. Brenda cursed and squirmed. Had she known this was the result of throwing a plate, she would have thrown a plate on the first night. Instinct pushed her legs apart in anticipation of the next stage.

SexPressions

Rudy kiss hard on the palm of her hand, and then began sucking with mean force. He held as much of her breast in his palm as he could and squeezed. Rudy allowed Brenda to move her into a more comfortable position. She pushed her head back as far as she could and tossed her arm around Rudy's neck. Rudy continued sucking, using his tongue to agitate the tender surface.

"Stop moving!" Rudy ordered.

Brenda instantly froze. Rudy went back to his task of fondling and sucking. Brenda wondered if this was what it felt like to be devoured. A ticklish sensation ran down the back of Brenda's legs.

"Don't laugh, Bitch!" Her version of Rudy's voice warned internally. Rudy stopped his suction with a popping sound to punctuate the movement.

Each of the three women rubbed the palms of their hands as Brenda allowed them to survey the results of Rudy's work. A pang of jealousy momentarily shot through each of them.

Rudy looked at Brenda for a second. A smile, unconcerned and defiant, dressed her mouth.

"Yeah you like this shit, don'tcha?" Rudy asked, slightly releasing Brenda's hand from the twisted position.

"Hell yeah, is what I wanted to say." Brenda told her friends, returning to the living room area with a new bottle of wine.

Bruised

"So what *did* you tell him?" Joani asked.

Brenda waved her hand across her body at a Rudy that wasn't there.

"No you didn't." Joyce said in disbelief.

"Yes I did. Gurl, I ain't punk." Brenda answered, unwittingly rubbing the hicky that was the result of her answer.

Rudy yelled as the loud ringing in his ear was replaced with a rough warmth on the side of his face.

"What the fuck is wrong with you?" Rudy said, rubbing the cheek Brenda had just slapped. Brenda began a verbal protest to the treatment (even though she'd soaked her panties she told her friends) just as Rudy applied greater force in twisting her arm. The force was enough to cause Brenda to lean side-ways, in her body's own attempt to alleviate the pressure.

"Okay you wanna play rough."

Brenda's vagina tingled quickly. Brenda watched the look on Rudy's face change from controlled anger to a menacing grin. He moved his head up and down slowly. And before Brenda could protest, he led her to the table. Knocking everything from atop of it, he forced Brenda to its surface. Rudy pushed down on the small of her back and smacked her raise ass cheeks with rough force. Brenda tried to look over her shoulder and yell, but all she could manage was an open mouth gasp. She was through playing hard to

SexPressions

get. He could *get* all he wanted. Brenda gripped the edge of the table. She searched her mind for the very moment she realized she liked rough sex. The answer to that was since losing her virginity, announced itself as Rudy snatched her back to reality

"He bit the shit out of me." Brenda said to her friends as they now sat quiet as mice. "I thought I was going to pass out."

Again laughter swarmed through the room.

Rudy growled as he eased the force of his bite. Brenda lay atop of the table trembling. A rogue orgasm swept through her body, making her stiff nipples feel foreign and uncomfortable beneath her. Brenda was frozen. She felt Rudy's hands moving under her, working their way toward her pant's securing clasp. Brenda lifted her pelvis, aiding Rudy in his accosting of her.

"Why the fuck didn't I wear a dress." She asked herself.

Rudy snatched at her pants, moving them from atop of her large rear and down her legs, finally pulling them, along with her soaked panties, off and tossed them on the floor.

"Wait. Ya'll was still in the kitchen?" Mesha cut-in, frowning slightly.

"Dayum Bitch, will you let her finish." Joyce snapped, the effects of the alcohol showing their effects.

Bruised

"Like that's gonna stop yo' greedy ass from eating over here." Joani added, turning back to Brenda.

Rudy could see the fresh teeth marks on Brenda's ass. He smiled at his handiwork. Rudy leaned forward and kissed the spot, then began sucking with terrible force. Brenda tried to scoot away, as a moan flew from her throat. Rudy continued sucking hard; using his tongue to accent the action randomly. Brenda pressed her face into the table's lukewarm surface, as Rudy roughly kneaded her soft ass cheeks between his palms. Rudy broke contact and watched as the love bruise slowly grew larger and puffier. He smiled as he moved his eager mouth over Brenda's large ebony ass. He teased her plump cheeks with curt movements of his tongue. Brenda slowly pushed her ass higher into the air. Rudy used slow, forceful circular motions to manipulate Brenda's ass. Rudy placed his hand on her warm cheeks and slowly spread them apart. He placed his thumbs on the sides of her brown rear hole, covered his thumbs with his mouth, and sucked hard, before tracing the sensitive area with his tongue. Brenda's toes curled and she wasn't sure if they'd ever straighten again.

"I damn near fell off the table." Brenda howled with laughter, as she lay on the floor reenacting the position for her friends.

Brenda howled loudly, tightening her grip on the table. Her toes tingled furiously, while the feeling of being light-headed overcame her. Rudy continued sucking softly and licking; drawing tears from Brenda's eyes. Brenda tried to move some muscles, while muscles she ordered to stay frozen, twitched and jittered. Rudy drew tight slow circles

SexPressions

around Brenda's hole, forcing curse words and prayers from Brenda's surprised mouth. Naked from the waist down, Brenda felt overdressed and rude.

"How dare I keep all these clothes on, denying this man and his tongue the pleasure to freak on me?" Brenda thought to herself, nipples throbbing fiercely.

Rudy moved his tongue lower toward Brenda's throbbing and forgotten vagina. He kissed her roughly on her creamily damp labia, navigating his tongue through her pubic hair, and against her swollen clitoris. Brenda moaned and lightly pounded against the table. She tried to peek around her ass at Rudy. Brenda frowned in pleasure; the feel of Rudy's tongue against her sex caused her to slowly squirm. Brenda gasped as Rudy moved the tip of his tongue inside of her vagina; brushing against the rough ridges of her flesh just past her labia. Brenda cursed wildly. Her head began swimming. She tried to control her breathing. Rudy worked his tongue faster, nose brushing against her sensitive ass cheeks. Brenda tried to move from the table again, but a quick swat of Rudy's hand across her ass held her in place. She felt kisses land onto her skin, then the feel of Rudy's hand.

"So this *is* the type of shit you like." Rudy shot, standing up behind her.

Brenda could hear the sound of Rudy's belt being unbuckled, tingling and chingling a warning. She wanted to resist. Brenda wanted to get up from the table and kick Rudy's skinny ass out of her house. But all she could muster was a demand.

Bruised

"You better have a rubber!" Brenda said, as she tried to sound tough as she lay on her kitchen table; naked ass in the air.

Rudy removed his shirt and shook his head in disbelief.

"Still acting tough, huh?" Rudy thought pulling a condom from his pocket. Brenda smiled, folded her arms, placed her head atop of them, and eased slowly backward, trying to brush her ass against Rudy's erection. She tried to gauge the situation. See what type of weapon Rudy had brought to the fight.

Rudy's penis throbbed slow and powerfully. His sex was hot and thick, small veins running along his shaft like roads on an ebony map. He pulled the condom, black and thin, down along his dick. The latex sleeve came to an end just before the base. Rudy smirked and grabbed Brenda's ass cheeks roughly. Brenda stood on her tip-toes as Rudy slowly pushed himself into her. She bit the inside of her cheek as Rudy eased his body, slow but close, against her. Rudy placed his hands on her shoulders and rotated his hips. Brenda grunted and tried to squeeze her inner walls around Rudy's girth, but Rudy pushed her forward causing her to fall over the edge of the table, scraping her forearm and elbow.

"So that's a real bruise, huh?" Joyce asked, surveying the damage.

"I bit my tongue, too. But it was worth it." Brenda laughed, looking down at her badge of horny. "Anyway..."

SexPressions

Brenda tried to return upright on the table, bracing herself on the chair in front of her. She winced as the searing heat of the fresh scar began.

"You okay?" Rudy asked sarcastically, slowly pulling himself backward.

And before Brenda could answer, or regroup she felt his palm slam harshly against her ass.

"But you tough. You can take it." Rudy sneered and began stroking.

Brenda's breath was stolen instantly. Rudy grunted curse words; moving with beastly determination. He barked orders and cadences as if he were angry at Brenda's pussy for being so tight and inviting. Rudy allowed his blood to flow with sexual hate.

"Bitch!" The word seeping wickedly hot from his mouth as he shifted from side to side.

Brenda grabbed the edge of the table and braced herself. She welcomed the roughness that raided her body. Brenda knew she needed the sexual kinks to be worked out of her. Rudy's penis was curved downward, pushing deliciously against the roof of her womb. Her vagina had become sadistic. Her vaginal walls taunted Rudy.

"Gimme more, punk!" It yelled. " Hurt me, Daddy!"

Brenda pushed backward. Her body challenged Rudy's. Soon each shouted and grunted challenges at each

Bruised

other.

"OOOOO, fuck me! Brenda ordered, the force of their motions testing the strength of the table.

Rudy's frowned overtook his smile. He felt his orgasm growing strength from allover his body. When it came, he'd be ready.

"Turn over!" Rudy said, pulling his thick penis from inside of Brenda's demanding warmth.

He sucked on his teeth and ran his hand over his chest and stomach and watched Brenda slowly turn over atop of the table.. He nearly laughed at Brenda's amateur contortionist act began and end. When she finally finished, Rudy pulled her to the edge of the table. He marveled at how her dark skin complexion stayed even and smooth all over her body. Rudy decided to add a few blemishes to her landscape. He, first, eased himself inside of Brenda, then leaned forward and began sucking on her breast. Brenda grabbed him by the back of his head and dug her nails into his skin. Rudy stopped applying suction for the hicky long enough to grunt his approval. He pushed deep and hard into Brenda, forcing moans from her mouth with the end of each stroke. Rudy placed a hicky after hicky against Brenda's stomach. Brenda's breast brushed against Rudy's chest, sending tremors throughout her body. Her body trembled and radiated with her impending orgasm. She moved her nails and their torture lower, and held onto Rudy's back. Rudy placed his hand on the sides of Brenda's head, supported himself over her and stroked. Brenda still welcomed the punishment. She beckoned for Rudy to pump

SexPressions

faster and harder. Soon he stood over her, held her legs by the ankle and pushed himself into her. They grunted and moaned sex filled insults at the other.

"Fuck this pussy!" Brenda shot.
"Take this dick!" Rudy demanded.

Neither heeded the warnings of their orgasms. Rudy's struck first. The head of his penis became filled with electricity. He held Brenda's ankles together; level with his face. Brenda held her large breast from tidal waving against Rudy's chin. Her stomach rumbled from her stampeding orgasm. She'd held her eyes closed but open them in time to see Rudy freeze, then shudder. She felt delight as his orgasm's force created his fuck face.

"Yeeeeaaaahhh!" he moaned, still stroking with slow movements.

Brenda pleaded for him to continue. Her orgasm was poised to erupt. Her heartbeat ferociously inside of her ribcage. She tingled and froze; body temperature fluctuating from extremely hot to bitterly cold. Brenda shook her head "no" as the word "yes" ejected itself from her lips. She pulled on her nipples and exhaled harshly, and before she could warn Rudy, her orgasm banged against her sexual windows. Brenda hummed and moaned as her vagina coached Rudy's penis to stroke slow and deep. She reached upward toward Rudy. Her fingertips were either numb or tingling; a few were both. Rudy slowed himself to a laboring stop, and then pushed backward from Brenda.

"Dayum." Brenda said in a rough celebration.

Bruised

Rudy leaned against the sink and stared down at Brenda and their aftermath.

"Ain't so tough." He shot at her.

"Fuck......You.' That's what I told him." Brenda said, giving Joyce and Mesha high fives. "After that we took showers and did our thang in the bedroom." Brenda finished, sipping from her glass.

Each woman sat back and absorbed Brenda's story. The four women instinctively moved their hands over their personal sexual ignition spots, each woman mentally praying for their cellular phones to ring with a *"booty call"* to save them. The yell of Brenda's doorbell caused each of them to jump before laughing at their own horny fear. Brenda sprang to her feet, moving to answer the door.

"Who is it?" She asked into the intercom, still giggling at herself.

"It's me, Bren." Rudy's voice sprang from the speaker in return.

The entire room burst with female laughter. Rudy walked into the room a few minutes later. He removed his coat, spoke, and took a seat near Brenda. Each woman instantly spied the large bruise that covered Rudy's neck. They all exchanged glances before breaking into fits on laughter.

"What's so funny?" Rudy asked nervously, involuntarily rubbing his neck, sending the into

SexPressions

uncontrollable fits of laughter.

"Nothing baby," Brenda said, kissing him on his confused lip, "nothing at all."

OLD FRIENDS; NEW LOVER

"So did you bring what I asked for?" Lee asked Renee. Although he saw the large purse that more than likely held the items, he didn't have anything else to say. He'd talked to Renee over the telephone and they had decided that a get-a-way was in order. But now standing in front of her, everything changed. Now Lee knew things were for real. *For keeps.*

Renee smiled as she stepped inside of the room past Lee. A sweet scent of perfume teased his senses.

"What's that scent you're wearing?" He asked, as his sex drive began to slowly fill his penis.

"It smells nice." Lee's voice quivered as he spoke.

"It's called 'Green'. Its a body oil I bought at the African shop. Do you like it?" Renee said.

SexPressions

She tossed her purse onto the sofa, before placing her hands on her sexy round hips. Lee swallowed hard. Everything about Renee was sexy and inviting. She was tall without being gangly with thick long legs. Lee often dreamt of falling asleep with his head resting on those beautiful ebony-toned legs. Renee's breasts were full and round, slightly hidden beneath her silk blouse. He held out his hand to Renee and suddenly he saw her eyes, as if for the first time. He'd seen Renee many times before but never really noticed she held the same look as he held. The look that said, "We're not young anymore." The look told Lee she was *'all woman'*. The look that *was* for right now.

"What took you so long?"

Lee pulled Renee to him. He fought off the urge to melt. His body nearly betrayed him. Renee was warm and seductively soft. Lee felt himself grow long, large, and hard within his pants. He was too excited to care.

Renee hoped the light trembling she felt deep within herself, wouldn't give her away. She'd been trying to conceal her cavalryish desire to seek Lee out, but to avail. She could lie to the girls at the office, and even maintain the lie around her friends. No, it was that bitch in her mirror who demanded the truth. And the truth was Lee made Renee want to throw caution to the wind. It was that antagonistic woman that lived over her sink who teased her every morning. So as Lee pulled her deep within his grasp, Renee thanked the mirror lady for keeping her honest. Renee closed her eyes and welcomed Lee's embrace. His hands were small, yet strong. Each fingertip igniting its own fire. Renee held on tightly to Lee, not wanting to fall. She

Old Friends; New Lover

hummed softly to her own inner music. It was the music she heard and felt each time she saw him. Lee, with that smile so stupid it no choice but to be liked. Lee, who was short and comfortable looking. Renee even liked that Lee was slim; his tight muscles hidden beneath his casual clothing and easy demeanor. Renee held Lee tighter still, as the heat of his bulge grew against her leg. She had chosen a skirt that displayed her lovely legs, and allowed for her to get a preview to come. Lee moved his hand slightly and kissed Renee cautiously on the neck. A small tremor awakened itself and ran down her spine. She finally would have Lee to herself. No more hoping he would notice her, she would have what she wanted. Renee tilted her head back and allowed Lee to kiss and suck from one side of her neckline to the other. His kisses slowly made her grow moist and warm. Renee cursed softly. She held Lee's head half guiding, half refusing.

"No wait!" Renee panted, "Not yet."

Lee gave her one last kiss. He held her face within his hand and looked through her. He smiled, using that smile that made her wonder why he was single.

"Okay. We have all the time we want." Lee said through that smile. "Besides I made dinner and you're going to need your energy."

Lee couldn't believe that he was sitting across from Renee this long. He had used all of his will power to stop from kissing her. Dinner seemed to be a test of that same will power. Although it was filled with lively conversation, Lee felt it went on forever. Really all he wanted was to pull

SexPressions

Renee across the table and have his way with her. He was tired of flirting with her; trying mask it as fun. This was their time and Lee would have to make the most of it.

After dinner, Lee poured them both a glass of champagne. He then turned on the radio to the slow jazz station. After two glasses each, they both knew the time had come. Lee showered first. He washed himself slowly and methodically. He fought the urge to masturbate. He refused to cheat himself. He stepped from the shower and toweled himself dry. Normally his penis would be shrunken by now, but now it hung proudly between his legs. It knew. It knew that Renee was different. She was special. Lee took great pride as he dabbed his sexual tool dry. He had always thought about the things he heard about size and if it really mattered. Lee knew it did. His penis throbbed its eight and a half inch concordance. He rubbed an easy coat of musk body oil over himself, before pulling on his soft black pajama bottoms. He stepped from the steamy brightness of the bathroom into the cool candle lit room. Renee turned the lights low and lit a few candles. The soft scent engulfed the room. She smiled as she carried her large purse into the bathroom.

Renee stood beneath the shower's hot steamy spray, frozen with delight. She showered twice before she had left home, creaming her panties each time. This time was more symbolic than anything. She washed away the old side world and readied herself for Lee; also it didn't hurt for a woman to make a man wait.

Damn, she thought, why did Lee have to be such a good cook? Dinner was a light pasta salad with chicken and

Old Friends; New Lover

mushrooms. Renee quivered after each mouthful. Now she hugged herself tightly under the showers heat. She wondered if she could keep her composure. Lee and his cooking skills definitely made that hard.

"I hope that isn't all that's hard about being around him." Renee thought as she rubbed her sexually swollen breast. Renee shook off the jitters and began to lather up. Since Lee prepared such a good dinner; she give his just desserts. Renee smiled as the thought filled her head.

Lee lay on the floor of the bedroom. He did a few push-ups and sit-ups to get his heart pumping. Although seeing Renee made that sexual ritual obsolete, he liked how his muscles tightened and presented themselves beneath his brown shell. It also made Lee feel that much more sexy, that much more enticing. Lee took pride in the fact he was a good lover. He liked he could dominate, "No", he corrected himself as his muscles began to burn, "I love that I can dominate." A smile curled across his lips. Lee thought of the look on the faces of the women he took to bed. The look of *"what-the-fuck?"* That look of sexual defeat. He used to wonder what women were thinking during sex. But that look talked to him. It said "I should've brought help to this fight. But I'm glad I didn't!"

Lee loved that look. It made women feel special. Because you couldn't get "that" look just any and everywhere. Lee also had a look he gave women. Lee's look told women, *"This ain't luck."* It said, 'This moment was special because she was special." It also said, "You should've brought help to beat this dick!"

SexPressions

Lee counted himself closer to the last of his push-ups. Arms growing more and hotter. The bathroom light shone over the floor beneath Lee, before the sight of Renee's intricately painted toes moved into his line of vision.

"I could get used to having a man at my feet." Renee said, standing over Lee. He continued on with his quick work-out, pausing long enough to kiss and lick Renee gingerly on the feet. Renee moaned as the delightful surprise of Lee's tongue and lips taunted her. Lee felt his heart rate quicken and reach it's desired pace. His body felt loose, yet hard. He pushed out a few more, treating himself to the added treat of Renee's pretty feet.

Renee stood over Lee enjoying the sight of his slender athletic body. His back looked as if some sculptor used a slab of light chocolate and created a man. Renee remembered toweling off completely, but even though she had done that, she now felt thick wetness between her legs. She believed she could watch him kiss her feet the entire night, but she wanted to have him. She wanted to finally feel Lee inside of her. And now she would. Lee moved higher along her leg, kissing and biting Renee gently on her ankles. She tried to swallow the moan that sat at the top of her throat, before releasing its soft sound into the room.

Lee slowly kissed his way up Renee's long thick legs. He stopped along the way to raid her cache of shiver inducing spots. Lee's hands moved along the back of Renee's legs, while his tongue stalked over the front. Renee ran her hands over Lee's head. His hands and mouth worked wonders, causing her to wonder if the items in the bag were necessary. She secretly hoped so. Lee softly pushed his lips against the back of her knees and held her sex cushioned ass

Old Friends; New Lover

cheeks within his arms. His heart pounded feverishly in his chest, sending new blood to fill his penis. He forced himself to be patient. Lee waited this long to have Renee and he wasn't about to rush anything. He kissed Renee softly on her thighs, before slowly rising to his feet. He stood back, taking in the full sight of Renee. She stood, legs spread, hands hanging before her. She wore an emerald green three piece ensemble. Her large brown breasts tested the strength of her lace and satin bra. Her cleavage's deepness invited Lee's tongue to dive in. Lee lowered his eyes to Renee's large shapely hips. The bikini cut panties, arrowed down from her hips to her sexual trapdoor. Renee stood before him like an erotic goddess.

Renee watched Lee as he fondled her with his vision. She slowly twirled giving him a complete view of her. She pulled her long shirt tight against her ass, teasing Lee with its roundness. She could almost hear him salivating. She completed her twirl to see Lee with his eyes closed, mumbling softly under his breath, as if he were praying.

"You better pray." Renee thought, her vagina's voice filling her head. "Because this pussy doesn't take prisoners."

Lee opened his eyes, reassuring himself he wasn't dreaming. She stared back at him smiling gently and slowly shaking her head.

"Never had a man pray before sex." She said partly probing, partly joking.

"I never had a woman I wanted to pray over." He retorted.

SexPressions

Lee placed his hands on her shoulders. He tenderly kneaded the tension from her knotted muscles. Renee's eyelids drooped before closing completely. She serenaded Lee with soft moans. He opened his hands, including the nape of her neck inside of message's radius. She craned her neck, welcoming the creeping relief of her muscles. She slowly began relaxing each sore spot. First her neck and shoulders loosened; then her back and thighs. Her calves joined the relaxing revolution. Finally her toes curled into a quick fist, before expelling the tension with a series of small pops and crackles. Lee ran the grasp of his hands delicately, as if he were holding a rare flower; scared to apply anymore pressure. He pulled her face close to his and kissed her on the lips, easily slipping his tongue between Renee's full lips. Her mouth was warm and sweet. Her tongue soon greeted his. Soon their tongues began a passionate waltz. Renee commanded her eyes to stay shut, while Lee's hands moved over her curves. His touch was firm and commanding. It ordered her body to tingle and shiver. Lee pulled Renee close to him and kissed her just under her chin. She tossed her arms onto his shoulders and ran her fingers across the nape of his neck. Lee smiled and continued kissing Renee's tender neck. He drifted his way down her neck to her tempting cleavage. Lee kissed Renee just above the edge of her bra. The each hummed in delight. She felt Lee's hand caressing her thigh and she allowed him to guide it up and around his waist. He felt the heat of her sex against his abdomen. He couldn't believe a person could produce so much warmth. He grabbed her buttocks, before moving her other leg around his waist. Renee locked her ankles behind Lee and leaned in to partake of his earlobe. Lee turned and carefully placed Renee onto the bed. She held her leg lock him. Renee ran her hands over his strong back, raking her

Old Friends; New Lover

nails over his smooth skin. Renee could feel the density of his sex as it brushed against her swelling labia and clitoris. Lee began to grind slowly as she; not wanting to be outdone, slowly rotated herself beneath him. He liked the sound of Renee in his ear. He kissed her across her neck. He moved his hands over her breast teasing her nipples through the bra's thin fabric. Lee ran moved his kisses lower and kissed each breast. She felt her nipples grow firm and tingle. Her internal temperature quickly became unbearable. Renee wiggled her arms free of the shirt and sat forward to start on the bra.

Lee slid his hand behind her and unclasped her bra restraint. He moved his hands to her hips and tugged lightly on her panties. Renee raised her pelvis and welcomed the feel of his lips against the cusp of her pubic hair. She felt free; as if she were flying. She sat up just in time to see Lee's head move lower. Next she felt his lips brush over her sensitive labia. No longer was Lee her play brother, he was now her serious lover.

Lee felt himself hum softly. The taste of Renee filled his mouth. Her legs began to grow tense around his head. Lee held her firmly in place by her butt. He drew slow circles around her clitoris with her tongue. He barely noticed the bulge that grew beneath him. All he wanted was to indulge his hunger for her. Lee order himself not to rush. He lapped at Renee's creamy thickness; alternating every other lick against her surprised brown eye. Renee watched him work. His tongue brushed against her vagina as if it were an intimate stranger, tweaking her tender places that seemed familiar and unknown. A sexual de ja vu. Renee ran her hands over his head, making meaningless patterns. She knew she could easily allow him to push her closer to climax with his tongue, but she wondered what else he had to offer. Simultaneously, Renee pulled Lee's head higher, while pushing his pajamas down with her feet. He quickly gathered the idea and began inching higher as well as wiggling free from his only piece of clothing.

Lee crawled over her until they were face to face. Her rapid breaths rushed past his face. His manhood throbbed, and then pulsated as it came into contact with Renee's vagina. Their hands moved quickly to assist him with moving his thickness inside of Renee, who won out. She guided him slowly toward her breach and eased him into her. His penis was greeted with an even more intense heat as he filled Renee. Slowly he moved himself deeper into her welcoming warmth. With each slow tender thrust, her sex walls massaged Lee's thick shaft. She-He-They grimaced with erotic surprise from the tight fit. Lee moved his pelvis with a sleek, smooth motion. This was just how he imagined it in his dreams. Renee cursed herself for wondering if other women got this treatment.

"No!" She panted in his ear, but scolding herself. With each deep insertion, she knew this was only for her. She'd lusted and longed for this. This time was special.

"No!" She moaned again, digging her fingernails deep into Lee's back. A soft tide began to swell deep within her. She didn't want to be so near to an orgasm so soon. Renee moved her legs up a long his waist, arched her back and tried to apply downward pressure as she rotated her hips. She shook her head "no" as the word "yes" leapt faster and faster from her mouth. Renee didn't hear herself moan and

Old Friends; New Lover

pant aloud. She blossomed with erotic warmth, as she shook from deep within.

One thought crossed her mind. "I should've brought help for this dick."

Lee felt sweat begin to coat his body. He couldn't remember when he started moving with such force. He tried to command his body to slow down, but some how Renee had hi-jacked his movements. Her vagina had taunted him, each thrust pushed him closer. Lee knew his orgasm was mounting but he tried to fight it off. She assaulted him with both pleasure and pain. Her nails dug deep into his back, turning him, surprisingly, on. While her tight vagina shamed him with the pain of his sexual defeat, he felt his toes begin to curl. His ass cheeks tightened as well, both sure signs of his orgasm. A prickly sensation overtook the head of his penis. His orgasm began its march slow and gained speed, driving him deeper and faster in Renee. His pants became uncontrollable now. An inaudible rumbling shook through Lee. His orgasm splashed hot inside of her, leaving him with one thought.

"This was a war," his own voice whispered, "and you just surrendered."

Lee collapsed next to Renee unaware of the look of exhaustion on her face.

Renee lay with her head on Lee's chest, dejected. She had experienced good sex before, but not this. This time the pleasure was immediate and long lasting. Renee couldn't make up her mind on the appropriate mood, so her face held

SexPressions

the neutral look of bewilderment. She kissed Lee's chest and told herself, it was good sex, no matter how long it lasted.

Lee lay back on the bed, with an uncontrollable frown across his face. He knew without hearing her say what she thought.

"Don't worry, Lee. It happens to everybody sooner or later." That's what her voice would carry to his ears. But he could do nothing else but worry.

His penis still throbbed between his legs, reminding him of his shortcoming.

"But she moaned." He told himself, "Hell, she damn near screamed." His own voice reassured him. "That has to matter."

Lee wanted to ask Renee how she felt but couldn't muster the nerve. Plus he could hear her breathing slow to the rhythm one only gets from sleep. He'd ask her another time or show her he could "hang" when she woke. Sleep soon overtook him. A smile crept across his face as the thought of the items he'd asked Renee to bring ushered in his dreams.

Renee's dreams were crowed with the intrusive smell of coffee. Even within her sleep she felt herself smile, as the sweet dark aroma escorted her to the land of the conscious. Slowly the entire room came into view; croissants, that Renee hoped were still warm, piled on a plate; two roses, neatly placed with a simple crystal vase; a large tempting bowl of fruit; mainly strawberries; finally the rest of the room came into focus, and after that Lee. Although her mind

Old Friends; New Lover

had nearly erased traces of him, her body fully remembered Lee. Her body was eager for another confrontation.

"Morning, sleepy head." Lee said, still naked.

Renee nodded in response and took in the sight of Lee. Trying not to gawk, she inspected every inch of him. Her eyes caressed his small defined chest. His powerful looking legs and the thick muscle that hung between them. Although it wasn't at its full length, Renee was impressed by the size and shape. The head appeared larger than the shaft. Fatter was the word that came to mind the more she studied it. She reminisced about the snug fit they shared. She wanted to touch him again; to have him touch her.

"Can a lady get something to eat?" She asked, her nipples becoming nervously erect.

Lee slowly poured two cups of coffee, placed croissants and strawberries on a saucer, and moved next to Renee on the bed. He plucked a few strawberries from the saucer, and held one between two fingers.

"Say Ah!" He moved the sweet morsel toward her lips.

Renee hummed and opened her mouth slowly to accept his offer. Lee allowed his finger to linger as he placed the strawberry just past her teeth. She chewed seductively as Lee continued to feed her. Renee slowly ate the offered food trying to erase the thing growling in her stomach. She hummed and moaned as the sweet, buttery taste of the pastry mixed and filled her. She felt the food slowly energize her.

SexPressions

She ate while Lee watched. She brought the coffee to her lips. The hot mocha liquid swept over her taste buds and gave her system a caffeine induced charge. Before she noticed, Lee watched her devour two croissants and a large cup of coffee. She used the food and drink to chase away one feeling while ushering another. Soon her body tingled with next-day sexual excitement. Lee sipped slowly from his cup. His penis lay against his leg like a proud lion. She smiled and again studied his features. She cursed and became irked with herself for not having a camera.

"Why are you looking at me like that?" she asked, trying to divert attention from herself."

"I'm wondering how long that glow will last." Renee blushed, not seeing the actual glow he referred to, but felt it all the same. Still she lied trying to evoke more sexual banter.

"What glow?" She asked, unaware of the quick flutter of her eye lashes.

"The one that started here." Lee whispered, leaning over to kiss Renee on her stomach. "And here." He kissed her again between her breasts. She nearly suffocated herself as she inhaled and exhaled simultaneously. She reached to caress Lee's head, but he moved just out of her reach, causing her to wonder if the gestures were genuine.

"Well stop that before you start something you can't finish." She giggled. Renee feigned anger at Lee's teasing, while still trying to urge him on. She slowly wondered about the reason for his staring. Where else am I glowing, she

Old Friends; New Lover

heard her body ask.

"So what's the plan for the day?"

Renee turned on the bed and faced Lee. She rested her head in her palm. Giving Lee what she thought was some of his own medicine.

"Well finishing breakfast, then I'm going to fuck you. Lunch and more fucking," Lee started in a matter-of-fact tone. "Then dinner and a movie. After that more fucking."

Renee sat mouth open; offended, shocked and ultimately turned on.

"You're so sure all that will happen?" She quizzed, forcing herself to frown and raise her voice.

"Not really," Lee said. He grabbed a handful of strawberries, a croissant, and moved from the bed. "We may not have time for the dinner and a movie." He playfully tossed a small strawberry at her before disappearing into the bathroom.

"Bastard!" She laughed, trying to swat away the fruity projectile. "You ain't shit." The sound of her voice bounced around the empty room.

Lee smiled at himself in the mirror. The minor throbbing in his loins told him things would be different his time. Not only did his body alert him to the difference; Renee looked different. He no longer felt he needed to ask if she enjoyed the sex. Her body told him she did. She had a

SexPressions

glow that Lee recognized. It told him that a high level of pleasure had been obtained. Lee hung his head and smiled. An erection grew been his legs. Lee lifted his head and grinned at himself in the mirror.

"Be sure to get down how you live dawg!" His reflection said.

"I will," Lee said, stepping into the showers hot stream of water, "I will."

Renee lay naked on the bed eating strawberries. She giggled at the way Lee's sexual confidence made her feel. She could barely lay still. Her vagina tingled with shameless glee. She smiled and slowly fed herself. She relished in the feeling the taste gave her. Even as a little girl, Renee always liked how eating strawberries made her "coo-coo" tingle. Renee slowly moved her hand between her thighs and searched for her clitoris. She used her pointer and ringer fingers to expose her hidden sexual target and her middle finger to slowly rotate it. Renee could hear herself hum and moan, not sure if it was because of the taste of the strawberries or the feel of her clitoris. She swallowed the sweet bits of the fruit and pushed a twinge from her black pearl; she told herself she didn't care. She popped herself another in her mouth and moved her finger lower. She slowly chewed the fruit as she found the entrance to her love hole. She moved her finger in slow unison with the mouth. She felt a small easy smile blossom across her lips. She delighted in the sticky warmth that covered her delicate extremity. A deep breath slowly ribboned from her mouth. Renee chewed and fingered herself into a personal nirvana. Again, she used the tip of her finger and moved it over her

Old Friends; New Lover

clitoris using short firm circular motions. Renee used her free hand and caressed her lonely, jealous breast. Her nipples, sat up erect and begged for attention. Renee felt her toes slowly curl. A deep moan pushed across her tongue. She held her eyes tightly closed. Renee hardly noticed Lee, who stood at the foot of the bed slowly stroking his thick manhood. She pressed harder and faster on her clitoris. She tugged roughly on her breast. The brutal feeling woke her senses. Renee reached out for the bowl, so she could eat herself into an orgasm.

"Let me help you." Lee said, just as she began opening her eyes. She wasn't sure how long he had been standing there watching, but she was glad he was there now. Lee crawled over her, kissing softly as he went. He took her hand and placed her sexually soaked fingers in his mouth and slowly filled her womb with his thickness. She held her mouth open so Lee could continue feeding her. *"Sex and strawberries; what could be better?"* Lee pushed slowly into her until their bodies kissed. He felt her shift internally around the head of his penis. Renee moved her legs together beneath him, forcing him to lay spread eagle atop of her. He gasped loudly at the added snugness. He pulled himself partly out, before slowly submerging himself again. She grabbed by the small of the back; lightly patting him on the upper portion of his ass cheeks. He placed his hands on the sides of her head and gained sluggish momentum. She dug her nails slightly into his flesh, urging him on. Lee slowly lowered his head and sucked on her breast, devilishly hoping to leave a hicky.

"Yes! Yes!" She moaned, answering a question only his sex asked.

SexPressions

Chills ran down Lee's back. His abdomen muscles tightened and slowly began to bum. She moved her legs outward, unable to stand the friction any longer. He moved deeper still. The backs of her knees itched. She opened her eyes and studied his face. She had never seen anyone so determined to please. If her orgasm wasn't so close she believed she would have faked it to reward him.

Lee felt sweat lightly begin to cover his back. The salt bum the fresh scratches Renee made. She slowly moved her hand over his lower back and ass. Her moans became high pitched pants. She slowly lay atop her she felt very soft beneath him. She grabbed the back of his head and whispered into his ear, before nibbling on the lobe.

"I love you."

Lee slowly moved to her warmth. He leaned to the side and entered her at an angle. Her breath began to come faster. A heated sensation settled in her head. Her body began gently shaking.

"I'm cuh...cuh...cuh...," was all she could muster before her body tightened around his.

She shuddered harshly as he took no heed and continued stroking. His own orgasm was too close; too near; too tempting to slow down. Lee increased his pace. He felt his own body begin to tingle and itch. He layover her, hands on her hips and moved faster and deeper. He made on last push before his body stiffened. He bit down on the inside of his mouth, as his body pumped hot fluid into her. She held her breath before welcoming the comforting explosion. She

Old Friends; New Lover

had often wondered about children. Mainly she wondered about the faces they would combine to make. She pulled him completely onto her, refusing to let him escape her. She listened to him breath. She found the bowl and fed herself as Lee's heart calmed itself. Soon he rolled to one side and snuck back to the arms of the Mistress of Slumber. She smiled and continued with her small daydream of their offspring until sleep took her as well.

Renee awoke slowly. Good sex had a way of knocking a person out. She thought about the last time she was "put" to sleep. Smiling, she caressed the side of Lee's face. He grumbled a smile in his sleep, and then nestled closer against her warmth. Renee wished she hadn't waited so long to date Lee. She'd grown up chasing behind him and her brothers and along the way she fell in love with him. She wanted this to last. She could no longer stand having him come to every family function with a "friend" of his. Now that she had him, she wouldn't let him go. She checked the clock on the night stand and noticed that the last episode had lasted nearly two hours. Renee decided she would pay for another night in the hotel; another day with Lee. They were worth it. She could even swim a few laps in the pool. She hadn't been swimming since high school. She slid from beneath Lee and got dressed quietly.

The scent of Lee still covered her body. Renee grabbed her purse and quickly began searching for her small change purse. She snatched her large over-night bag and stuffed her hand in. The first thing she came across was the brown paper bag, containing the items Lee told her to bring. She raised an eyebrow in recollection. A sly grin slipped across her face.

SexPressions

"I almost forgot about this stuff." she thought, stuffing the bag back. She decided to take the entire bag along with her. If she had forgotten then so had Lee.

Lee woke and looked around the room. He hoped Renee would still be lying next to him. Seeing her gone, he pulled her pillow close. The smell of "Green" filled his nostrils. The smell was uniquely sexual as was Renee. He allowed his smile to transform into a timid giggle. He hugged the pillow and rolled over in the bed. Lee lay on his back and smiled at the ceiling. He thought about Renee. She had definitely grown into a beautiful woman. She was no longer the brat who wanted to tag along with the boys. He no longer had to hide his affection with jokes and innuendos. He could love her openly.

Lee rolled over and noticed Renee had been shopping, leaving him to wonder how long he had been sleep. Next to the shopping bag was a small paper bag, knocked open from being dropped. Lee peered in the bag and saw the items he asked her to bring. Lee grinned as he told himself to get familiar with each and every item. He placed each one on the night stand and recounted how he planned on using them.

"This should be fun."

The contents were the average things people used during sex, but he thought about how un-average this situation was going to turn out. He lay back in the bed and waited for Renee to return.

Rene's chest burned, but she continued with more laps

Old Friends; New Lover

because she loved swimming.

"Plus Lee already messed up my hair." She thought before diving in the pool's luke-warm water. She let the door close behind her and walked into the room tilting her head, trying to clear the water from her ear.

"Hey Pretty Lady." Lee said, wrapping his arms around her from behind.

A soft moan painted the inside of her mouth. She reached over her shoulder and pulled his face softly against hers. Renee wondered if the smell of chlorine would ruin the moment. She felt his kisses on the back of her neck and didn't really care. She let her body sink back into his.

"This feels good." she hummed. He pushed her hair out of his lip's path and moved his kisses higher.

"Go get in the shower and meet me in the bed." He whispered, so only she could hear as if the room were being bugged.

His lips moved just over her eager skin; the air from his words tickling her fine hairs. She steeped away from his warmth, telling herself to breath. The swim had drained her of all her reserve energy, leaving her body weak and sensitive in more places. She turned and kissed him. Renee liked how soft and thick his lips were. She moved her tongue pass his lips and brushed his warm tongue.

'This is too good." Renee thought again.

She slowly removed her tongue and kissed him three

SexPressions

soft times on his wonderful mouth.

"Okay! It's a date."

Renee softly patted him on his ass and danced toward the awaiting shower.

"I paid for another night, so we can take our time." She said over her shoulder.

"Good. We're going to need it." He responded.

Lee sipped the champagne slowly and thought about Renee while she showered. She had worn a t-shirt over her bathing suit. Her amply shaped ass cheeks hinted at their presence, teasing Lee. He wanted to tell himself it was the sweet bubbly alcohol that forced him to have an erection but he knew damn well it was the sight and feel of her. He listened to the sound of the running water. Lee tried to imagine the path the water took down her body to the drain. He wondered if the water splashed roughly against her body and then caressed her breast. If it took it's time over her stomach, easing its way down her thighs. He asked himself if the water found her hidden clitoris. Lee, himself, rubbing his thick bulge, smiled at his slight jealousy of the shower's stream. He poured himself another glass of champagne and reassured himself that being jealous wasn't so bad.

The swim had done her some good. The shower was adding to the sensation and she hoped Lee could do an even better job. She poured shampoo in her hands inhaling the apple-vanilla scent, and vigorously began working the gel in her hair. Her hair was thick, nappy if you wanted to be

Old Friends; New Lover

honest, so she dug deep. Renee raked her nails across her scalp. She moaned at the secret feeling of having her scalp massaged. She smiled and gently swayed her hips to her own sexual sound track. Renee leaned into the water's stream and wondered how long it would take for her to have an orgasm from having her scalp massaged. Maybe Lee could help her find out.

She shrugged her shoulder and thought. "Maybe he could."

She applied more apple-scented shower gel to her loofa, and slowly scrubbed away the feel of the un-sexual outside world. She made sure to get those *"hard to freak"* places and those places she hoped Lee wouldn't forget to freak again. Renee reached between her thick thighs, and scrubbed her vagina. Her eyes instinctively rolled toward the back of her skull. She parted her labia and exposed her clitoris to the treatment. Renee cursed at the lightheaded feeling that flushed her brain. She often told people she didn't masturbate. But she did admit to washing herself for long periods of time. Renee knew she had gotten by on a technicality. She "washed" herself close to orgasm before moving on to the rest of her body. She didn't want to cheat her or Lee out of any fun. She smirked, thinking she didn't bring that stuff in the bag for nothing.

Lee heard the water stop and moved across the bed to wait on Renee. After his own shower, he oiled himself down and now could smell the soft scent of the musk oil. He could hear her rummaging around the bathroom, before he opened the door and stepped into the room. Lee had always liked how hotel rooms positioned the bed so that a person could

SexPressions

see into the bathroom in the mirror that hung on the opposite wall. He wondered if the room's designers were aware of that little voyeuristic flaw; maybe so, because it was like that in most hotel rooms. He watched Renee walk from the bathroom, adjusting the towel she wrapped around her body. No need for that, he thought, it barely hides assets. She moved from the steam and around so Lee could see her. He blew her a tender kiss and waved her forward. Renee moved to the bed and slowly stalked over to him. He shivered as her breath passed over his exposed skin. He moved his hands to her thick hair. She kept her eyes on Lee now. She felt like a panther. She had always wondered how it felt to stalk one's prey and if it felt anything like this, then panthers were lucky. Lee tried to look away, to maybe halt the attack. She grinned a knowingly seductive leer.

"No where to run honey." She thought."

Lee watched her slowly move over him. He rubbed her head, softly massaging her scalp as he coaxed her higher, not wanting her to stop along the way. His ebony thickness, pushed against the restraint of his underwear. She moved higher still. He puckered his lips and awaited the feel of hers. Renee delicately kissed his chin, before sucking. And that's how the fun began. Lee held the sides of her face. He slid his hands between her skin and the towel, searching for the makeshift knot. He liked how her naked skin felt against his own. He loosened the towel and wrestled it free. Her body was noticeably warmer than Lee's. His body gasped in surprised delight. He searched for Renee with his mouth and held onto her like a dazed boxer. She carefully began grinding against him. She could feel his stiff penis pressing against her labia. Her wetness coated the head of

Old Friends; New Lover

his penis. She knew he was ready, but she wanted him to beg. She began toying with him as if he were an ebony, sexual mouse. She pushed up from Lee and straddled him. She slowly rotated her hips and tenderly clawed at his chest. He squirmed beneath her felinistic touch. Renee saw the items arranged on the night stand.

"Don't move." She whispered. Lee licked his lips and nodded in agreement.

She grabbed the blindfold first. The she snatched the small chain so that it didn't make a sound. She tied the blindfold over his eyes. Lee smirked as the room went black.

"Hands off." She ordered.

Her voice changed slightly. It became more dominate. Lee took quick notes and obeyed.

"She was in control." He told himself. "For the time being anyway." Renee placed the padded alligator clips to his nipple. She found pleasure at the sight of him wincing. She pulled the chain tight. The middle of the chain held smooth beads. Renee made three loops with the beads around his penis and attached the other clip to his free nipple. Lee squirmed, wiggled, and feigned protest. His penis grew long and wide in its restraint. She removed a condom from the night stand and placed it over his bead-covered erection. He wince became a polite smile as Renee slowly stroked his sex. Lee sat confused and excited. He opened his mouth wide, exhaling slowly. The chain tugged at his innocent nipples with each movement. He opened and clinched his fist. His palms tingled and burned lightly.

SexPressions

Renee, gently at first, slowly moved her hand along his long, brown sexual muscle. She allowed giddiness to well up in her. She thought she would soon have to use two hands. The pearl beads rolled with her grasp. She cursed inside of her head. She wished she had brought a ruler. Because there was no way his penis could grow as large as it felt. If it was, she had to have it in her.

"Hands Off! I said." She spoke aloud, as his hands slowly moved across her naked legs.

He closed his eyes and smirked with embarrassment. She stroked his length and tugged softly on, the chain.

"Damn." He spat, each letter tasting tart and robust as it left his tongue. Lee held his eyes closed as Renee stroked him. He slowly rolled his hips beneath her grip. She could feel his orgasm bubbling and growing hot beneath his skin.

"This is my dick." She told him in a domineering tone.

Renee gently kissed him on his stomach. She tasted the traces of his maleness. They quivered from the touch of her lips and tongue. She moved higher over his body. She reached his nipples and ran her tongue over each of them Lee jumped from the eager intrusion. Words ran through Lee's head but none of them could reach his mouth. All he could come up with was ass-clenching grunts. She gripped the base of his pearl bound penis and sucked the area just below his neck. Thick wetness moved between her thighs. Fear asked Renee if she was ready.

Old Friends; New Lover

"No." Renee answered, "I'm scared of this dick."

Renee moved higher onto Lee. She kissed his neck and chin; finally, she kissed him softly on his mouth.

A tear softly whispered, "I love you, Lee", as it slipped past her lips.

Lee welcomed the feel of Renee atop him. He cheered the slight pain at his nipples. He felt exhausted, yet alert. Only the promise of good love making brought on such a feeling. He defied her orders and caressed her ass cheeks. He knew he loved her. He knew that it from the first time he heard her speak with an adult voice. Love draped itself over them like a light blanket. Love now told Lee to savor the moment. It commanded that he not worry about other nights; those belonged to her husband and family.

"She is yours tonight." Love said, "And that's all that matters."

Lee gasped and held onto her as she guided him into her warmth. Lee/Renee felt the pearls push her walls; gently rolling over several sensitive spots all at once. He pushed himself further into her; Renee grinded softy and slowly against him and his pearled penis. He pulled downward on her shoulders, causing her to sit up. Now the chain taunted her clitoris from within. Smooth latex covered beads brushed the ridge sensitive area just inside her vagina. He clenched her breast in his palms, caressing each with hunger and appreciation. He kissed each swollen nipple, bit them delicately, and then transferred the small clamps on them. Renee sneered in disdainful glee.

SexPressions

"MuthaFucker!" She silently yelled, reaching behind her to caress his frightened scrotum, as she slowly started riding his erect penis. Lee pushed up into her, cursing the soft blindfold that didn't allow him the sight of her passion in action. He felt her body twitch with each upward penetration. He tugged at the chains, forcing high pitched moans to splash against his chest. Their tempo had increased. Sweat lightly covered her forehead. He smacked her ass cheeks, before grabbing them roughly. A small tremor was born deep within him. Renee's vaginal walls kneaded and massaged his penis. The pearled chain enhanced the sexual taunts.

" This pussy is too much for you!" Lee heard in his head.

"You can't handle this monster." Renee heard at the same time.

She placed her palms on his upper abdomen and worked her pelvis. She could feel her thighs quivering; threatening to lock. Her nipples slowly began to swell, pushing the small clips further open. She leaned forward and began sucking hard on Lee's neck and shoulder's. He grabbed her shoulders, his orgasm was surely coming. The tremor that had been small and cool, had now grown large and fiercely hot. He only wanted to expel the feeling. The blindfold had worked its way higher on his face, allowing Lee to peek from beneath it. He saw the look of determination on Renee's face. She bit her lip and held a scowl of fierce disapproval on her face.

"A bitch shouldn't have to work this hard, to feel this

Old Friends; New Lover

good." The look said.

She dug her nails into Lee's skin. He fought his natural urge to wince. They spat a quick cadence of *'damn's and 'yes's*. She felt her asshole pucker and a sweet hot flash consumed her. She told her body to stop moving and allow the orgasm to have its way. But her sexual inertia was too strong, and Lee wasn't a part of her body. She felt her pelvis slowly continue moving over his stiff penis. She was sure she asked him to give her a moment's rest, yet he continued moving; his own orgasm gathering just below the head of his penis.

Lee felt possessed as he kept pumping. Why wouldn't Renee stop rocking? He wondered. He could barely stand it. He pulled the clamps from his nipples. He wanted to be free of the sweltering sex waves that were deep within him. He guided Renee from atop of him, and then tossed the blindfold from his eyes.

"Damn this!" He thought.

Renee slowly heeded his silent orders. She wanted to rest; to sleep if possible. She limped off of his body, still quivering and jumping, then slumped forward. He pulled the condom and pearl chain from his length, freeing the thick bulge. He moved behind her. He warned her with a gentle well-placed kiss at the small of her back. Renee realized it was too late. She felt his hand slowly moving her ass cheeks over. Her sexual entrance was presented to Lee as if he'd spoken a magical word. Lee gripped the base of his penis and slowly moved it into Renee's exhausted vagina. She balled the sheets into her fist and accepted her fate. She felt

SexPressions

him move past her thick sexual lips. The head of his penis felt extremely hot, as his blood were boiling. She secretly wondered if his penis were angry. She hoped it was. She rested her head against a pillow, as he slowly filled her. He felt larger, he went deeper. The feeling of his orgasm caused him to rush his movements. After two slow introductions strokes he began moving. His scrotum swung forward and hit her clitoris. Soon he felt his stomach begin to tighten. Primal grunts roared from his throat. Renee exhaled and panted with each movement. Aftershocks of her orgasm had begun. Renee tried to open her eyes but couldn't. Lee held her by her waist and pushed and pulled them together.

"Damn!" Lee grunted as his orgasm rushed forward. His body shook, and then froze as his penis pumped hot sperm deep into Renee. She gasped and slowly moved back into him, coaxing every drop from. Lee gained control and slowly moved himself into her. His thick manhood slowly pumped and twitched. Lee felt his tongue began to itch as his extremities tingled. He was sure his pinky toe had gone numb. He slump forward and collapsed next to Renee. They faced each other; eyes locking. They wanted to talk. He had things he wanted to tell her. She had feelings she had to reveal to him, but they just lay within each other's space only touching with their eyes and hearts. Soon they kissed. More bouts of love-making and sex were present. That would be for later, their eyes agreed for now they only wanted to lie next to each other, as OLD FRIENDS AND NEW LOVERS.

Yellow and the Drum

Paul pressed the stop button on his small tape recorder, blessing Professor Thomas for allowing him to record her lectures, although he had already planned to secretly record the sessions with or without her permission. It was much easier having the recorder placed on his desk in plain view, especially given the fact that a couple of times he'd fallen asleep. Paul quickly jotted down study notes for himself and the study group. They didn't meet for another day, but it was always better safe than sorry. He's He had been studying, but hated being unprepared even more. Plus he liked being the older, smarter guy. The rest of the members of his study group were younger women. He laughed at the thought of being a dirty old man at thirty--five.

"So did you enjoy my class Mr. Myers?"

Professor Thomas stood next to Paul's desk as he organized his belongings. A soft, sweet scent surrounded him and introduced her sexuality to his senses.

"So it's Mr. Myers now, huh?" He laughed, stopping his actions long enough to smile then wink flirtatiously at

SexPressions

the Professor. She smiled and moved close to him. She placed her hands on the desk, displaying her deep cleavage.

"So have you thought about my invitation?"

"Wouldn't miss it for the world, Charity." He said, singing her first name. "Wouldn't miss the new you that you've been telling me about."

"Okay. Remember you said it. Be at this address by eight o'clock, and please don't be late." She hoped she sounded commanding as she handed him her address.

Professor Charity Thomas walked away slowly, her size 22 frame swaying sexually to an internal melody.

"Wouldn't miss it for the world." Paul whispered to himself.

Paul checked his watch as he pulled into the long drive and smirked at his early arrival. He had to admit it; he was anxious to see what Charity has had in store. He and Charity had dated when they were younger and had lost contact. Actually her father made them lose contact. Now fifteen years later, Paul *just happened* to find her teaching a course in African American studies. They went out on a few dates, reacquainting themselves with each other's lives. He told her of his life in the Army's Special Forces. She filled him in on her living throughout Africa, and that's how the invitation came about.

"I'm a daughter of the Wuntu tribe." Charity said. She sipped her wine. The light from the candle danced in her

Yellow and the Drum

gray eyes. Paul was hypnotized. He nearly missed the part about Domination.

"Not like the Europeans." She laughed softly. "It's hard to explain, you have to see for yourself." So how could he turn down a chance to learn more about his African culture? A chance to see a more sexual side of Charity Thomas, a far cry from the awkward, naive woman he knew before. Also it was a fantasy of his to sleep with his teacher. Charity told him of how the Wuntus were a female dominated society, where the women were the leaders. They were the scholars, musicians, and artists. And the role of the men was that of hunters, defense and sex. "Mostly sex," He remembered her saying as she slowly caressed his hand causing him to giggle, and then laugh. He continued the dinner trying not to seem distracted. He nodded his head as she spoke, secretly visualizing her braided quaff dangling above him as she slowly moved atop of him. She had gained some weight since he last saw her, but it only enhanced her sexuality. Paul rewound the impromptu history lesson, thinking of her as her new self. He could easily see how something like the Wuntu Tribe's lifestyle appealed to her. He remembered himself slowly placing forkfuls of food into his mouth and shaking his head in affirmation. Although, she asked him multiple and various questions, most of which were not of the "yes or no" type, he only heard two.

"Will you come to our gathering?" and "Do you think you can submit to me?"

The second question Paul remembered her asking in a hushed tone as he held her close to him, later that night.

SexPressions

"Yes I can." He told her *and* himself as well. "I could very easily submit to you."

So as he sat in the driveway, he smiled. He could feel himself glowing with eager enthusiasm. He truly and honestly wanted to belong to a woman. He was even happier at the fact that the woman would be Charity.

I'll submit to you." He whispered it quietly. Now it was an oath, his new battle cry.

Paul stepped from the car and stood in front of a large Colonial-style home. The house was a fair distance from the street, but the long drive way enhanced the look and feel of a majestic estate. It appeared to Paul to be well maintained. It definitely showcased a woman's touch. It was well lit without being over-bright. Cozy was the word he felt in his throat. Even with its size, the place seemed cozy and welcoming. Paul glanced around then stepped onto the porch. He checked his watch then rang the doorbell. A loud harmonic series of bell chimes sounded throughout the house and could be heard clearly on the outside of the home. Soon the sound of a woman laughing then yelling to be heard neared the other side of the door. Paul unconsciously dusted his clothing, just before the woman peeked through the small window to the side of the door. She smiled politely allowing the curtain to fall close.

"It's him!" She yelled back into the house. Paul naturally assumed someone else answered with," Who?" Because the woman yelled back, "Who else?"

Yellow and the Drum

A series of clicks and clacks were heard, and then the door was slowly pulled open.

"Hello. I'm Paul Gordon, and ..."

"We've been expecting you." The woman answered, holding the door open for him "Sister Camara is getting prepared." She ushered him into the house, smile growing in size and friendliness, as if it were holding back a laugh or giggle.

"Thank you." He said, lowering his voice.

"I am Limbe Akili. If you need anything before the ceremony, just ask me. You can wait here until Sister Camara is ready." She pointed to a small room to the left of the atrium. Again Paul thanked her and moved into the room. He took a seat on the large sofa and let his mind drift. What was this ceremony? He couldn't wait to find out.

Joyce Mitchell, known to her sisters as Limbe Akili, nearly burst with joy. She thought about the happiness in Camara's words when she told the Daughters about her beau. She could see why now. He had a gentle look, but the way he stood, told her that he was strong, he had a warrior's strength, a strength only known from carrying around a lifetime of heavy burdens. Joyce was happy for her. She had told the entire tribe about him and even then her face was bright with happiness. Limbe (Joyce) knocked on Camara Bunmi's door; smile never diminishing.

SexPressions

"He's here!" She said, slowly pushing the door open. Limbe eased inside of the room and slowly closed the door behind her.

"I see why you're so happy." she said, before scanning the room for Camara (Charity). Limbe called her name and moved to the small bathroom. Limbe could hear soft sobs coming from the bathroom as she neared the door. She called out Camara as she neared the door. She stepped inside of the bathroom and her heart was broken immediately. Camara's back was to her. She stood naked in front of the sink, head hanging. Her body shook as deep sobs erupted from her.

"Sis what's wrong?"

Camara raised her head and look at herself in the mirror. Her arms were loosely embracing her body. She was wearing, what Limbe thought to be the cutest she'd ever seen, lilac bra and panty set. Tears lightly moistened her face as she tried to respond to Limbe's question.

"I'm scared." She said, moving her hand to wipe her face. "He'll be my first. He has always been my first."

Limbe moved forward to comfort her. "She's going to collapse." Limbe thought.

"He'll think I'm fat. Just look at me." She said, and flung her arms out. "That was the first thing he said, that I had gained weight."

Yellow and the Drum

Limbe wrapped her arms around Camara as her knees buckled. Camara's body heat strengthened Limbe's muscles like the warmth of the sun's rays. Camara began to babble as tears fell against Limbe's shoulder. Limbe had never seen Camara so unsure of herself before. She wasn't used to this side of her. Limbe guided Camara out of the small bathroom to the bed. Holding her mentor/sister/mother by the head, she allowed her to cry. She whispered comforting words into her ear. She had to, that's what Camara would do for her. Limbe wasn't embarrassed by the tears; just as she knew Camara wasn't embarrassed to shed them. Camara had spent many a night doing the same for her and the other sisters. Camara was the tribe's Mother of Fire. She watched over them. She was their sense of comfort, security and love.

"He'll love you just as we all do." Limbe said, her heart pounding, "With his entire heart." Both of the women tightened their embraces.

Paul stood before the full-length mirror, inspecting his clothes. He couldn't remember the last time he'd felt this way: frightened, nervous, and unprepared. He had dated many women before, some of important status and prestige. But this was *Charity Thomas*. No! Professor Charity Thomas. She was his "Eve." She started his history of women. Charity didn't know it, but he had lost his virginity to her. The uncomfortable feeling of nervousness overcame him as the re-run of that day played in his head. He had no recourse but to giggle at the sound of his inexperienced sexual questions echoing in his memory. He wanted dearly for her to be pleased with him. His penis grew warm and firm against his leg reassuring him. Again he heard her

SexPressions

question from across the dinner table. His entire body shook as his memory played his answer again.

"Now man up!" His body whispered. He'd never willingly allowed himself to be broken, and here was his one true love asking him to not only give up, but turn himself completely over to her. The idea of surrendering had never sounded so appealing. He felt like a virgin all over again.

"What about her other men?" A spiteful voice asked from inside of him. A frown crept across his face. He hadn't really given that side of the matter any thought. Paul paced around the room refusing to let his mind wonder. He could do that later. Now he just thought about how to make Charity happy. "Fuck' em. If she has other men then they should worry."

Paul heard a small, quiet commotion outside of the room and out of his view. He could easily make out the voices of happy women; one "shushing" the others, yet another trying to muffle a high-pitched giggle. He couldn't get as an accurate number of how many there were. So all he could do was wait. His heart pounded in his chest. Paul licked his lips and waited. When what felt to him like a lifetime had passed, the room's double doors were slowly and quietly pushed open. The small-framed woman who has had greeted him stood in front of a group of women. Paul counted nine, all different in size shape and complexion, all smiling, yet serious.

"You've been invited to this house as a guest." The woman Paul knew as Limbe said. "You've come this far, yet

Yellow and the Drum

you have quite a way to go." She stared directly at Paul. Her words were warm and stern. She spoke to Paul as if she were in control.

"She is." Paul's heart said.
"You were asked a question along with your invite. Repeat it."

"Can I submit?" The words came from his lips filled with anxiety.

"Now repeat to me and my sisters your answer."

"I can submit to her. I *will* submit to her." Paul added the last part for effect. The woman nodded in affirmation as her entourage smiled behind her. Paul saw how happy they were to hear this.

"From this moment forth you are hers."

Limbe Akili stepped forward until she was directly in front of Paul. He wondered if she saw him flinch. His blood raced hot through his veins.

"You must be prepared. Please undress completely." She pointed to a large gray robe that lay across one of the sofa's arms. "I'll be outside of this door. Knock when you are done." Limbe turned and walked softly out of the room. The small group of women quickly dispersed into the house, each happy and excited. Paul stood in amazement. His body was awake and eager. His thick penis grew long and scorching against his thigh. Paul turned to began getting undressed. He heard the doors close slowly behind him. He

SexPressions

unbuttoned his shirt. Then behind him he heard the doors softly open. A sliver of light cut into his dimly lit room.

"Thank you for coming." A voice said. "She deserves a good man." It was Limbe Akili. "My sister has yet to choose anyone and now you. She deserves to be happy as well, and she is very happy about you being here." Paul heard the doors closed behind him. He wondered if either of them knew how happy he was to be here. He listened to the sound of Limbe moving softly around outside of the door.

Paul quickly undressed. He slipped into the robe and tightened the belt around his waist. He mouthed the words *African Dominatrix* to himself and finally allowed his sexual mind to wonder. It would be good for an old dog to learn a few new tricks. He knocked lightly on the door. This time Limbe opened the door with assurance. She smiled at Paul. Her face was bright. She was dressed in a soft purple colored skirt and white raw cotton shirt. No words were exchanged. Paul saw it in her eyes; things had changed. It was serious now. She led him down the hall. Her pace was fast and full of authority. Paul struggled to keep up and held the robe securely. He felt like a private fresh out of basic training. Limbe never checked to see if she had lost him. He knew she was aware of his presence. They turned another corner and stopped in front of another set of double doors. Paul suddenly noticed how quiet it had gotten. He could actually feel the hush, as if even the walls were paying attention. He wanted to speak, and then realized his words would sound small and useless. So he stood naked beneath his robe, intimidated by this woman and those doors.

Yellow and the Drum

"Stay here." She said over her shoulder, "I'll announce you."

Paul didn't answer. None was needed. He did what he was told. Limbe stepped through the doorway, leaving Paul alone wondering if he'd ever had an erection as intense as the one he had now. With that he thought of Charity. He wondered what part she played in all of this. He knew it didn't really matter. He was very much in love with her. If she had asked him to come here and walk over hot coals, then he would. A soft chuckle washed over his lips, as he wondered how true that might turn out to be. He thought about how sure of herself she had become. Confidence was always something he found sexy in a woman, even more now because it was Charity. Habit overcame Paul as he look at his wrist to check for the time, finding no watch at all, he was left to do was wait. He fidgeted and sang softly to himself. He placed his ear against the door and tried to listen. All that accomplished was giving him a cold ear and a feeling of spying. Finally the door opened and a woman of average height and build stepped out and closed the door. She smiled at Paul and moved quickly past him. Paul watched her disappear into a room halfway down the hall. She reappeared after only a few minutes, carrying a large vase and a large terry cloth bath towel. She vanished back into the room's dimness. Paul exhaled loudly, clearly the sound of an impatient person. He would wait, but he wouldn't like. Soon Limbe opened the door.

"Don't speak until told to do so." She said, ushering him into the room. Paul nodded his head and stepped forward. He moved into the center of the room and slowly took everything in. Although the lights were off, the room

SexPressions

was still bright due to the amount of candles. He wasn't sure if the mood was meant to be intimate or solemn. He settled on the latter. The room was either a large dining room or a small ballroom. He could see how an event like an old fashion coming out would be held here. Paul quickly counted thirty women, not including Charity and Limbe, before losing count; he believed the number was fewer than one hundred. He was suddenly overcome with a powerful feminine aura. All these women of different sizes, shades, and ages, stood around him. They all wore white blouses with skirts of different colors. Charity's was red with an orange hem. He assumed the colors had some importance. The women wearing red and orange skirts, Paul counted fifteen of them, stood toward the front of the semi-circle. Paul finally rested his eyes on Charity and welcomed the warmth in her eyes. Charity took a deep breath and softly began to speak.

"You know me as Charity Thomas. Although that is my birth name, here, I'm known by another." She stared past him now. Unsure if she should make eye contact. From somewhere in the room the sounds of drums played. The tempo was slow, yet powerful. The drums spoke to her, strengthened her. Calm moved across her face. She was a beloved and honored matriarch of this family.

"When you're inside of this house. Inside of these walls you will address me as Camara Bunmi. "

Paul softly repeated the name trying not to move his lip. "The name has different literal meanings, but for me, for this tribe." She paused and looked around. "For my sisters and daughters, it means *Teaching from experience is my*

Yellow and the Drum

gift." Paul swallowed hard. He took this for exactly what it was; a history lesson. "I am the one who brought this way of life to them. I taught them the tribe's way, what was taught to me. We are the Sisters and Daughters of the Wuntu tribe."

She began walking around the room stopping to hold hands briefly. A few of the women wiped tears. Others nodded in agreement to an unasked question. As if by looking at them Camara was asking them to verify her words, to lend credibility to her speech. This is the truth, their faces said, the utter and complete truth. Paul watched her move around the entire room. She spoke of the Wuntu tribe's history and the history of the house itself. She spoke to the women, past and present; to him as well. She wasn't the oldest of the women, but she clearly was the most respected. Paul saw that they loved her, just as he did.

"So let's begin." She said as she returned to nearly the same place she had began. "There are some things you must do before I can accept you as my own. Will you do what I ask?"

"Yes." He answered.

"From this moment forth will you take my words in your hear heart and wear my colors?"

"Yes." The single word felt heavy and empowered leaving his tongue.

SexPressions

"Just as I have taken on a different name, so shall you." She moved toward him. She used her eyes to reach out to him.

"I'm nervous and scared." Her eyes said.

"You're doing fine." His eyes answered. They stood for a second silently comforting each other.

"There are two reasons for the name; one, so that you have a constant reminder that in this house things are different. We are different here. Do you understand?"

"Yes."

"The other reason and the one I believe is the most important, It give it connects you to your African self. The person you may have been if you started off there. It connects you to the entire tribe; The men of the past and those of the present."

Paul nodded he understood without having to be asked.

"You will be known as Gamba Kayode. It means the warrior who brought joy. My sisters chose the name. I know it doesn't roll off the tongue, but it's yours."

A series of soft chuckles swept through the room.

"It's the name I'm giving you. Do you accept it?"

"Yes." Gamba repeated the name to himself and replayed it in his head. A warm feeling was born in him. He

Yellow and the Drum

felt as if he was changed slightly. Like getting a well needed haircut, or a tattoo with a very special meaning.

"Gamba Kayode." He whispered to himself again.

His body began to slowly heat up. He felt new and pure.

Camara nodded her head slightly, signaling the two women, one on each side of him, to step forward.

"Now you must be presented to the tribe, so that no matter where you are you will be known to be mine."

Without warning the two women pulled the robe from Gamba's shoulders, exposing his nude physique to everyone present. He felt himself gasp. His penis hung, half erect, between his legs. He held his chest out and head up. He knew an inspection when he saw one. He was proud to be her man. They should see that he was worthy. The entire room surrounded him. A few requested he lift his feet but mostly they took him in visually. They moved their eyes over his scars. They saw his muscular, hairless chest, his strong warrior thighs. A few read the Latin words tattooed on his back. They inspected his jaw and visually reviewed his hands. No one touched him. No brushing against him. No mockingly smacking his buttocks. No caressing his developed arms. He wasn't for them. The pleasure of his touch was Camara's and hers alone. Finally they returned to the other parts of the room and watched.

"How do you find him, Sisters?" Camara asked.

SexPressions

Limbe looked around before stepping forward. "We find him well. We have all seen him and will know him from any direction."

"Thank you, Sister." Camara said.

She turned and retrieved something from a small table behind her.
"These are my colors; one necklace and one bracelet."

She held her hands out before her and allowed a beaded necklace to dangle from her right hand and a bracelet from her left. There were two large red beads in the middle then smaller red ones, three on each side. Orange beads were then connected; those were edged by a yellow bead on each end. This pattern was repeated on the bracelet, although the beads were somewhat smaller.

"If you'll notice, red is the dominant color. Outside of these walls, outside of this tribe, it has many interpretations, some good and others not so good. Here, it is the color of passion and life. It is also the color of the heart. Notice I didn't say the color of love, but of the heart. It is a very important color to me."

Her voice was steady. She didn't speak low, nor did she yell. She spoke as if she were using the words to leave a mark, and the entire time she did this, Camara held the jewelry in front of him.

"The color was chosen for me by the Mother of my tribe. I was then as I am now, the heart of my house. Just as these other women are." She glanced slightly toward the

Yellow and the Drum

women standing closes to them, near the front. "The other colors you see are orange and yellow. Orange is the color of comfort and flame. It signifies my station as the Tribe's Mother of Fire. For a lot of the women present, I am a source comfort. I'm a warm kind word. I am their protection from an often cold world."

A slight chill danced across Gamba's body.

"Yellow is the color of nourishment. It is the color of the sun. For us, it is the color beauty. "

She smiled now and for the first time he noticed all the women wore something yellow. Most of the accessories were small; a ribbon here, a scarf there. Earrings. Fingernail polish. Watches. They all wore something yellow. They all were beautiful in some way. His eyes repeated what his brain and heart had just learned. Camara smiled in acknowledgment.

"The colors that you don't see but are present are black and brown, simply because these are the colors of the people. And black was the color that was there before we were. Do you understand what has been told to you?"

"Yes."

"Good. Now the bracelet must be worn at all times, just as you would a wedding band. It is how you carry my name. The necklace is to be worn inside of this house. You may wear it outside but you <u>must</u> wear it inside."

SexPressions

Gamba felt his heart beat growing stronger and stronger. It beat in time with the drums. It rocked and moved his entire body. Then he realized it wasn't his heart. It was his very erect penis. He was extremely aroused. What man wouldn't be aroused standing naked in front of all these beautiful women?

"Need to get a copy of that drum music." He thought to himself.

"If I ask you to wear the necklace when we are alone outside of this house, you must. If these are ever broken, you must return to me and this house and have them replaced." He nodded his head. She lifted the necklace higher while he lowered his head. She gently draped the necklace around his neck and positioned them softly against his chest. Then fastened the bracelet around his wrist. He welcomed the warm weight of the colors. He liked how they felt against his skin, against his heart. She moved closer to him and stood close enough for him to feel her heat.

"You are mine. We now belong to each other."
And before he could answer, she kissed him. Her touch set off sexual explosions through his body. For the first time that he could remember, Gamba nearly fainted.

"Sister I present to you Gamba Kayode Bunmi. My first man; my Adam."

Suddenly the sound and presence of the large number of women washed over them in a wave. There was clapping and cheerful laughter. The lights were turned on. Some of the women thanked him, while others waved and smiled.

Yellow and the Drum

Nearly all of them hugged or kissed Camara. She held his hand tightly. She steadied her emotions with his touch.

"Please follow Sister Limbe," she told him softly. "She'll show you to my room.

Limbe stepped forward. Her contagious smile alive on her face.

"Please wait outside. I'll take you up."
They all watched him move through the jovial crowd and out to the door. Once the doors were closed, a roar of laughter and cheer erupted throughout the room. Limbe quickly hugged Camara again.

"I can see why you were happy to see him. Sure you can handle all of him?" She joked.

"I'm surely going to try." Camara raised her left eyebrow and laughed. A large bottle of wine was opened and passed around. Camara was offered the first glass which she took gladly. "Damn his dick is big," she whispered to herself, hoping Limbe didn't hear her. She gave it some thought, swallowed the wine in one gulp and requested another.

"So how do you feel?" Limbe asked, as they walked down the hall. She neither walked ahead, nor behind him.

"I feel good. If I had known I was getting married I would've told my family." He joked. "But I feel good. I feel new."

SexPressions

She smiled her head slightly. She knew the feeling.

"Most of the men feel that way. To be honest the ceremony is usually shorter."

"Why all the extra stuff?"

"Because she wanted to do it right. Plus you only have one first man." Gamba rocked his head in an "umm-okay" manner. They stopped in front of a door and faced each other. "Here we are brother. Make yourself comfortable. She won't be long." Limbe turned to walk away.

"One last question."

"Okay." She said, slowly turning to face him.

"I was wondering about the little inspection. What was that about?"

She exhaled softly and suppressed laughter.

"Two reasons... One, she was showing off. You're a handsome, well built man." She tried her best not to gawk. "Secondly, so no one will have an excuse. We've all seen you naked. So none of the sisters can say that didn't know you were her man. We all know what you really look like. We try and express sisterhood, but we ain't fools. Now like I said brother, she won't be long."

They both laughed. He disappeared into the room and she down the hall.

Yellow and the Drum

Gamba Kayode stood with his back to the door. He used his entire body to absorb the room. Camara had decorated and arranged everything with passion in mind. Whether that passion be meant for her or someone else. He took small cautious steps. The bed was large. It was covered with fluff and comfort. The room smelled of lilac and sandalwood. There was a large mirror against the wall that was used as a headboard. A large orange and red throw rug covered the floor between the bed and a hutch. Two orange three-wick tower candles sat in opposite comers. The flames cast shadows that welcomed him further into the room. Next to the nightstand, was a doorway that opened to an adjoining bathroom. He stood in the middle of the room and slowly turned. He tried to take everything in. Closing his eyes, he mentally blindfolded himself. He could taste the contrasting scents of the incense. He listened to the comforting invitation of the bed as he ran his hand over the blankets. He smelled the intimate lightning of the candles. This comfort was for him.

"Is it to your liking?" Camara asked, easing into the room.

He nodded and softly answered, "yes," without opening his eyes or turning around to face her. He felt the warmth of the room.

Camara moved past him into the bathroom.

"Come in here." She said.

He opened his eyes and followed her. From his vantage point he missed the full bathtub. He noticed the

SexPressions

wisp of steam rising from the surface. Camara sat on the side of the large tub and waved him over. She let her hands play slowly in the water; testing it the temperature. Gamba covered the short distance and stopped in front of her and the tub. He leaned forward and kissed her softly on the forehead. A soft masculine smell greeted his nose. He noticed the small oily circles floating in the water. Gamba eased himself into the bath water, exhaled softly, and slowly he rested against the back of the tub.

Camara wet a large sponge and quickly rubbed soap across it.

"Surprised?"

"Yes. Pleasantly. I thought I was going to meet a few of your friends." He laughed, filling the small room with the sounds of a man.

"I'm just glad you're happy."

Without lifting his head or opening his eyes, he raised his thumb and gave her the "thumbs-up". This little gesture sent them both into a playful laughter. She felt free. She was no longer nervous. Her heart no longer pounded. It sang. It was no longer heavy. She knew he would carry the burden of their love.

She placed the sponge on his chest and paused for a brief moment. She wondered if he felt her shaking; if he felt her trembling. She moved the sponge over his chest and neck, then his arms. She gently scrubbed his back and along his sides. She had him stand so she could wash his lower

Yellow and the Drum

half, his thighs and buttocks. She washed his knees and calves. She left his penis for last. She held his black pride in her hands and felt him grow stiff. She cleaned the head carefully. Then she wiped and stroked his shaft repeated. He thought she were was giving him a soapy hand job. She lifted his dangling balls and wiped them as well. Smiling, Camara repeated the entire task again, this time ending by cleaning his butt hole. She washed his hair. Massaging his scalp, dragging moans from his mouth.

"Okay." She whispered.

He stood, allowing her to rinse lather him completely, then rinse him. He kissed her softly on the lips and held her for a brief moment.

"
I love you," his embrace said, "I always have, and always will."

Camara kissed his chest and allowed his him to guide her to the other room. Gamba stopped in front of the bed and stood behind her. He kissed her neck and allowed his hands to roam across her body. They both panted and moaned softly. He slowly traced the outline of her breast. His palms caressed the bottom of her large curves. He was slightly embarrassed by the intensity of his erection, and then shook off the thought. He pulled her blouse quickly over her head. He hadn't seen her naked in years. The sight of her partially exposed body gave him a warm feeling. He placed his lips against her neck softly. She shuddered from his sexual attention. Camara reached behind her and pulled him close to her. She needed his heat. He removed her bra. He held her large breast in his palms. He paused for a second as if they were being photographed. He needed this moment to last for an eternity.

Finally he flexed his fingers leaving nothing but palms against her nipples. He slowly moved his palms in circular motions, barely touching her happy nipples. He continued kissing and licking her exposed back. He moved his lips and tongue lower on her back until he kneeled behind her. Camara leaned forward on the bed, nearly collapsing. She cursed as the warmth of his mouth and gentleness of his touch caused her body to jump and buck. Gamba slowly pulled her skirt and panties from her ass and thighs, then down her legs and off her feet. He felt like he was moving too fast but he couldn't stop himself. He'd been holding back for too long and could, would, no longer restrain himself.

Gamba let his hands drift from her breast, down along her back to her ass. He spread her ass cheeks and forced her to her tip toes by pressing his tongue to her exposed vagina. Her taste was mild and comforting. She was dry, and then grew wet with each pass of his tongue. Staying on her tip toes, Camara spread her legs slightly and placed her face onto the bed's softness. She knew he couldn't hear her moans and squeals if she did that. Gamba buried his face further and further into her cheeks. His tongue tapped at her sexual liquids while his nose tickled her rear hole. She tried to stop her knees from jumping. Camara pounded her hands against the mattress and babbled sexual declarations. She turned her head slightly and began crawling further up on the bed. She had to get away. She needed to regroup. She tried to catch her breath. Her body rose and fell from her attempt to breathe. Gamba crawled over her. He kissed her

Yellow and the Drum

ear. His hot erect penis brushed against her ass, slowly moving between her cheeks. He slowly lifted her by her pelvis and slid himself inside of her. She bit her lip and resisted the loud moan swelling in her throat. She questioned the feeling.

"Is this what I've been waiting for?" Then answered her own question. "This is what I've been waiting for."

She stopped moving and allowed his motions to take over. He held her by the waist and slowly moved inside of her. His thickness and heat sang to her body. She waited until his body asked hers to join the moment. She accepted and slowly rocked her pelvis and buttocks back against his pistoning sex. She heard him curse and exhaled roughly. Her breast swayed beneath her, nipples brushing against the sheets. The years of absence from his touch flooded her brain. She wanted to touch him, to hold him. Camara pushed back against him hard and with him still inside of her, she rose to her knees and leaned back. His chest welcomed the feel of her back. She swayed her hips as if she were dancing. His penis brushed against the rest of her vagina. He ran his hands along her sides. All the while he moved his hips. Being inside of her felt familiar and new. He held onto her breast, leaned forward, forcing them to fall on the bed. He kissed the back of her neck and moved from her vagina. He rolled her on her back. Gamba kissed her breast, then her soft lips. He held her left hand with his right and guided his penis into her with his other hand. Instantly Camara felt one with him. She felt their souls become intertwined. She could hear and feel the ceremonial drums with each stroke. She urged him further into her womb. She

SexPressions

moaned as the ticklish erotic feeling of his penis made her skin dance. He kissed her and hastened his pace.

"Please." She asked his body with hers.

She looped her hands around her shoulders and pulled him closer. His muscular arms began trembling slightly then shaking violently. She watched as he grunted roughly then felt the extremely hot splash between her thighs. She silently thanked his body for surrendering and humped upward into his body. Her excited clitoris soon ignited her orgasm. She grabbed the back of his head attempting to stabilize herself against the violent sexual warmth that flowed from deep within her. They both kissed and touched. Years of missed chances danced through their heads.

"This is how it should have been." They both told themselves. They continued kissing until their bodies were re-awakened. Camara kissed his cheek then straddled him.

"Now, I'm in charge." She whispered, before guiding his thickness inside of her. Gamba smiled and watched her body move over him. The snug fit coaxed him into an erotic blackness. The last thought he had before drifting off into sexual bliss was how beautiful the color yellow appeared as her necklace dangled over him, then the feeling of his toes involuntarily curling. He continued smiling as his eyes closed.

Camara watched his eyes close and grinned. She'd waited a long time to be with a man, this man, and now that he was back in her life she surely wasn't going to let something like sexual euphoria get in her way. She eased

Yellow and the Drum

down until she felt the tip of his penis touch against the back of her vaginal walls. She slowly gyrated and rocked. She allowed her movements to become random and without rhythm.

"I dreamt of this dick." She whispered, tossing her head back. He responded by stretching his grin further. Her clitoris quivered sending an aggressive feeling of sexual invincibility. "You ready for me to fuck you?" She whispered, although to him it sounded like a soft growl against his ears. Camara felt *nasty* and basked in the ill-tempered warmth.

"Yes." He finally answered, grin still across his face.

"Say it then. Tell me to fuck you."

His penis grew harder as he repeated her request. A slight thrill rushed through her as he twisted his face into a grimace with each word. She felt stronger as he grew inside of her. He belonged to her and she couldn't help but want to please him. she placed her hands onto his chocolate-carved chest, moved her legs and squatted over him.

"Grab my ass." She ordered.

His touch was still hot and powerful. He grabbed her thickness and held on for his sexual life. Camara started slow. She concentrated. Her vaginal muscles contracted around his shaft and molded herself around his shape. She lowered herself halfway down and raised herself a quarter of the way up. His penis was thick, veined, and straight, a brown masculine rod. The contoured head of his penis felt

SexPressions

like it was an attachment. Like his dick was built instead of given to him at birth. Camara eased down completely on her new pleasure and was assured that the term "Mother Nature" was precise, because only a woman would construct a feeling of such pleasure and beauty. She positioned herself until the head of his penis moved against her sexual trigger, and then she moved up and down on him. Camara again heard the drums. She rammed herself onto him. The spiritual tempo reached a steady pace, mesmerizing her. Now there was only the sound of the drum and the feeling of his dick. She forgot about the thin walls as her moans turned into rough screams.

Sounds of the drums and the feeling of the dick; she didn't care about the sweat or her weight, just drums and the dick. She ignored the fiery tingle of her orgasm. The drums pounded inside of her chest. He dug his nails into her ass cheeks and pushed upward into her. The feeling of his dick sang to her. Finally it was her turn to fall into a blissful euphoria. Gamba kept moving beneath her as she froze then shook violently. Her hands spasmed and her fingers were locked. She felt her stomach muscles tightened, and then her vaginal muscles tried to expel him. The only thing that resulted was rapid waves of electricity and hot liquid warmth. Her body twitched and quivered. Her head swam in a pool of cerebral warmth. She leaned forward, kissed him then rolled to his side.

"You got me lying in the wet spot." He whispered. She giggled and kissed his cheek. She tossed her thick leg over his, placed her head on his chest, and listened to the drums fade.

Yellow and the Drum

"Thank you for coming." She whispered. Smiling, he kissed her on the forehead and pulled her tighter against him.

Paul sat in the library going over his notes. He checked his watch and wondered how long his study group would stay. Unconsciously, he played with the beaded necklace and listened for the drums. The last two nights were filled with their sound. He and Charity had gotten closer. He didn't feel like himself. Not like Paul Gordon, anyway.

"Ya' know Professor Thomas has a brace bracelet like that." One of is his study partners said.

"Yeah," he answered, feeling empowered and secretly naughty, "she told me where to get one like hers."

Trouble with Hanna

Tavon hated arguing. He hated arguing about the bitch who, even now lay upstairs in his bed. Most of all he hated arguing with himself. On one hand Bridget was his wife. And what hurt her, in theory, should hurt him. If this wasn't Hanna, Tavon knew it would be an easy choice. But it was Hanna, so it wasn't that easy. Hanna was there during his long nights at school. It was Hanna who brought the two of them together. Hanna had even helped him fight a few times. He loved them both. Eventually he'd have to choose. Tavon hated that little fact. Bridget was his wife and Hanna was only a friend. A friend who he loved just as much as he loved his wife.

"So what do you mean *she's* upstairs", Bridget snapped, "you told me by the time I got home that *BITCH* would be gone!"

"Don't call her that. Her name is Hanna." Tavon said, moving his finger to his lips. Bridget placed her bags at her feet. She'd left two weeks ago. She needed a breather. Part vacation; part cooling off period. Mainly it was to get away from Tavon and his bitch. Why couldn't he see what she was doing to their marriage? Even Dr. McCoy said that the

SexPressions

problem was Hanna. She'd already given him an ultimatum. It was her or the bitch. Apparently Bridget had lost. But she wouldn't go without a fight. She had an attack plan. There was no way she was going to lose her husband. This was war. She outlasted his buddies. She defeated the weekly visits to the club, and this would be no different.

"Okay Baby." Bridget said, a tight smirk easing across her face. "But, before I leave I just want to show you a few things."

Bridget closed the front door and stepped completely into the house. Tavon folded his arms and watched as Bridget tossed her coat onto the sofa. She'd been wearing a long trench coat and disappointment slipped over him when he saw she was wearing a heavy sweat suit.

"So what do you have to show me?" He asked.

Mocking him, Bridget placed her finger to her lips.

"No more talk." She whispered.

Bridget walked to the middle of the spacious living room. She kept her back to him and slowly began to lift her heavy cotton shirt. The first thing Tavon noticed was the bronze toned skin. It seemed the Caribbean sun had touched Bridget all over. No tan lines. Tavon's body reminded his mind and most importantly his sex, that it had been entirely too long of a time since he'd held her close. The second thing he noticed was the butterfly tattoo that covered the small of her back, a small inscription that read, *Your Pleasure.*

Trouble With Hanna

"Does that Bitch have something like that?" She asked, peeking over her shoulder. Sexy bedroom eyes punctuated her point. Tavon shook his head "no" and wiped his mouth. She smiled knowingly at him. "I didn't think so." She thought.

Bridget bent slightly at the waist and started lowering her sweat bottoms. Her bronze-toned ass peeked out before being revealed. Three heart-shaped tan outlines decorated her tender ass. Tavon's mouth watered from the sight of her naked body. Her little get away had done her body a lot of good. He eased his eyes over her. Bridget stepped from the pants and stood naked in front of him. Part one of her attack plan was a show of force. Let him know what he was up against.

"Tee, this is what I wanted to show you. Me!" She said, slowly tracing the curves of her body. "You can't have us both." She raised her long delicate arm in the air and nestled her head into her bicep.

"But... "

"But nothing."

She knew it would be a bad idea to let him talk. His voice was smooth, yet very light. He often sounded as if he were singing. She didn't want to be hypnotized. She moved close to him and slowly moved her hand over his frame. She could feel that bitch, Hanna, in the house. Tavon stood his ground, bracing himself against her warm frame. His penis grew thick and warm against his thigh. Bridget was thin, soft

SexPressions

and brown. It had been two long weeks since he'd touched her and that was only a last ditch effort for her not to leave. He turned his head slightly and exhaled secretly. She even smelled new and refreshing. No matter what pretty fragrances he bought Hanna, she never smelled this good. And even if she did, they were only friends.

Bridget ran her hands under his uniform shirt and kissed him along his neckline. She slowly, yet purposely pulled his shirt open sending buttons flying one after another across the room. He tossed his hands in the air in protest, but was ambushed by her warm tongue against the thumb on his left hand.

"Does she do this?" She asked, looking down as momentum shifted in his eyes. "I bet she doesn't."

He wasn't sure if she were talking to him or to herself. But either way she was right. He'd never touched Hanna. Not in a sexual manner, anyway. In some places or in another life, he would've fucked her like the school ho' on prom night. The thought of having sex with her even made him sick. She was pretty, but just not his type. She was just his friend. Plus her boyfriend was German and would probably kill Tavon if given the chance. Bridget ran her tongue down the middle of his chest until she reached his navel. She felt a small trembling run down his back. She softly sucked just above his navel, before returning her way back toward his chest. He glanced down and ran his eyes over her naked frame. His thick inches pushed against his boxer briefs, begging to be free. She quickly undid his belt and unzipped his pants. Her hands savagely opened the front of his pants and roughly pulled them down along with his

Trouble With Hanna

boxers. He breathed in misguided relief as his penis flung itself out toward her. She grabbed the thick muscle by its base, feeling it pulsate in her hand. He tossed his head back and closed his eyes. He pushed an elongated exhale toward the ceiling as she slowly drug her tongue over the head of his penis, before covering that part in the warmth of her mouth. She sucked softly, placing her tongue over his hole, tickling the area around the tiny exit. Bridget stroked the length of his sex, slowly rotating her hand. She ascended then descended along his shaft. She slowly swallowed him until his brown sex nearly filled her mouth and throat. She reached her free hands between his legs and slowly caressed his ass cheeks. She continued sucking and stroking, as she pressed a random finger against his brown rear opening. Tavon felt himself levitate to the tip of his toes as at the pressure from her finger. He shivered and cursed himself for the pleasure he got from the sensation. He reached forward and braced himself against her head. Bridget peered up at him. She wanted to see the effect she was having on him. She made loud slurping noises to drive home her new enjoyment of the taste of his sex. She slowly stroked and pumped his shaft. She fought the urge to laugh, as he made, *woo-woo* noises. Bridget listened for Hanna's movements upstairs and heard none.

"The bitch probably lying in my bed." She thought, dragging her teeth across his penis for punishment. "I can't do this for you if that *bitch* is here." She told him seductively, emphasizing the word she used for Hanna. Tavon shook his head and moaned in compliance. She gave his head one last swallow, ending with a loud pop and soft kiss for good measure. She stood to her full height and kissed her husband on the lips.

SexPressions

"Let's make a baby." Bridget whispered into his ear. A smile crept across his face. He'd been pushing Bridget to stop taking her birth control for sometime now, but with no luck. Now here she was giving him what he always wanted. That was something Hanna couldn't do; carry his child. Besides he hated using condoms with his wife. He followed Bridget to the love seat. She bent over and smiled back at him. Tavon slowly guided himself deep into her. Her vagina was warm and inviting. She started with slow lengthy movements. He placed his hands on the small of her back and pushed her forward. This angle put friction directly to her g-spot and eased the feeling from his most sensitive areas. Bridget moaned as his stout penis moved across her ridged sexual center. He kept his hand on her back, maintaining her position. He smacked her sharply on her ass and increased his tempo. He felt his orgasm nearing while she gave him head, but now that feeling had subsided. He grimaced from the tight fit. He felt himself slowly reach his full length and smiled. She wasn't really fond of the doggy style position. He knew she only did it to get her way. She would, but not before he made his point. He continued pumping, pushing moan after breath stealing moan from her mouth. She buried her face into the plush cushions. Her orgasm was teasing her with it's approach, all the feeling of an oncoming explosion, without the fireworks at the end. She held her breast to stop them from swaying. She wasn't sure how long it had been since she'd felt this way during sex. Her hands and feet tingled. She locked her knees to absorb the pounding Tavon was giving her. Hanna or no Hanna; Bridget wanted more of this, but one thing at a time. First she had to win this battle before she picked any more fights. Bridget felt the lightheadedness of heavy orgasm. She

Trouble With Hanna

bent at the knees to relieve the pressure from her clitoris. Tavon groaned, either from pain or pleasure. Bridget wasn't sure which; she believed it was both. She slowly began to push back into his charging sex, countering his strokes.

"This is war." Bridget thought again. "The Battle of Booty Hill."

Tavon felt his orgasm mounting. Within a few strokes he'd have what he'd always wanted. He grabbed her large butt cheeks and held her in place. Bridget had won out. Hanna would just have to understand. She would if she were a true friend. Hell, he thought, he couldn't fuck her. If everything was cool maybe she could live with the German and his family. And as he neared his orgasm, he no longer cared. Let her have her way and get rid Hanna. That was the only way. As his life fluid rushed through his shaft, he pulled his penis from her awaiting womb and placed it between her butt cheeks.

Hot, life splashed across her back. He smiled and slowly tugged along the shaft. A small yelp escaped Bridget's mouth.

"We'll start making babies after you've run out of those pills."

He laughed as he smeared sperm across her ass. Bridget lay across the love seat's arm. She reached behind her and dipped her finger into the thick milky consistence cream and brought it to her mouth. She liked the sweet taste his cum had to it. As far as the rest on her back, that's what

SexPressions

showers were for. All that mattered was she and her husband would be rid of that bitch Hanna.

Tavon pulled his pants up and sulked up the long flight of stairs. She could hear the brief exchange between them. Bridget grabbed her clothes and moved to the bathroom. She couldn't stomach being around her for a second. Bridget peeked out the door and watched as he led her from the house. Bridget could hear her crying as she went. She felt a pang of remorse. Tavon was a good man, but he already had a woman in his life and he no longer needed her.

Tavon turned the music up, drowning out the sadness. He had already decided Hanna would have to go. Having Bridget come home only solidified the choice. He could tell Hanna was upset with him. He could look in her eyes and read that. But this was something he had to do. He pulled to the stoplight beside a minivan. Hanna turned her head and faced away from him and sighed. A small, quick horn toot jolted Tavon from his thoughts of fun with Hanna that had long since passed.

"Excuse me mister," the young driver of the minivan started, "What kind of dog is that?"

"Terrier Collie mix." He said back.

"My kids would love one like that. Do you have any puppies?"
"
No." Tavon started, smiling from ear to ear. "But pull over and maybe we can work something out."

Sunni and Lorraine

Fred felt like a little kid. He hadn't seen his cousin Carlos in years, After college they both did their own thing and time had just passed them by. But watching the cab pull in front of his house brought back memories. Fred stood in the doorway, smiling like a proud father. He watched as Carlos stepped from the car. He ran down the stairs to help with the bags, when he noticed the sweetest set of legs he had ever seen. The sister they were connected to was a lovely ebony-toned queen, tall and well built. Fred barely noticed the hand Carlos extended.

"Cuzzin." Carlos said, pulling Fred into a hug.

"Hey family." Fred replied, returning the hug, although his mind was still on those legs. Fred hoped he didn't poke Carlos with his little greeter. As the two men looked over each other, Carlos' friend joined the group.

"This must be Freddy." She said. Her voice sounded as if her vocal cords were laced in honey." So I guess that makes us Cousin-in-laws!" She said as she hugged Fred. Fred felt her braless firm breast press against his chest.

"Ya'll keep that up and we gone fight." Carlos laughed. "This is my wife Sunni. She's my little surprise."

SexPressions

"And what a surprise." Fred thought as he stared at his favorite cousin's favorite lady.

"Let's go inside." Fred said, turning toward the house, "And where ya'll bags?" He asked over his shoulder.

"Uh the hotel room." Carlos answered. "We didn't want to get in ya'lls way." Fred scolded him as they walked into the house. Sitting in the living room Fred made drinks while Carlos rolled a joint.

They talked, rehashing old times and stories well forgotten. After a few drinks and more joints, Fred realized Sunni had unbuttoned her top some and was staring at him. Actually he noticed she was staring at his dick as it pressed against his pants. Damn he was horny. He wished Lorraine was here. Then at least he could relieve some of this pressure he had built up. He couldn't take his eyes off those sweet brown legs of hers. They were the color of chocolate. He nearly came in his pants thinking of her. Sunni passed the joint to Carlos, stood and asked which way to the ladies room. She giggled and her nipples were erect against her blouse. And now Fred did cum in his pants. When Sunni was out of the room, Carlos leaned across smiling at Fred.

"If you stare any harder, you'll be able to see through her clothes."

Fred smiled an uneasy smile. Carlos laughed and sat back in his chair.

"It's cool, bruh. She's down with it. Let me set it up."

Sunni and Lorraine

Carlos winked at Fred. Fred puffed from the joint and wondered if he was in heaven, and as if on cue, Sunni returned from the bathroom. She sat next to Fred on the couch. She smiled and licked her lips. Now it was Carlos' turn to leave the room. He went to the kitchen to get more beer and ice. As soon as he was out the room, Sunni rubbed Fred's leg and whispered softly in his ear.

"I hope you ain't gone be scared to touch me... because I'd be sad if I couldn't have a little of that big dick of yours."

Carlos returned passing out beers. Fred couldn't believe his luck. The only thing that would make this better was for Lorraine to be here. Carlos sat on the couch creating an erotic trio sandwich.

After a few sips of his beer, Carlos began rubbing Sunni's breast. He kissed her on the neck. Fred was getting hard again. He watched as Carlos released one breast, then the other. Sunni's breasts were as beautiful as he had thought they'd be. While Carlos rubbed and kissed her breast, Sunni let her hands roam, she found the rock-hard dicks of both men. Using skillful hands she unbuttoned their pants, she removed the ebony rods and gently stroked them in unison; she twisted her hand at the top, Fred couldn't take it anymore. He leaned in and began kissing and stroking her breast. Sunni moaned. She felt like a freaky queen. She was wet and wanted out of her clothes. Sunni stood up and began removing her clothes slowly. Each man followed her lead and undressed. Sunni stood in front of them and posed. The two men were as eager as their dicks were hard. She decided to give Fred what he wanted first. She pushed him over and began kissing him on his thighs. She kissed her way up to

SexPressions

his soft sweet sack. She placed Fred's balls in her mouth and softly sucked. Fred leaned, eyes rolling and sucking hard for air. Sunni gripped the base of his manhood and licked the under side of his penis. Carlos sat back and watched the show as Sunni licked the head of Fred's dick. She glanced up at Fred with soft eyes to witness what her mouth and hands were doing to his manhood. Her eyes talked to him through each lick.

"Don't worry. You're in good hands...and lips." Fred stroked Sunni's hair, as she slowly took him into her mouth, only halfway at first. Then the warmth of her mouth shocked his senses. Sunni sucked softly on his top half, still using her tongue, she licked around the top. After a few half strokes, she slowly took Fred in. Fred inhaled hard. He was nine and a half maybe ten inches and thick around and Sunni was swallowing him whole. Although she moved faster, Sunni maintained a tender touch. Fred felt his body harden and his toes curl. He was close. Sunni felt him nearing orgasm.

"Not yet." She mouthed. Sunni rose and stood over Fred.

As if by magic, she produced a condom. Placing it in her mouth she again squatted. Taking Fred back into her mouth she slowly draped Fred's rod with the love glove.

"No hands." She said as she winked at him.

This time Sunni turned facing away from Fred, and straddled him. She was tight and the fit was snug. Sunni leaned forward and worked her pelvic area only. At this angle Sunni moved slowly over Fred's thick curved

Sunni and Lorraine

blackness. Now it was her turn to moan. Fred held onto her tight ass cheeks and pumped up at her. Driving himself deeper into her heat. Fred's girth massaged the sides of Sunni sweetness. Sunni leaned forward, adding a soft tender pressure to her black pearl. Her body tingled. Fred slowly kissed the small of her back as she sat forward. His stomach went from being slightly wet to being coated in Sunni's juices. Fred wrapped his arms around her and guided her back to him. He held her against his chest, as she rotated her hips. They moved in unison.

Carlos sipped his beer and smiled. Even though it was his wife and another man, it was a pretty scene. They meshed with-into each other like an erotic ying and yang; his light skin and her dark skin; her moan against his groan. He slowly stroked and rubbed his onyx-toned manhood, and to himself Carlos wished Lorraine was here as well.

Sunni's body began to tremble. Lying within Fred's arms and against his chest, she felt his warmth. He was still growing inside her, or at least she thought so. She continued to move her hips around her size. She bit down on her lip. She would be cumming soon. Fred kissed her neck sending ecstatic waves through Sunni's body. Fred whispered in her ear some erotic declarations. Sunni smiled and rose off Fred, barely able to stand. Fred stood and they switched places. Sunni laid on the couch, one leg on the head rest and the other Fred held against his chest. Fred crawled atop Sunni. He kissed her breast softly. Slowly he eased the full length of himself into her. Sunni gasped as her body welcomed Fred. Starting slow Fred stroked smoothly. Sunni looked at him and spoke again with her eyes said panted. "Damn this feels good," her eyes said. Sunni moved softly. She held

SexPressions

onto Fred shoulders. She breathed in his manly smells. She couldn't hold off any longer. She wiggled slowly under him as the first tremor began to take over her body. She was having two twin orgasms, one between her leg, where his sex labored, and the other along her spine into her brain. Sunni shook suddenly as she exploded. Fred felt her tighten under him. Placing the leg he held to his chest down, he placed his leg over it. Sunni gasped for air, the entire length of him now moved deeper into her, she grabbed his buttocks, not wanting to stop him, but praying he wouldn't go on any longer. Well not in front of Carlos anyway. Tears ran from her eyes as she urged Fred on and another wave shook her. Fred stroked and adjusted his angle. Sunni was tight against him. He moved her from left to right. He was close. Leaning forward he kissed her lips and held her against him. His body tightened; then trembled. With one last power thrust, Fred exploded. He bit his lip as he pumped the last of his juices into her. For what seemed like an eternity, they laid in each other's arms.

"Damn Cuzz-o." Carlos said, breaking the erotic bond.

Fred slowly rose off Sunni and slumped back against the softness of the couch, exhausted and spent, Sunni lay where she was, still cooing slightly and holding herself.

The phone rang, Carlos answered on the third ring.

"Hello. Yeah, this is Carlos. Oh hey family... Yeah he right here." Carlos handed the receiver to Fred.

After a brief conversation, Fred hung up the phone.

Sunni and Lorraine

"Lo's on her way home." The entire room smiled.

Lorraine had come home from work eager to meet Carlos and Sunni. She and Sunni had spoken on the phone secretly. it was nice to have them in the house finally. She couldn't ignore the smell of sex and seeing the lazy look in Fred's eyes told her he had been half on the action. She was slightly pissed, closer to miffed than mad, but didn't really let the situation bother her. The goose and gander thing came to mind. She and Fred had a flimsy agreement about things like that. Now it was her turn to cash in. Carlos was sitting across from her and Sunni. She had tried her best not to stare at him, but had given up on that when Sunni raised an eyebrow and smiled. Carlos nor Fred hadn't really noticed they were either laughing or watching the television. Lorraine wondered if Carlos's dick could make her gag. She had always found dark skinned brothers more sexually attractive. There were a few but never up to her stereotype of a mandigo style fuck buddy. Carlos looked like he could change that. She needed a chance to try him out. To ride that large bulge pushing along his pant leg.

"Hey baby, I need some more to drink." She said to Fred who gave her a look that said he knew.

"Yeah no thang, Lo. What ya want," He answered back.

"Dick in a black bottle she wanted to say but settle of something a little more tactful.

"You know my drink."

SexPressions

Fred nodded and smiled. Carlos tried to stand to follow Fred out the door.

"Nah Cuz, I'm straight. I'll stay here and chill."

Carlos shrugged his shoulders and flopped back into his seat. "Whatever," he grumbled. He tossed back and watched Fred walk out the door.

Carlos couldn't help but stare at Lorraine. He couldn't figure out what turned him on more. Her breasts were large and firm. She was of average height, but with long, well-toned brown legs, and thick lips that surrounded the most beautiful smile. Carlos' penis grew along his leg as he decided it didn't matter. He stared at her lips, as she sat across from him talking with Sunni. Fred had gone out to buy more refreshments, leaving Carlos alone with the women. The sat and talked as if they were old friends. The conversation was mute to Carlos' ears until a few words brought Carlos alive.

"So is his dick as big as it looks?" Lorraine asked staring at the large bulge that had grown within his boxers.

"Bigger!" Sunni giggled." And it's thick too. Show her baby!"

Confused for a second, Carlos stood and removed his black muscle from his boxers. It pointed out from his body. Lorraine smiled, reaching across the table and stroking it slowly. Her soft touch teased Carlos. Lorraine slowly moved around the table, not taking her hand from Carlos' length, and sat in front of him. She stared up at Carlos with soft

Sunni and Lorraine

bedroom eyes. Using both hands, Lorraine she stroked Carlos to his full length. She kissed the head gently, before slowly taking him into her mouth. The warmth of her mouth made Carlos weak. She stroked the bottom half as she sucked the top. Carlos wanted to scream. His body began to tingle. Lorraine used her tongue with each stroke, seeming to wrap it around the head. She slowly inched more of him into her mouth until finally Carlos full thickness was swallowed. Carlos stroked her hair and muftled soft curse words.

Sunni lay on the couch watching the show. She worked one hand between her legs while the other stroked her breast. Sunni and Carlos smiled at each other as they both neared orgasm.

Lorraine had slowly picked up her pace. She added a slight turn at the apex of her movement. Working only on the top half, she licked and sucked Carlos until he could barely stand. Carlos' knees buckled, as his body trembled. Without missing a beat, Lorraine continued at her erotic task. Carlos shot hot sex fluid into her mouth. He slumped back into the chair as Lorraine watched him with her soft bedroom eyes. They'd finished in time to watch Sunni bring herself to full pleasure.

"Your turn!" Carlos said as he pulled Lorraine to her feet.

Carlos softly kissed her belly letting his tongue peek out upon contact. Lorraine moaned softly as he drew circles around her navel. Soon Carlos kissed a trail around to the small of her back. He kissed his way to her lovely ass. His

SexPressions

kisses landed tenderly against her warm cheeks, as he slowly Carlos slow massaged her cheeks apart. He couldn't resist. He held her cheeks apart and blew softly against her 'brown eye,' before delivering a few quick darts with his tongue. Lorraine nearly fell forward from the unexpected surprise. She moaned and reached back for Carlos. He slowly licked his way back to her cheeks. He traced kisses along her spine. Carlos felt Lorraine shudder as he reached her neck and ears. Trailing kisses along her neck, Carlos arrived at her lips. He tasted his own sexual musk. He finally reached her large honey toned breast. Her nipples were warm and erect. He placed one after the other into his mouth. Carlos teased, pampered, and caressed each breast. Lorraine tingled with electricity. This was almost new. Fred knew each of her spots, but Carlos had to discover as many as he could, and he did a small celebration, as each spot was unearthed. The *sexpense* was killing Lorraine. Her thighs were glazed with her own wetness. Carlos finally reached her belly button, completing his circle. He trailed soft kisses down past her pubes. A harsh pant signaled he was in the right place. Sex marks the spot. Carlos placed Lorraine's left leg on his shoulder. He reached under her and held onto her buttocks, as he brushed his tongue across her swollen black pearl. Carlos tenderly attacked Lorraine's sweetness with his tongue. She squealed in sexual surrender. Her small white flag waved against Carlos' tongue.

Fred had come back and slipped in quietly. Lorraine's eyes were closed and he legs hovering over them both. Sunni lay in the couch and slowly rubbed her clitoris and hummed. Fred didn't know if he were more turned on by his wife naked and moaning or angry about them starting without him. Decided it didn't matter. It was a sexy sight.

Sunni and Lorraine

Lorraine felt two cool hands against her breast. Fred stood behind her, caressing her warmth-filled breast. Carlos moved his hand between her ass cheeks, teasing that hole as well. Lorraine was on the verge on exploding. Fred whispered soft encouragements into her ear.

Carlos licked greedily between her thighs and sucked softly at her sweet spot. Lorraine's body betrayed her, as an erotic eruption shot through, nearly causing her to faint. She shook as Carlos licked away at her sexual cloud. Lorraine shivered from a small aftershock. Carlos licked and sucked until he was satisfied that she was through cumming. Lorraine slumped on the sofa next to Sunni. She softly stroked the sensitive area in erotic disbelief. Carlos sat back in his chair, letting Lorraine's flavor linger on his tongue, before sipping on his beer. The four of them sat around talking and touching. Fred smiled at his cousin approvingly. Suddenly Lorraine sat up, whispered quickly to Sunni. The two women rushed past the men, mumbling, leaving them slightly confused. Carlos stared at Fred as a flash of understanding struck him. Fred pulled puffed on the joint and passed it to Carlos.

"She said 'Toys!" Fred smiled as he reclined in the chair. The word danced around in Carlos' head. He hit the joint and smiled to himself.

Carlos couldn't remember falling asleep. His last thought was of Lorraine's sex. His member throbbed in drained bliss. He pulled himself from a sex and alcohol induced nap, hoping to see Lorraine's naked body. But to his surprise neither Lorraine nor Sunni were there. He assumed they'd made another run to the store until he heard Sunni's

SexPressions

orgasmic moans. Carlos wiped his eyes and tried to gather his bearings. Was that Sunni? Then her unmistakable moan whistled throughout the house. The realization that the women were having their own party woke Carlos fully.

Carlos wanted to see the show for himself before he woke Fred. He crept up the stairs, careful not to cause any early warning creaks of wood. Once at the top not only could he hear Sunni's moans, he could also hear the distinctive sound of a vibrator's hum. The sight that captured Carlos' attention was of Sunni doggy style and Lorraine using a large golden vibrator to fuck her. Lorraine held the pleasure device as if it were her own unit. Moving it in unison with her hips. Carlos grew half stiff in his underwear. Although he'd seen his wife with other women, there was something about this time that was more entertaining. More erotic. More secret.

Carlos wanted to let Fred in on the show but he couldn't tear his eyes from the scene. Carlos let his hand drift to his black joy muscle and slowly began to mimic Lorraine's movement. If Lorraine's stroke was slow and full, so was his. When she worked only the vibrator's tip, Carlos teased the sensitive head of his sextremity. Carlos heard himself moan. Watching his wife being dominated by someone as lovely as Lorraine drove a shiver through his spine. Carlos became jealous of the encounter. And his manhood grew harder from the new sensation. But not only had Lorraine overtaken Sunni's body, she had him in her spell as well. She tugged at his strings like an erotic puppet master. Carlos felt his hand clench tighter around the shaft of his dick. He exhaled louder than he thought. He hoped no one heard him. He hoped he hadn't disturbed them. He froze

Sunni and Lorraine

as Lorraine turned and made eye contact. She smiled, quickened the pace of her hand strokes, and then smacked Sunni on her beautifully raised ass.

"Take that!" Lorraine whispered through Carlos's lips.

He saw Sunni begin to tremble as Lorraine smacked her after each thrust.

"Beautiful, ain't it?" Fred asked from behind.

Carlos wondered how much of the show his cousin had seen. The smile on Fred's face told him he'd seen more than enough. Carlos turned his attention back to the show as Lorraine slowly removed her golden "dick." Sunni panted and collapsed onto the bed. She smiled at her husband and his cousin, wondering to herself if they were enjoying what they saw. She let her hands move across her body. Her nipples were erect and sensitive. At Lorraine's urging she spread her legs and welcomed her tongue against her queasy clitoris. Sunni closed her eyes and exhaled slowly. She held he breast firmly and teased her nipples. She'd been with women before, but this was better. Lorraine had taken possession of her. She wrapped her legs around Lorraine's neck and pulled her tongue deeper. She lost count of her orgasms and tried her best to hold back from cumming again. Her body burned with pleasure. Sunni felt the bed around her sink beneath her due to added weight. She opened her eyes to see Carlos's throbbing third leg. She let her mouth fall open and closed her hand around him/it. Carlos was warm inside of her mouth. He was close to exploding and Sunni welcomed its arrival. She sucked softly on the head, before inching him deeper into her mouth.

SexPressions

Carlos began to slowly rotate his hips. A rebel breath exhaled itself from his lips. Sunni eagerly fucked him with her mouth. She was the conduit in an a sexual power line.

Sunni tongue danced gingerly around Carlos's dick and Lorraine licked and kissed Sunni's pearl tongue. Carlos hunched his back and gave up his sexual resistance. Sunni shook violently as Carlos's life juice splashed against the inside of her throat. Lorraine lapped at the sweet love syrup that leaked from between Sunni's thighs. Lorraine smiled t herself, as the tremors that ran from Carlos through Sunni through her, had now began to run through Fred; who had eased himself deep into her. The warmth of Fred's erotic exhaust greeted her slight shivers. Fred buckled at the sensitive feeling of the head of his dick. Sunni sipped at the last drops of Carlos's still stiff member. Her body quivered as she let Carlos slip from her mouth. She pushed Lorraine from between her legs and forced Carlos to the bed. She kissed him soft on his chest, then his lips.

Sunni sat up and wiggled her hips as she guided her husband slowly and deeply into her. She exhaled as his full length reached into her and seemed to grow from the feeling of her warmth. Leaning forward, she slowly bounced and rocked. Sunni felt a hand caressing her anxious breast and glance down at Fred, who lay next to them under Lorraine. Fred's face reacted to Lorraine's kneading of his sensitive sex member. Fred arched his back and pumped at Lorraine. With one hand he continued to massage Sunni's breast and with the other he rubbed Lorraine's ass. He used Lorraine's wetness to lubricate her tight rear hole, before slowly inserting his finger. He pumped his finger alternate of his pelvic thrust. Lorraine's walls clenched onto Fred's member.

Sunni and Lorraine

She begged her body to release her impending orgasm's grip. She opened her mouth to speak but was muffled by her powerful orgasm. She felt the warm stickiness run between her thighs and spread over Fred's abdomen. Lorraine felt dizzy as she collapsed on Fred. She turned her head and watched Carlos and Sunni have twin explosive orgasms. Lorraine dipped her finger in mixture of their loves juices.

The four of them lay drained, exhausted and pleased. They soon drifted to sleep; side-by-side; first the men, then the women.

Sneaking Off

    Dean checked his watch and saw that there was another thirteen minutes left in class. It always amazed him how the class material being taught, ran out before the actual class. Teachers surely knew how to waste your time. But seeing how it was sneaking off day, he didn't care. He had waited the entire week, so he could easily wait a few more minutes. Today was the day he and Rebekah could sneak away and be together, alone. They usually just had sex; which was very cool with him. He liked Rebekah. Everybody used to call her Bugs, because of her teeth. That was until Dean broke Tony Frazier's nose. After that, no one called her anything other than Rebekah. Sneaking off didn't used to be such a big deal.

    They used to spend as much time as they wanted together. Then Rebekah's mother caught them having sex. She told Dean to keep his "thing" in his pants and his pants away from her daughter. Bitch! Damn shame what two people have to go through to be together.

    He looked across the room at her and waved. He couldn't get past how pretty she looked. She always dressed nice when they snuck off and today was no different. She wore a pink skirt that stopped a little above her knees, with a

SexPressions

white blouse half buttoned down the front. It was tight so her large breasts teased Dean from across the room. Her skirt hung loose and free around her thick brown legs. Dean smiled to himself, reminiscing about how soft they felt against his face. She was the first girl he had ever eaten out. That happened the first time they snuck off. She moaned so loud, he thought they would get caught. All that noise they made and no one came. No teachers. No students. Damn sure no parents. No one. That time they hid in the janitor's closet on the third floor. It was on a Wednesday morning. That was also when they realized neither of them had a class for fourth period. After that everything fell into place. No need to go to dirty ass motels. No hoping that their houses would be empty. All they had to do was wait until Wednesday. There was a classroom that Dean found unlocked. Since they'd been sneaking around, they had both stashed blankets in their lockers. No one ever came around so they wouldn't get caught. It was too easy.

Dean smiled across the room at Rebekah, who by now was watching the clock as well. She started rocking in her chair some. Dean couldn't help but stare at her legs. She told him she wanted to get a tattoo of a panther crawling up her thigh. He often masturbated thinking about such a beautifully powerful animal on the leg of such a powerfully beautiful woman. He even began calling her his "Beautiful." Mainly because of the song he heard on the radio. She thought he looked like that guy Pharrell, too.

"Ten more minutes." Dean told himself.

Watching Rebekah had made him get an erection. He always thought of what it would be like to have her when

Sneaking Off

ever he wanted. He already decided he would ask her to marry him. They had already turned eighteen this year, so why not? He would work with his father and come home and make love to his Beautiful wife. Who now was just his Beautiful girlfriend. He wondered if she was wearing panties. Sometimes she did and other times she didn't. But that was only on sneak off day. All the other days she wore granny panties. She had a few she wore when she wanted to feel sexy. His favorite pair was her purple bikini pair. They were lace and silk with a flower pattern sewn on the front. He liked those pair because she had stuffed those in his pocket after they had snuck off the third time. He used to sniff them at night before bed. They smelled of her perfume. He could smell her pussy juice on them too. He gave them back so she could wash them. Even he knew that was nasty after a while.

The long clanging of the bell snapped Dean back to reality. "Finally," He thought. He sat in his seat awhile longer. It was always best to be patient, he told himself. Rebekah stood and adjusted her skirt, which had worked its way up her thighs while she sat.

"What a tease," Dean whispered to his penis. She called it his love muscle. He thought that was cute. Actually Dean thought everything about her was cute.

She stopped to talk with her two best friends and began walking by him slowly. He was so engrossed in her smell, he almost missed the note she dropped on his desk. He palmed the tightly folded paper and stood. He paused long enough to allow his hard-on to soften; he'd cum in his pants once thinking about her, and then moved out into the hallway. They always took different routes to their hiding place. No one ever noticed them when they weren't together, but as soon as they started walking down the hall together, it too, became every kid in school's business. That was her idea. Dean was glad she had thought of it, he would absentmindedly hold her hand when they walked together. He didn't care if people said he was pussy whipped; he was in love. And as far as he was concerned, everyone should know what real love looked like. They were special, he and Rebekah, and so that made their love special.

Dean stopped at his locker, stashed his books and grabbed his blanket. He glanced around the crowed hallway to see if anyone noticed him. As usual, no one did. Good. He couldn't use being noticed today. High Schools were funny like that; no one ever paid attention, unless they needed something or wanted to do something mean. Dean ignored them when they called him names. He cared less if some six-year football player thought he was a nerd. He had a beautiful woman. So 'fuck 'em,' is what he thought.

Dean stuffed his blanket in his backpack and turned down the hallway. He fixed his clothes and dusted the front of his shirt. He slid his hands in his pockets. Dean felt the note Rebekah slid him and smiled. He nearly forgot about the note. His hard-on returned as the scent of her perfume floated from the paper.

Hey Baby,
Can't wait to have you to myself, I shaved my pussy just for you. It looks cute. I wanted to surprise you.

Sneaking Off

Love Your Beautiful
P.S. Since you like orange, I have a surprise for you

Dean slowly refolded the note and moved through the rush of people. He let his head hang and his smile to develop. With a woman like Rebekah, who wouldn't be frantic? Who wouldn't want to sneak off and see her?

Dean made it to the end of the hallway and turned to go up the stairs. He wanted to run, but took his time. No need to rush. He moved up the first flight and turned up the next when he heard his name. He lifted his head skyward, exhaled and rolled his eyes. Stepping into the second floor hallway, Dean looked around to see who wanted his precious time. He scanned the floor until he came eye to eye with Coach Levelle. Everyone called him Sarge, but Dean just called him Coach.

"Hey Coach." Dean mumbled, as he stood in the middle of the hallway fidgeting nervously.

"Don't 'Hey Coach' me." He growled. "You study that book?"

"Yeah Coach. Maybe I'll use my bishop more during matches." Dean was on the chess team and was close to taking city. Coach Levelle wanted him to stop using his knights so much to attack. Who cares? Dean was good.

"No '*maybe*' about it. Get on to class."

SexPressions

Coach Levelle stuck his hand up high for Dean, who gave it a quick slap and turned to walk away.

"Hey Dean, where's that pretty girlfriend of yours?"

Dean froze. He wondered if Coach Levelle knew they'd been sneaking off. He didn't want to turn around. Couldn't look coach in the eye and tell him a lie. He would if he had to. Dean mumbled a half answer.

"I always see you and her together. Just wondering where she might be?" Coach waved at Dean before disappearing into his classroom. Dean allowed his breathing to return to normal. He pushed fright from his body and welcomed sexual mischief. He liked sneaking off to be with her. It made their time special and different. Dean turned and moved up the stairs. When he reached the third floor, he slowed his pace to make sure the coast was clear. A few students moved to classes on the far end of the hallway. Nowhere near the classroom, he and Rebekah used.

Dean turned into the classroom and moved toward the back. He removed the blanket and spread it out. He quickly ate a breath mint, you can never be too sure, and waited on Rebekah. Dean closed his eyes and thought about his life with Rebekah. He thought of their home. Wondered if they would have children? Dean hoped they would. If they did have children, he only asked that they be normal; ten fingers, ten toes, two eyes and one nose kind of normal. He didn't care if they were ugly at first. You could grow out of ugly. That's what his mama had told him. So all he asked God to give him was normal. Okay, and a very nice truck to drive his normal family around.

Sneaking Off

"Hey Baby."

Rebekah's voice bounced around the room's emptiness. She spoke softly, although her voice was heavy for a girl. It sounded very sexy to Dean.

"Hey Beautiful." Dean smiled as he opened his eyes and looked up at her face. "I couldn't wait for today. I missed you."

Rebekah dropped her blanket and crawled next to him. He smelled her soft perfume just as she leaned in to kiss him. Rebekah wore a light coat of lip gloss and Dean could taste the sweet strawberry flavoring as their lips met. The first kiss was always just lips, no tongue. That's how first kisses should be, Rebekah told him the first time they'd done this. She had taught him a lot about being in love and even more about how to make love. She told him not to say he loved her until he really and truly did, anything before that was bullshit and would only make her mad.

"I missed you too, baby. Had to wait for Dina to go to class. She so nosy." Rebekah slowly pulled of her light jacket. Her breast pushed against her white blouse and Dean couldn't do anything but stare.

"So what's the surprise you have?"

Dean was anxious and eager. The last surprise she had for him, kept him happy for a week. Dean loved her surprises, and he loved her.

SexPressions

"I took pictures for you to look at when I'm not around. Wanna see?" Rebekah was already looking through her purse before he could answer.

"Dina took them for me so you don't have to worry. I took some of her for her man too." She turned from her purse and handed him a stack of pictures. Dean really wanted to know where she got them developed, but really didn't care. Rebekah smiled as Dean looked through the stack of photos. She could see the desire in his eyes. She wanted to spend the rest of her life looking into his eyes. Her mother didn't know about that look. She didn't know how it made her feel. So he didn't have everything. That's why she continued sneaking off with him; that look. Rebekah knew that look meant he loved her. Even before he spoke the words, she knew because of that look.

"I love 'em Beautiful. You look very sexy and pretty." Dean said putting the pictures back into the envelope.

"That's not all I wanted to show you."

Rebekah stood in front of Dean slowly began rocking from side to side. She slowly unbuttoned her blouse, revealing her large breast and the silk and lace bra that held them against her chest. Rebekah pushed Dean, who had begun to reach for her, back to the floor. He lay on his elbows; eye's smile bigger and brighter than the one his lips held.

"That's not all."

Sneaking Off

Rebekah tossed her blouse over the back of the closest chair and reached behind her and slowly unzipped her skirt. She slowly pushed the sides down. Her large ample hips held skirt's hem snugly before releasing it from her thickness. Rebekah let the skirt fall then stepped from the circled bundle. Beneath her skirt she wore a pair of bikini panties that matched the bra. Dean missed the part where she told him her cousin took her to buy them last week, she'd been wanting to show him for an entire week.

"Do you like them?" She asked. Dean shook his head slowly up and down. Rebekah smiled, and then slowly turned slowly so he could see that her large ass cheeks were divided by soft material. She wiggled before turning to face him. She kneeled and crawled into his embrace. She greeted his lips then pushed her tongue roughly into his mouth. Peppermint greeted her efforts. She hummed and fell completely on him. She searched for his hands, found them, and then locked him in her grip. Rebekah kissed Dean with rough passion, before guiding his hand over her nearly naked body. His touch was tender and smooth. It was hard to tell they were sneaking. He touched her body as if they had all the time in the world, and to them they did.

Rebekah ran her hands over his body as well. His body was soft and hard at the same time. She liked to call him pudgy, with muscles though.

She pushed her crouch against the bulge in his jeans and felt her labia spread slightly. She didn't have to touch her sex to know there was a thick coat of anticipation. Dean had told her she had a bland taste, yet sweet.

SexPressions

"Like bananas." She heard his voice say in her memory. Rebekah kissed Dean softly on the lips then his left cheek. Her body began to become filled with teenage lustful heat.

"Take this damn shirt off." Rebekah said, pulling and tugging at Dean's shirts.

Dean crossed his arm in front of him, reached to the hems of the shirts and pulled them over his head together.
Rebekah grinned shyly. She always felt new and beautiful when they were naked together. She kissed his exposed chest and stomach. She hated that they had to rush. So she always kissed him slowly when he started undressing. She wrestled at his belt; finally pulling the two ends free. Dean unfastened the button and unzipped his jeans.

"Thank you." Rebekah whispered, and then kissed him on the down slope of his stomach. She could smell his manhood now. Her mouth watered. She knew she couldn't "suck" on him for long, but she had to at least taste him, hold him in her mouth and savor his manly taste. Dean lay back completely and closed his eyes. He was bigger than she was but always trembled beneath her when she did this. Her tongue traced the edge of his penis head. Precum slowly seeped from the tiny opening. Rebekah looked up to see his eyes. She needed to see his eyes and feel that look. When their eyes met; she smiled.

"I love you Beautiful." Those eyes said. Rebekah licked the base of his shaft and raised her head and let his penis stand free of her mouth.

Sneaking Off

"Put the rubber on baby." She whispered. Dean pulled his pants and boxer free and fished the condom from his pocket. Rebekah had taken her own underwear off and was completely naked. She crawled atop him, kissed him on his neck, and then slowly guided him into her. They both winced; then moaned. Rebekah wiggled side to side, and then found her own comfortable rhythm. Dean held her thighs and pumped upward and into her. "This is how what love feels like." He thought. Rebekah started slowly. She wanted him deep inside of her. When they were married, she would ride him like this, only then they wouldn't have to sneak. They wouldn't have to use condoms, either.

"And have normal babies, too." She whispered as her swollen clitoris rubbed against her excited labia.

She moved faster and rougher. Rebekah leaned forward and forced a large breast into Dean's mouth. He sucked and licked her breasts and nipples. Rebekah forced his stiff penis roughly against her "spot." No time to tell him, she did it herself.

Dean bit his lip and stiffened. Rebekah knew he was about to cum. She didn't know how long they had, so she always made him cum fast.

"That means it's good." He told her once. And she wanted him to like having sex with her. Rebekah lay atop of him and furiously worked her pelvis into his. She fucked herself speechless. She wanted to tell him about her orgasm, but not yet, so she kept working. She felt his heavy hand palm her ass cheeks. "He's coming!" She thought, "My man is coming."

SexPressions

A soft wisp of air kissed her sweat-covered ass. She wished she had remembered to cover them with her blanket. Her head began to swim. She felt Dean kissing her neck. Her stomach rolled itself into knots. Her orgasm could no longer wait. Rebekah felt far away. She felt Dean tapping her on her ass cheek and heard him cursing from far away.

"... the fuck". He said; voice deep from the dreamy distance. "What the fuck."

Rebekah loved when he cursed during sex. Her orgasm held her entire body hostage. Her toes curled. Her hands locked themselves around his head. Her vagina gripped his penis and coated it with her liquid sex.

"Beautiful... please stop." Dean whispered. "Please stop." He begged her now. Their passion had made him weak. She could hear it in her voice. Rebekah ignored him. she rocked herself into him.

"Rebekah! Stop!" Dean yelled.

She froze now. What was wrong, She wondered. Then asked. "What's wrong baby?" Rebekah whispered, still engrossed in their sexual aftermath. She kissed Dean's face and opened her eyes. "What's wrong?" She repeated.

"What the hell are ya'll doing?" An angry voice growled from behind them.

It was Mr. Levelle. Where did he come from?

Sneaking Off

"I tried to tell you..." Dean started, but Rebekah didn't let him finish. She grabbed at her clothes and crawled behind Dean. Her tears came next.

Mr. Levelle and the new security guard, Ms. Annie with the big booty and short hair, stood staring at them. She closed her eyes and let the tears come. Mr. Levelle yelled at Dean. She felt hurt and ashamed. Rebekah knew she had gotten them caught. Ms. Annie grabbed Rebekah's clothing and held them out to her. She could hear Mr. Levelle yelling even louder now. Dean was quiet. He dressed with his back to her. Mr. Levelle told him to face the wall. She wondered if Mr. Levelle was jealous of how big Dean's dick was? Mr. Levelle turned and yelled once more over his shoulder at her.

"What were you and Dean thinking? What were ya'll doing?"

Rebekah wanted to answer. But she couldn't. Not aloud anyway. Mr. Levelle asked her the question again. "Sneaking off." She whispered to herself.

Mr. Levelle and Ms. Annie walked them to the principal's office. Everyone saw them. Dean held her hand and never made a sound. She could feel them making jokes. Some people pointed; others laughed. But everyone watched the two retarded kids being taken to the office.

Rebekah's mother got there first. She found out later Dean's Uncle Gus came after school. They all blamed Dean. Even he said she had nothing to do with it. Rebekah hated them for ganging up on her man, on her husband.

SexPressions

"And you better stay yo' ass away from my daughter!" Her mother yelled. Rebekah hated her mother. She thought she knew everything. But she didn't know everything. She didn't know about Dean and she didn't know about love.

"Why would you do this?" Mrs. Garner asked, the principal asked, Rebekah.

Her word came slow at first.

"He says I'm Beautiful." Rebekah mumbled.

"Speak up." Her mother snapped.

"Won't this bitch shut the fuck up?" Rebekah thought.

"Because when we sneak off, I'm Beautiful." She answered. She was strong and defiant now. She had to be; they were picking on her man.

"When we sneak off, I'm Beautiful to him. I'm not a wetard, or slow. I'm just Beautiful Rebekah, and it feels good mama. His dick feels good in me."

Rebekah added the last part because her mother didn't have a man. She didn't have anyone to love. She didn't have anyone to make her feel special.

"When we have sex we can be normal, Mama. That's why! Because we can be normal and not special or wetard."

Rebekah saw the hurt in her mother's eyes.

"Good." Rebekah thought. "Leave my man alone."

The First Time

Rachel's heart pounded quickly behind her ribcage. Jake's voice was deep and smoothly rolled from his tongue and over his lips. It was the same voice he used to introduce himself with. The very same voice he used when he proposed, and it was the same voice she was now allowing herself to dance with.

"It's our floor baby!" Jake said voice silhouetted against his smile. "Ours and ours alone."

Rachel stood to her full height, which was only five feet, and allowed her new husband to guide her to the dance floor. After a few steps Jake slowly turned Rachel, her white wedding gown billowing around her. Rachel felt Jake's hand easily pull her close to him. His touch was warm and light, yet it was dominating, guiding her, and them, slowly around the room. Rachel pushed her head deeper into Jake's chest and listened to the sound of her new husband; the sound of her first and only lover. Rachel slowly nestled her cheek into the soft fabric of Jake's tuxedo. The single tear that ran from her eye now moistened his lapel, before disappearing into the jackets soft color.

"I love you!" Jake whispered as Rachel closed her eyes.

SexPressions

Rachel took one last look at herself in the mirror. She held back the rush of tears that welled up in her eyes. She'd finally found the man of her dreams; her very own Prince Charming, tall, brown, and to die for. So if anyone deserves a night this special, it was her. Rachel ran her hands over her body as she watched herself in the mirror. Her entire body buzzed with sexy electricity.

"Mrs. Rachel Conner." Her new name floated from her lips and up to her ears. Rachel hugged herself tightly. The smooth feeling of her silk gown and robe against her skin calmed her feeling somewhat. Rachel wore virgin white. She tried to tell herself she'd chosen the color but finally decide the color had chosen her. The gown was long and flowing. It hung low in the front, exposing her deep smooth cleavage, with thin spaghetti straps. Rachel looked down at her glass slippers and smiled. This was her very own fairytale and she didn't want to miss any details. Rachel gave herself a final check, although she missed the three tears that rolled over her cheeks. She felt as if she'd been reborn. Her nipples burned with the anticipation of Jake's touch. She'd waited her entire life for this night. No more sleepless nights wondering if the pillow between her legs felt anything like a man's body. She finally would find out it didn't compare. She turned to open the door and enter her new life. Her married-having-sex-when-she-wanted life, and just as her hand reached the door when, a soft tap at the door sent her emotions in a whirlwind.

"Are you coming to bed," Jake said, "Or do I have to come in after you?" Rachel's body pulsated with the sound of each word. A soft tremor began from between her thighs. "I'm coming honey!" Rachel sang in return. She looked at

The First Time

her reflection once more. This would be the last time she'd see her virgin self.

"Don't be skurd!" Rachel whispered to herself as she stepped from the bathroom.

Rachel and Jake chose to honeymoon in the Caribbean. And the room they'd been given came with a balcony that overlooked the ocean. Rachel stood recording the moment. The moon hung full and bright, just over Jake's shoulder. He was dressed in raw white cotton slacks and shirt. The sky behind was a perfect jewel blue, etching Jake's physique across her vision. With the clarity of the sky Rachel believed she could see well into their future. And she saw their love lasting forever.

Jake moved slowly toward Rachel holding out slender champagne flutes. The light bubbly beverage mirrored Rachel's feeling. She took the glass from Jake's hand. A transfer of electricity passed from Jake to her. She gasped deeply. Trying to hide her trembling hand, Rachel sipped from the glass. Jake kissed her hand and moved closer to her. She inhaled his soft manly aroma. He continued further up her arm. Each touch of his lips pushed Rachel further into frenzy. His lips caressed the tender skin on the inside of her elbow. Jake allowed his tongue to peek from between his lips, as he reached the top of her arm. Rachel held the slender glass with two hands, as Jake moved behind her. She sipped from the glass, trying to masquerade the fact she'd been holding her breath. Rachel felt lightheaded. Her equilibrium began to betray her. Rachel knew she'd topple over.

SexPressions

"Relax baby." Jake said, whispering from behind her." I'm right here."

His strong arms wrapped around her. Rachel opened her stance and softly floated back into Jake's body. Her lips trembled as Jake softly kissed Rachel's neck. The erotic force pulled her legs apart and caused her inexperience sex petals to blossom. Rachel pushed air from her lungs. Jake worked his hands over her breast in alternating circular motions. Rachel felt herself begin to moisten. She lifted the champagne glass to her lips, before realizing she'd allowed it to slip empty from her hands. Jake trailed his kisses along Rachel's jaw line and moved his hands to caress her face. Joyous tears moved from the comer of Rachel's eye. Rachel stared blankly at the Caribbean night. She slowly rocked from side to side. Jake's manhood slowly grew against her thinly covered buttocks. She shivered at the thought of his length deep within her. She'd never been this close to Jake's sex. She hoped he'd be happy with her naive sex, and if as if reading her mind, she heard Jake whispering for her not to worry. That she was in good hands.

"I know!" Rachel replied." I know I am." Jake slowly turned Rachel around and looked deeply into her eyes. Rachel didn't believe people when they said they were lost in another person's eyes, but as she stood before her new husband (she didn't think she could ever get used to saying that word) she had no clue where or who she was. Rachel stood awestruck. Her emotions glued her to the floor. She watched happily defenseless, as Jake leaned in to kiss her. His lips were soft and not very thick. Although they'd kissed before, now it felt new. As if this was their very first encounter.

The First Time

"This is how a husband kisses." Rachel thought. Jake slowly slid the robe from Rachel's shoulders. He continued to kiss Rachel deeply and fully. Their tongues playfully moved in new erotic union. She held onto Jake not wanting to lose contact with him. She moved her hands under his shirt and pulled them, her to him and him to her, closer. Jake's skin was hot to her touch. Rachel moaned softly and welcomed the heat. She lifted her head so that Jake could kiss her. He kissed her softly on the lips, and then sucked gingerly on her neck. She wanted to giggle, but only pulled him deeper to her. Jake eased his tongue lower; kissing and sucking as he went. Rachel pushed her fingernails deep into Jake's back as his tongue found the virgin wonders of her cleavage. She closed her eyes and let her head fall back. She held the picture of Jake, now naked standing silhouetted against the Caribbean sky. Rachel wanted to think of it as a Virgin's sky.

Jake delicately removed Rachel's breast from the gown. Her nipples stood erect from the center of their light brown surroundings. Jake cupped them as if they were fragile, slowly easing the tip of his tongue under her nipples. He heard Rachel pant softly. Jake licked upon each nipple with erotic determination. Since he wasn't a virgin, he wanted to give Rachel his full attention. Jake felt himself begin to grow slowly erect and wondered if Rachel felt it as well. The head of his sex muscle began to throb soft and slowly. Jake continued his labor of lust until he covered Rachel's large breast with kiss after passionate kiss. Rachel held her eyes closed, causing Jake to wonder what she dreamt about.

SexPressions

"This very moment!" A soft voice sang deep from within him.

Jake eased Rachel's gown further down her body until it fell, crumpled over her glass-slippered feet. A soft breeze caressed them as Jake kneeled before Rachel's naked body. He kissed her on her stomach before drawing circles around her deep navel. Rachel held the back of Jake's head. Shivers overtook her naked body. She bit down her lip and tried to brace herself. Jake kissed, licked, and bit his way around to Rachel's side. She giggled a moan, as the foreign feeling of a pre-orgasmic tremor touched her. Rachel held Jake's head against her and turned herself over to him. Jake stood and guided Rachel over to the large bed.

"Leave your shoes on." Jake whispered, "I like that." Rachel smiled as she stepped from the gown. She slid back onto the bed and watched as Jake slowly removed his clothing. She smiled at the pleasing symmetry of his nakedness. Rachel loved how Jake looked without his clothing. He definitely made staying a virgin very difficult. Her heart thumped with passionate panic as his manhood fell free from his pants and hung between his legs. Jake pulled Rachel toward the edge of the bed. Placing his hands under and around her thighs, he kissed her on both knees. Rachel giggled in delight. Jakes slowly parted Rachel's legs as he lowered himself closer to her virgin sex. Jake could smell Rachel's moist heat. He decided to take his time. Rachel deserved this. She deserved for her first night to be special. Nights like this only come once in a lifetime. And Jake swore he would make it the greatest night of her life. Jake raised his head and tenderly kissed Rachel's stomach again. He hadn't noticed before but she was trembling.

The First Time

"And crying." His inner voice told him. "And so am I." He told the voice.

Jake trailed kisses from just under her navel to just above her vagina. Rachel gasped hard and whispered Jake's (her new husband's) name. Jake kissed Rachel flush on her labia with soft passion. Her taste was sweet. It was the taste of "new." The taste of the untouched. Rachel fought against Jake's grasp as he moved his tongue across her swollen vagina. Rachel cursed as her body shuddered then froze. She tried to speak but Jake's busy tongue licked away her words. Jake used his tongue and parted Rachel's sexual doors. A soft thick juice greeted Jake's tongue. Rachel felt heavy and light. She held onto Jake's head for dear life. Scared he'd stop if she released her grip. Jake inserted the tip of his tongue into Rachel's sex. She inhaled hard. Even that small amount of him caused her some discomfort. But it was also nice. Rachel tightened her buttocks and braced herself against Jake's experienced tongue. Jake hummed as he moved his tongue over Rachel's sexual place. He began to massage Rachel's tender cheeks. Rachel quietly began to pray. She pleaded for this to be as she had dreamt. She prayed that it was as good as she was told. Most importantly she prayed that this was love.

Jake continued licking. Rachel tried to wiggle away. Her heart rate quickened. She was frightened. Rachel lay numb and horrified. *Was this what a heart attack felt like*, Rachel wondered. Jake continued licking her toward the edge, and suddenly her body turned against her. Rachel felt herself screaming, but her ears heard no sound. She thrust her hands down to repel Jake from between her thighs, but found herself holding him to her. Rachel felt her extremities contract. Her hands instinctively balled into fists. She wanted to fight, but couldn't. Her feet curled into themselves, and finally Rachel found her voice.

"Ja... Jaaheyke! iieee 'm cub cub..." She started, "I think I'm cumming baby." Rachel moaned pushing the words from her. She loved the sound of those words. Her vagina tingled intensely. If Jake were still licking at her black pearl, Rachel could not tell. She lay on the bed lost in her own virgin sky.

Jake stood over his new wife. He watched as tears slowly moved down her face.

He watched as her wide mouth smile attempted to grow even wider. Rachel trembled and moaned. Jake was sure she didn't hear these moans, or even fell feel the trembling. Jake loved her that much more. His sex had grown to its full length. It throbbed slowly, as Jake lightly and gently stroked himself. His body buzzed with excitement. He dearly wanted to please his new wife. He smiled at her glowing face. Plus, he never slept with a virgin. Jake believed himself to be the most blessed man in the world.

Jake crawled over Rachel, until they came face to face. Her breathing slowed to a trembling rhythm. Jake kissed her shyly on the forehead. He held her face in his hand and stared into her eyes. Where Rachel had lost herself; Jake in contrast found himself. He kissed Rachel softly on the nose, then her soft lips. Rachel lifted her head allowing pants to float from her mouth. Jake ran his tongue from Rachel's left earlobe, down and across her dainty neck. Rachel spread her legs, ushering Jake closer. Jake rotated his

The First Time

hips and began slowly grinding against Rachel's clitoris. Rachel wondered if his penis was as big as it felt against her. She could feel her sexual heat returning. Rachel ran her hands along Jake's back. She heard him whispering for her to "relax" or "not to worry" with each touch of their sex. Rachel nipples rubbed against Jake's chest. Her senses were mixed and jumbled. She wanted to absorb Jake. Rachel felt herself opening up. Although she was lying down, she felt light and nimble. She hardly felt awkward or clumsily as some of the women she worked with had said they felt during their first time.

"Husbands were skillful at things like this." She thought.

Jake kissed her breast. Rachel searched for words, but "damn" and "shit" was the only ones she could muster. Jake lifted her breast; kissed and *licked* the underside. Each touch of his mouth sent waves of cool shivers through her. Jake paid close attention to each breast before moving back to her throat. Jake ran his hands beneath Rachel's shoulders and slowly massaged her neck. He switched his pelvic movements from circular to back and forth. The head of his penis gliding over Rachel's tight opening. Jake's breath tickled her ear. Rachel felt the room begin to spin. Her only anchor was the sight of Jake; the sight of her new husband; her new lover.

Rachel whispered softly into Jake's ear that she was ready. She really didn't trust her words, but she did trust her heart, and her heart trusted her husband. Jake kissed her passionately on the lips and held her with the softness of his gaze.

SexPressions

"Don't worry." Those eyes said to Rachel.

"I'm not." Rachel's eyes answered.

Jake wiggled lower. He positioned himself so he'd be at what he hoped was the perfect angle. He circled her vagina with his love-hardened penis. He quickly worked Rachel into a sexual-juicy frenzy.

"I love you." He said, kissing Rachel again on the mouth. A single tear drifted from his eyes, as he slowly entered Rachel.

Rachel felt the tear that ran from Jake's face land softly on her nose and fell in love with him even more. She hugged him. The feeling of *him* close to her sex caused tears to well up behind her eyes. Then Rachel felt Jake began to move inside of her. They said love hurts, and Rachel immediately knew they were correct. Jake had breached the gates of her intimate fortress and her body wanted to repel the intruder. But surprisingly a few rebellious emotions welcomed the uprising. Rachel was angrily excited. Her breast cheered Jake's touch. Her legs and back cursed his arrival. But Rachel's heart swelled. Rachel hated herself for telling Jake to continue. His strokes were slow. Jake merely placed the very tip of himself into Rachel. She was past hot. Her sexual sanctuary was scorching. Rachel's face contorted with pleasure and pain. Jake would've stopped if not for Rachel.

"Don't stop!" She pleaded, "Please don't! But go slowly."

The First Time

Jake smiled at his new wife and moved gently. Rachel's sexual grip was tight, but soon eased allowing Jake to move from semi-slow strokes to full powerful strokes. Rachel's vagina throbbed. She didn't know if it was from an orgasm or from the pain. She was sure it was because of her husband; her "new" husband; Jake, her only lover. She dug into his back, as each stroke stretched her slighter wider. Rachel yelled his name. She'd closed her eyes and imagined the sight of them making love. The way Jake's body moved slowly over her. She pictured her body welcoming his pistoning sex. Rachel watched herself rub his head. She watched as she kissed his cheek. Rachel watched the couple in her imagination switch positions. The woman on top, slowly moving over the man. The man entering the woman from behind. Rachel liked the sight of the pair. The couple in her imagination caused her to forget about her pain. There was only her, Jake and the couple. Rachel felt herself smile. She continued smiling as Jake shuddered and froze atop of her. A soft warmth ran from Jake into her womb. Jake whispered softly into her ear. His head resting gingerly on her shoulder, and after a few sentences Rachel recognized what he was saying. Rachel hugged Jake deeply and kissed him on his lips. Rachel drifted off to sleep with the sound of Jake, her new husband, laying beside her.

Thug Love

    She sat on the porch watching him. She had held a crush on him since they were in high school. They had gone on a few dates, but nothing special, just some kissing and touching. She even sported a hicky he gave her like a badge of honor. The closest they had come to actual sex was his two fingers pushing inside her; nothing special. That's where it ended. So now all she did was watch him. Watch him stand out and do what he did. She wished she could change his lifestyle but if he did something else she wouldn't be able to stare at him. He was a thug, a drug dealer. She found that sexy. Who dreams about having sex with an accountant? He was a thug and she loved it. Yeah, he sold dugs, which pissed her off, but it went with the territory. That's what thugs did. He wasn't big time; far from it. He just sold enough to notice. She noticed him alright. She would always notice him. She often told herself she didn't care if he sold drugs. That was part lie. Really it was all lie. "But isn't that what a fantasy is," she asked herself, "a lie dressed for a date?" So there he was, the thuggish lie she dreamt about.

    Monica lifted her glass of pop to her lips before noticing she had already finished her drink. She smiled and allowed her body to awaken. Although it would be easier to

SexPressions

walk to the refrigerator to refill her glass, she suddenly wanted -no, needed- to walk to the corner store. Monica giggled to herself and hoped he would at least try and touch her ass. She knew it was childish and juvenile, but so was having a crush on the local bad boy. The only thing was, her body didn't care, and it yearned for his touch. As Monica stood, she felt a soft breeze wipe across her breast. She was glad the weather was mild enough that she didn't need a jacket. She wore a pair of her scrub bottoms from the hospital, and a T-shirt that was tighter than it needed to be. Add in the fact that her only clean bra happened to be thin enough to allow her nipples, now stiff, to be seen clearly. Normally she would be embarrassed and walk with her arms folded in front of her. But *he* was out, and this wasn't a normal situation.

"Damn," she wondered, "why didn't he just ask her to fuck?"

Monica stood and looked down at her size 18 framed body and knew he would touch her ass. The hug she would give him would ensure that.

Monica nearly danced as she moved down the stairs. She readied herself mentally and started toward the corner. She tried to concentrate on her approach. She made sure her steps were slow and steady. Monica knew the polite movement of her hips would attract his eyes. She crossed her arms as she neared the first set of his cohorts. Monica liked the feeling she imposed on them. Their conversation slowly quieted itself as she past them until the only words spoken were a mixture of flirts and gangster greetings. None of their words mattered to her, only his.

Thug Love

"When you gone stop playin' and marry me?" he asked her as she tried her best attempt to pretend not to notice him.

"Whenever you give up this corner and get a real job." She spat back, knowing most *real* jobs didn't pay in a month what he collected in a day or two.

"Aight then. Well at least let me take you to dinner. You work so much, you probably never get a chance to eat real food."

Monica had stopped in front of him and held his gaze. His eyes were the color of a deep brown marble. She welcomed his vision's ability to undress her. She wondered if he knew about the tattoo she wanted to get on her buttock. If not, she would have to tell him one day.

"I'll think about it. But like you said, 'I work so much."

"That's cuz you need a better man." He took a step away from the fence he leaned against. One more step would put him within breath-touching distance.

"Maybe I do," Monica conceded. Really, she could just use a man in general. "We'll just have to see, won't we?"

"I guess so. So you off too?" he asked, changing the subject, "And where's my hug?"

SexPressions

"I'm going to the store; I need a juice for my lunch." Monica spread her arms and welcomed him against her body and she pulled him closer. His hands held him against her body. She pulled him close. His hands were firm against her back before sliding lower and then caressing her butt cheeks. Monica's body temperature rose slightly as she acted as if she didn't notice. This is where she wanted to be. She could smell the faint aroma of beer on his words as he whispered the nasty things he could do if given half the chance.

"Really? I haven't had a tongue against my pussy in a long time." Monica answered, showing off her own bad and nasty streak. She wanted to laugh. "But let me go before one of your many women sees us. I ain't fighting over a man that ain't mine."

He pulled her closer and held her tighter before releasing her with a kiss.

"See you later, Ms. Monica."

"Okay, Mr. Steve."

Monica took a few steps and told herself it was okay to breathe. She could feel his gaze against her backside. She swayed her hips, hoping he was watching her ass. She stuffed her hand into her pants pockets hoping he didn't notice her hands trembling.

"Damn he was sexy." She thought.

Monica pushed an exhale from her lungs, calming her nerves. She peeked over her shoulder, lying to herself that it

Thug Love

didn't matter if he were looking (she hoped he was) at her. Monica caught a glimpse of Steve turning back to join the group of men. With him retreating from her, courage strengthened Monica. Now she stared. His sleeves were rolled up exposing his sculpted arms. Monica hummed to herself wondering if those arms were strong enough to hold her up against a wall. She floated to the store, and was still floating as she moved passed him and his friends on her way back. She couldn't look at him. If she did, Monica believed she wouldn't have made it to work.

"See you later, Monica," he said from behind her.

Monica didn't dare respond. Not only were her hands trembling, now her inner thighs quivered as well.

Steve lay inside of the dumpster trying not to gag.

"Where the fuck did the police come from," he thought. He knew he should've called it a night a few hours ago. He didn't really need the money, but it felt good to be out with the shorties. It was bad business, because they were so reckless. You can't gang bang and sell drugs. "But if they were out here getting this money," he whispered, "then I'm out here getting this money too." It all sounded good until the task force came. The unmarked cars had gotten too close. Somebody should've been on security screaming out,"Who-dee-who... Pinky," but they didn't. So task force had swooped in and started grabbing people. Steve had some very *real* reasons to worry. He already carried one felony on his record. The pistol stuffed in his pants was enough to send him away, and the 200 packs of crack would be the icing on the cake. If he got caught he wouldn't see the

SexPressions

streets until he was a very old man.

"What the fuck was I thinking," he cursed under his breath. Steve wanted to lift the lid of the dumpster to peek into the alley, when the sound of radio chatter made him burrow further into the trash. The smell was making him sick, but it was better than jail time. The sound of an officer's radio stopped in front of the dumpster. Steve froze, fear telling him he was caught. Thugs didn't get miracles; they got years. Then just as he thought it was over, a woman's scream (the second officer) made his heart rate slow.

"What the hell you scream for," the first officer asked.

"I just saw the biggest rat I've ever seen in my life," she shot back, "if that muthafucka's in that dumpster then he good."

The two officers laughed, although the first officer never moved from the dumpster. Then the sound of feet shuffling and the female's voice,

"Don't you run muthafucka." The male officer quickly began shouting into his radio before their footsteps faded down the alley. Steve decided this was his chance. He lifted the lid so he could see out; seeing that the alley was empty, he jumped out, grabbed the bag he stuff his contraband in and ran down the alley in the opposite direction. He was nearly at the end, when a squad car turned into the alley from where he had just left. They stopped, turned their light on the dumpster then down at Steve. It must've been the flinch, but the squad car's light cut through the darkness and the sirens began blaring.

Thug Love

"Shit," Steve spat. He hopped the nearest fence, tossing the bag before him. He knew he had to hide and fast.

Monica sat on the edge of the tub and checked the temperature of the bath water with her hand. The night had been a demanding marathon of bullshit. A patient had even tried to smack her. It was times like this, which made her wish there was somebody to go home to; anybody would do. She poured in the bath salts and let her thoughts drift to Steve. Maybe she would stop being a punk and let him take her out. She blushed to herself thinking, "I'll even let him think it was his idea."

She walked around her small home, turning off the lights and checking the locks. As bad as she wanted a man, she didn't need one sneaking in trying to rob her; or worse. She checked the back door, thought about the wild patient and shook her head. Her heart had just begun to slow down from the altercation.

"Crazy bitch," she laughed at it now, but it wasn't funny then. Pregnant or not, Monica wanted to knock the bitch out. She grabbed a glass and the bottle of coconut rum she had chilling in the freezer and headed back to the bathroom. She inhaled the sweet relaxing scent of the candles. This is what she needed; a hot bath, a good drink and a hot, good man to snuggle against. She let her bathrobe slip from her hips when a knock came from the front door. It sounded more like the window but it was definitely from the front of the house.

"Damn", she spat. "Who the fuck would be at my

door?"

Monica had told herself she would curse out who ever it was. This was another time that having a man would be handy. She stormed to the front door and snatched it open. The storm door was locked, preventing anybody from getting in. To Monica's surprise the only thing on her front porch was a garbage bag.

"Bad ass kids," she thought, looking back and forth. Then just before she closed the door a man ran from the side of the house, causing her to jump and nearly yell.

"Whoa, whoa ma'. The man yelled in a hushed tone. "It's me, Steve." He looked around now. Monica got the feeling he was sneaking or being chased. He had his hand on the storm door handle anticipating her unlocking it. "Please let me in."

"Boooy, it's late as hell." Monica readjusted her bathrobe and shifted her weight to one side (her right).

"C'mon Monica, the police are chasing me. They think I'm hiding in your back yard."

They stood there looking at each other, only the tough storm glass between them. Monica had never seen him like this. This scared; this desperate. "Fuck it," she thought. She didn't want him to go to jail. That wouldn't do anyone any good. She quickly unlocked the door and pushed it open. Steve grabbed the garbage bag and nearly ran her over. The full effect of the smell hit her and it took everything for Monica not to vomit.

Thug Love

"Ewww you stink."

"I was hiding in the dumpster..." he started. Steve moved past her toward the back of the house. "I'mma sit this by your back door. I'll throw it out in the morning.

"Who said *you* gonna be here in the morning?" Monica tried being tough again. She stared at him, thinking how good it would be to sleep next to him, even if it was for one night. He kept moving past her.

"Please Ms. Lady. I'll sleep in the front on the floor. I won't try shit. I just can't go back out there tonight. Not now." He looked at her. His eyes were cold, but not frightening. She knew he wasn't lying.

"Okay", she started "but put that bag by the back door."

And just then a hard knock came from the back door. Monica watched Steve freeze and stop breathing. She wasn't sure if she had done the same thing until she heard herself breathe again. The knocks came again. Steve motioned for her to not answer the door. The house was mostly dark. It looked to be empty. Like no one was home.

"Don't answer it." Steve mouthed the words and put his hand up. Monica snatched away before he could grab her.

"Who is it?" She said from across the kitchen, trying her best to sound brave and unafraid.

SexPressions

"The police Ma'am." A deep voice called back to her. Monica listened for the tell-tale sound of walkie-talkie noise, hearing it; she turned on the kitchen light and moved to the door. Steve had stopped moving completely now. Fear pumped through his body. He didn't know what to do, so doing nothing was all he could think of. Monica pulled back the curtain on the door and came face to face with two white police officers. They held up their badge nearly blocking themselves from her view. They were plain clothes and seeing their badges made her heart plummet into her stomach.

"Yes," she asked, trying not to give Steve up.
The two officers adjusted the weight of their vest. They looked to be about the same size with the same facial features. The only difference was one had blond hair while the other was shaved bald. That's who spoke first.

"There was a man standing behind your residence. We were checking the area. To see if you heard or saw anything."

Monica frowned slightly and shook her head. She was about to ask a question before being cut off by the other officer.

"May we come in a look around?"

"No." Monica shouted scaring herself. "I just got home from work and I'm trying to take a bath and go to bed. I said I haven't seen anybody."

Thug Love

Monica's heart rate was faster than she had ever felt. This being a crook was too much for her. Before the two officers could say anything else she let the small curtain fall back in place and walked out of the kitchen. She walked to the small hall and stopped in front of Steve and nearly collapsed. He was breathing again. His chest was heaving from the excitement, just as hers was heaving from fear. Monica stood watching his features. It was different from earlier. The urge to grab him and pull him close came over her. She wanted to hold him close to her. She wanted to protect him from the police. She felt the heat from his body and wanted to touch him. She wanted to kiss his worried lips and have his fugitive hands running across her body.

"If you gonna stay her tonight you have to take a bath." She finally said. "C'mon," she said moving toward the bathroom. "Get in the tub. I'mma get you a towel." She left the bathroom leaving him alone. She grabbed a large bath towel and a pair of shorts. By the time she came back to the bathroom, Steve had gotten completely undressed and sat in the tub. He had tossed his wet clothes in a pile by the hamper. Steve lay in the hot water with his head back against the tub. She could see him trying to control his breathing. She'd seen people at the hospital doing the same thing; usually they were trying to psyche themselves up about the pain. It looked the same to her. Monica leaned against the door and admired the sight of his street-sculpted body. Outlines of muscles flowed into outlines of other sexy muscles. Scars and tattoos of different skill levels covered his chest and arms. She wondered about the lower half of him, the half being covered by the soapy bubbles that floated on the water's surface.

SexPressions

"Let me wash you up," she asked softly. Monica didn't remember walking to the side of the tub and kneeling beside it. All that her brain registered was his body. So what did they say?" Steve asked. He opened his eyes, without lifting his head. *Like he belongs here*, she thought.

"They asked about you," she told him, "I told them my man scared him off." She lied. She knew he had heard the exchange but it felt good saying it. *My man scared him off.*

"So I'm ya' man now?" he lifted his head and smiled at her.

"Yeah, only my man can use my house to hide from the police."

He held her gaze for a few seconds then let his head drop.

"What's wrong?"

"Just kinda' embarrassed. I got the law chasing me to ya' house."

She didn't like him sounding like that way; sounding defeated. So before she could stop herself, Monica kissed him. She had to stop him and she couldn't think of any other way to stop him from talking than to keep his lips busy. As she kissed him, she savored the fact that his lips were thick and soft. She surprised him with the kiss, so it took a few minutes to register before he returned her affection. The taste of expensive cognac coated his tongue. She lightly moved her tongue around his, before pulling her kiss back.

Thug Love

First just the lips; with long passion filled touches. Then just light pecks until they both were just looking at each other.

"You don't have to feel bad," she whispered, "you can run here anytime and for any reason. Just don't let the police be the only reason you come."

Steve smiled and kissed her again. He pushed the robe from her shoulders and kissed her softly on the neck. Monica lifted her head, letting soft tension easing moans escape from her. A chill danced through her body as Steve drug his hands along her delicate silhouette, guiding her robe to the floor. It felt good to Monica having her nudity exposed to a man. Steve ran his kisses across the front of her neck while his hands caressed her back. He stopped his touch and randomly massaged different areas. Monica slowly melted. Tight, knotted muscles received some long needed attention. She felt the temperature between her thighs quickly increase. Her large breast swelled from his touch, her nipples became ultra sensitive. He moved his warm mouth down to her cleavage and began kissing between her breasts, forcing Monica to gasp. She held on to the back of his head and fought off the feeling of free falling. Steve kissed her one last time and stood.

"C'mon, get in and let me wash you."
Monica nodded her head, kicked the robe from her feet and stepped into the tub. She eased herself into the water's heat and Steve slid in behind her. The fit was tight, but Monica didn't care. She wanted to be that close to him. Steve's thick penis felt like a long, hot stone against her back.

"Lean back, baby," he whispered.

SexPressions

Finally Monica relaxed against his body. The dimness of the small, candle lit bathroom, along with the soothing heat of the water, coaxed her eyelids shut. A soft, delicate smile crept across her lips. Steve took the loofa and applied vanilla-scented shower gel and slowly started washing her. His motions were gentle, yet firm. Not rough like she thought he would be. Steve dipped the loofa into the water and squeezed the hot water against her neck and back, and then her breast.

"Stand up," he softly ordered.

Monica stood being careful not to slip, although she knew he wouldn't let her fall. She braced herself against the tiled wall while he wiped her legs, thighs and feet. Monica giggled and nearly fell from the attention. She'd never had a man wash her feet. It made her feel regal like a Sexy Ghetto Queen.

He lightly washed between her thighs and spread her curvaceous butt cheeks and washed there. Monica didn't feel embarrassed as he washed her between the small folds of her stomach and sides. His touch made her feel much sexier.

"He can sell all the crack he wants if he'll wash me like this," she told her nagging conscious.

He rinsed her body as she did before. Steve stood behind her and moved his soapy hands across her body. Monica felt faint and weak. She thought he touched her everywhere all at once. His hands were busy. His left hand playfully massaged her labia and clitoris, while his right hand rotated gently round her breast. Monica bit her lip and

Thug Love

tossed her head back. She reached behind her and took his stone like dick into her hands. She slowly slid her hand up and down his shaft, pulling soft manly moans from his throat.

"Damn girl." He tried to bite back the words. Monica's heart rate quickened and she unknowingly matched his pace with her hand. She let her head fall forward as her body shook. It wasn't an orgasm, not yet, but a sexual precursor. She released his penis from her grip and slowly spun in the small space of the bath tub. They were face to face now. His penis touched her just to the left of her vagina against her thigh. She returned her hand to its base and began stroking. She playfully kissed his mouth, sucking roughly on his tongue. She traced her kiss to his chest. Monica traced the outline of his chiseled chest and abdomen with the tip of her tongue. She even sucked softly on a "R.I.P. Jay Stone" tattoo just above his left nipple. She carefully kneeled in the bath tub. The water teased her clitoris with its heat as she submerged her lower half. Without stopping to look up at him, Monica gently eased her mouth over the first few inches of his penis. Steve gasped from the comforting warmth. Monica placed her tongue under his shaft and wiggled it against the smooth skin. She slowly rotated her hand and moved her mouth on to and off of his thick, dark penis. She placed a small glob of saliva over the tip, lubricating her efforts and quickened her pace. Monica began moaning as she fed inch, after thick sexual inch, into her mouth. She sucked and licked down both sides and returned to the head. She dipped her free hand into the water, cupped some into her hand, and held it against his dangling balls. She felt him quake from the *sex*quisite shock. Monica worked up a steady rhythm; pushing and pulling;

SexPressions

licking and sucking. A few times the tip of his swollen dick head touched the back of her throat. She fought the urge to gag and continued with the task of pleasing herself with his length. Steve spread his legs and held himself up by placing his hands on her shoulders. She took note of the fact that he didn't grab her head, smiled and continued. Nothing pissed her off more than having her head grabbed; it just fucked up her flow. She didn't often give head but when she did, she hated for a guy to fuck her mouth. Monica kept working her hungry mouth until she felt his penis stiffen and grow from just hot to piping hot.

"Not yet," she thought.

Monica slowed her pace, and then eased his penis from her mouth with a dramatic pop and slurp. It made her feel like a nasty slut and she liked the feeling. She kissed the tip, then slowly stood and kissed his neck, then trailed her kisses around to his ears.

"I want you to nut on my ass."

Steve raised an eyebrow and grinned. "Aight then, Ma,"

Monica trembled from her own invitation. The slutty words dribbled from her lips and slowly down her breast. Steve held her waist as she turned. She placed her hands against the wall and bent over.

"Damn you gotta pretty ass," Steve whispered.
He resisted the urge to smack it but still grabbed two rough handfuls. Steve held the base of penis and worked the

Thug Love

tip in her wetness. Her labia puckered, and then slowly opened, welcoming him inside her womb. Monica's breath rushed from her in an excited gasp. She rested her head against the forward wall. He placed his hands at her waist and slowly rocked from side to side. He eased forward, until his balls brushed against her labia. He worked his thumbs strongly over the small of her back, shifting his weight. He wanted to get accustomed to her fit; get accustom to her tightness and plush ness; to the heat against the tip and shaft of his dick; to the feel of her soft body beneath his hands. He did all this before he slowly started fucking her. Steve ran his left hand to the middle of her back and slowly began moving his hips. His sexual jabs were slow and full, and then gained a rough thuggish momentum. He never did half strokes. She had just held as much of his dick in her mouth as she could fit and thought about the feel of him floating inside of her wetness. But Monica didn't want it long and slow, she wanted it fast. Being clean, this clean, made her want something dirty and nasty. Right now she didn't want to be sanitary nurse Monica; she wanted to be his hood rat bitch. His "around the way girl". Monica placed her foot on the side of the tub and braced herself by holding the tub's faucet.

"Oh shit yes," she panted. Steve grunted. They both could feel the end. Monica pushed her ass downward as his grunts became more intense. "Yes, baby, yes."

Steve felt his body stiffen. Pulled his penis free just as hot white liquid shot from the head. Globs of whiteness shot across Monica's back and covered her raised ass cheeks. Steve used the tip and smeared the globs over her roundness. Monica felt giddy from the nasty, stickiness. She moaned

SexPressions

her approval. He kissed her neck, and then slowly washed away the sexual residue from her body. He washed her again then stood and allowed her to wash him. Monica rinsed his body and stepped from the tub. She grabbed a large bottle of oil and two bath towels.

"I want to rub you down," she said.

Monica felt free and new. She smiled at Steve as they both dabbed each other dry. She kissed him passionately, and turned to lead him from the bath room to the bed room. Then without warning her feet slipped on a wet tile. Monica had a feeling of falling before a warm pair of hands caught her.

"Monica…Monica… Monica. You okay?"

The voice was familiar but not the one she wanted or thought she would hear. Monica slowly shook her head then looked around to get her bearings. Slowly everything came back to her.

"I'm okay Gary. I just have to sit down."

She had passed out.

"You say you know that dude" Gary asked. He was a good doctor, but terrible with the comforting. "I think the police want to talk to you."

Monica shook her head again. She couldn't believe that was him. The worst part was his apology.

Thug Love

"I'm so ... embarrassed Ms. Lady. I'm sorry I had to see you like this. Then he smiled and his eyes rolled to the back of his head. Monica couldn't close her eyes. All she saw then was Steve's body, covered in blood, flopping on the white gurney. Her eyes burned as the tears began to flow. She watched the police officer walk through the door and sit next to her.

"Excuse me, Maam. I need to ask..."

"His name was Steven Green." She blurted that out, cutting the officer off. She was unsure if she could do it any other way. "I'm not sure of his address." Her emotions took over now and the tears rushed down her face. "What happened?" She yelled.

The officer swallowed hard, looked at his partner and began talking speaking.

"He was shot during a raid. He and another man tried to elude the police. He, your friend, fired on four officers, killing two. He was shot after a short stand-off."

Monica yelled and shook her head violently. Not him. Not Steve. Sexy ass Steve couldn't be dead, not *her* Steve. She placed her face in her hands. The officer began talking but Monica didn't hear him. All she heard was Gary ushering them out of the room. Two more nurses; Gail and Tasha, rushed in the room and sat on either side of her. She closed her eyes and shook her head. "He was gone," she thought to herself. *Her* man was gone. unsure if she could do it any other way. "I'm not sure of his address." Her emotions took over now and the tears rushed down her face.

SexPressions

"What happened?" She yelled.

The officer swallowed hard, looked at his partner and began talking speaking.

"He was shot during a raid. He and another man tried to elude the police. He, your friend, fired on four officers, killing two. He was shot after a short stand-off."

Monica yelled and shook her head violently. Not him. Not Steve. Sexy ass Steve couldn't be dead, not *her* Steve. She placed her face in her hands. The officer began talking but Monica didn't hear him. All she heard was Gary ushering them out of the room. Two more nurses; Gail and Tasha, rushed in the room and sat on either side of her. She closed her eyes and shook her head. "He was gone," she thought to herself. *Her* man was gone. Then a smile crept over her face. At least he took a one of them with him.

www.ingramcontent.com/pod-product-compliance
Lightning Source LLC
Chambersburg PA
CBHW031958220426
43664CB00005B/61